Understanding Conflict
and Conflict Analysis

Understanding Conflict and Conflict Analysis

Ho-Won Jeong

Los Angeles • London • New Delhi • Singapore

First published 2008

Apart from any fair dealing for the purposes of research or
private study, or criticism or review, as permitted under
the Copyright, Designs and Patents Act, 1988, this
publication may be reproduced, stored or transmitted in
any form, or by any means, only with the prior permission
in writing of the publishers, or in the case of reprographic
reproduction, in accordance with the terms of licences
issued by the Copyright Licensing Agency. Enquiries
concerning reproduction outside those terms should be
sent to the publishers.

SAGE Publications Ltd
1 Oliver's Yard
55 City Road
London EC1Y 1SP

SAGE Publications Inc.
2455 Teller Road
Thousand Oaks, California 91320

SAGE Publications India Pvt Ltd
B 1/I 1 Mohan Cooperative Industrial Area
Mathura Road
New Delhi 110 044

SAGE Publications Asia-Pacific Pte Ltd
33 Pekin Street #02-01
Far East Square
Singapore 048763

Library of Congress Control Number: 2007934279

British Library Cataloguing in Publication data

A catalogue record for this book is available from the
British Library

ISBN 978-1-4129-0308-0
ISBN 978-1-4129-0309-7 (pbk)

Typeset by Cepha Imaging Pvt. Ltd., Bangalore, India
Printed in Great Britain by Cromwell Press
Printed on paper from sustainable resources

Contents

Preface

In International Relations (IR), there is a long tradition of research studying inter-state behavior with a focus on decision making behavior. Back in the 1960s and 1970s, many IR scholars adopted advanced theories developed in various fields of the social sciences to enrich our understanding of foreign policy makers' behavior in a crisis and other inter-state conflict situations. In illustrating international conflict, our attention has been expanded to the analysis of inert-group dynamics, actor motivations and external constraints beyond inter-state rivalry and governmental decision making. There has been a growing demand for new knowledge about the emergence and dynamics of many conflicts embedded in a complex environment of national and international politics.

While many of these studies respond to the necessity of reducing the risks of unnecessary catastrophic wars, we have observed complex conflict phenomena at various settings along with the major changes in the international system. Even before conflict studies were well recognized by scholars in mainstream IR, new theories and conceptual thinking about structural, psychological, communicative and behavioral aspects of a conflict process were developed by Chadwick F. Alger, John W. Burton, David J. Singer, Johan Galtung, Theodore Lentz, Paul Smoker, Marc Ross, Milton Esman, Anatol Rapaport, Christopher Mitchell, Janice Stein, Kenneth Boulding, Nazli Choucri, Ronald Fisher, Dean Pruitt, Glen Paige, James Rosenau, Charles F. Hermann, Herbert Kelman, Morton Deutsch, Louis Kriesberg, Jurgen Dedring, and many other prominent scholars. In order to develop a major textbook in conflict studies, it is necessary for us to assess the current status of our knowledge about the topic with recognition of the existing intellectual traditions.

My aim in this book is to provide a solid, elaborate conceptual knowledge base that helps students be better orientated toward the analysis of contemporary conflict phenomena, ranging from ethnic and other inter-group conflict, international terrorism, and inter-state disputes. In doing so, it identifies major theories needed for a full grasp of real world conflict situations, their sources and dynamics. I began to realize the importance of this task more, when I chaired the admission committee of my program and reviewed many hundred files of promising applicants whose careers range from diplomats, high ranking military officers to NGO workers.

What many of our students aspire to have is the intellectual skills they can depend on for responding to many conflict situations. Most importantly, this capacity cannot be developed without a full grasp of how each conflict evolves and in what context. This book is designed to help our students be prepared for this task by devoting full attention to the process of conflict emergence, escalation, de-escalation and settlement as well as structural characteristics of interlinked conflict system, and modes of interaction between conflict participants. As an attempt to reflect past studies on behavioral, psychological, and structural aspects of conflict dynamics, the volume sheds light on the options and choices available to various actors, social psychological aspects of adversarial interactions, and behaviors constrained by such relational characteristics as power symmetry or asymmetry.

The objective of student learning should focus on building the intellectual skills of conflict diagnosis that is essential prior to any efforts to initiate conflict settlement and resolution. In the field of conflict studies, there has been much discussion about conflict resolution practice and skills, but research on conflict analysis and dynamics has been relatively less emphasized. The intent of this manuscript is, in part, to fill the gap in providing conceptual frameworks that are needed for putting forward our questions about key international events. A list of complex issues is explored to investigate a conflict system as a dynamic phenomenon.

A single volume cannot cover every aspect of conflict analysis and resolution, since it is a vast field of study. This manuscript does not specifically examine conflict resolution practice in domestic settings nor does it cover a long list of conflict management techniques unless they are relevant to the regulation of antagonistic relations. In addition, it does not touch upon other thematic issues such as globalization, development, peacekeeping, environmental degradation, and so forth, in great detail, as a few textbooks in conflict studies do. Although they may be helpful in understanding broad social or international trends, this book's desire is to provide a more tightly integrated body of academic knowledge about conflict.

By better comprehending the sources, situation, context, and process of a conflict, we can develop informed policy options. Frictions in the current world order have created complex pictures of international decision making processes. On the international scene, diverse actors emerge and play different roles, either destructive or constructive, in the maintenance of international peace and security.

Two decades ago, the IR field did not pay much attention to disenchanted ethnic groups, warlords, and terrorist networks. Over the last decade, the IR field has evolved to include analysis of internal conflicts, as they spill over to international arenas. The US entrapment in the war in Iraq and Afghanistan illustrates the importance of factional, regional politics and agendas. The topics covered in this project are relevant to illuminating the behavior of international actors, both state and non-state.

Although I am solely responsible for any content of this book, I am intellectually indebted to Chadwick F. Alger, John W. Burton, J. David Singer, Johan Galtung, Christopher Mitchell, Jurgen Dedring, Marc Ross, Daniel Lieberfeld, Charles Lerche, Denise Williams, Nadim Rouhana, Richard Rubenstein, Sean Byrne, Charles Snare, Daniel Druckman, Ronald Fisher, Dennis Sandole, Dean Pruitt, Kevin Avruch, Peter Black, Johannes Botes, Tamra Pearson d'Estrée, Janie Leatherman, John Darby, Luc Reychler, Jim Whitman, Jeff Pickering, Jacob Bercovitch, Marty Rochester, Christos Kyrou, Abdul Aziz Said, Anthony Wanis-St.John, Kent Kille, Anne Snyder, and Earl Conteh-Morgan. I also benefited from work done by my colleagues at the Institute for Conflict Analysis and Resolution, including Andrea Bartoli, Marc Gopin, Wallace Warfield, Joe Scimecca, Hazel McFerson, Mark Katz, Terrence Lyons, Agnieszka Pacynzka, Susan Allen Nan, Susan Hirsch, Mara Schoeny, Solon Simmons, Mark Goodale, and other faculty members and associates.

In particular, Christopher Mitchell, Charles Leche, Daniel Lieberfeld, Mara Schoney and Mark Stover have reviewed different chapters of this book and offered valuable comments. In addition, Kate Romanov, Sylvia Susnjic, Eleftherios Michael, Joshua Ruebek and other graduate students supported the various stages of this project with their intellectual skills. Mary and Nimmy provided the most valuable support for stimulating my thoughts. Finally, I would like to express great appreciation for the encouragement of the Sage editor David Mainwaring who brought my work to fruition.

Centreville, Virginia, August 2007
Ho-Won Jeong

Dedication

For my mother

Part I
Concepts and Analysis

Approaches to Understanding Conflict

1

Conflict dates from the beginning of human history and will probably never end. Our survival on this planet hinges on how we manage the various features of conflict that is fuelled not only by seemingly incompatible interests and values but also by hostilities. The most destructive types of conflict such as interstate and civil wars consist of a coercive, violent mode of confrontation among adversaries. Whereas conflict embraces personal loss and societal destruction, its many features are not limited to physical violence. Non-violent forms of struggle are also prevalent in pursuit of different values and scarce resources. In bringing about important social change, resorting to force is neither necessary nor inevitable.

In order to explore strategies of managing and possibly resolving conflicts, our goal needs to be an in-depth analysis of human behaviour and its surrounding environment. It is generally accepted that psychological and behavioural elements, as well as structural conditions for alienation, combine to fuel conflict (Azar, 1986; Burton, 1990; Kelman, 1972; Mitchell, 1981). The examination of motivational and perceptional aspects of human decision making is essential to exploring the dynamics of mass violence, arms races, and international crises. Perceived and actual threats originate from the misinterpretation of intentions or a lack of trust fed by opposing interests and power struggles. In assessing protracted conflict, major attention has been paid to the very nature of a system that reproduces incompatibility among social units. A large scale conflict arises from collective human action often precipitated or controlled by a structural environment.

Each year 20 to 40 armed conflicts of various size rage around the world. Some conflicts have been successfully managed, but others have brought about devastating consequences such as wholesale killing (Marshall and Gurr, 2005).

In Cambodia, the unheralded mass extermination of the regime's enemy classes in the mid-1970s was marked by more than a million deaths; in Rwanda, indiscriminate killings of civilians by militia groups led to the loss of almost a million lives. Civil wars in Sudan and the Congo represented the most brutal internal wars, involving the deaths of as many as four million people, caused both directly and indirectly by armed fighting. Bosnia-Herzegovina experienced ethnic cleansing, expressed in mass killing of the innocent Muslim population by Serbian militia groups. The wars in Chechnya have been responsible for the most horrific human rights violations, while the civilian populations in Iraq have become terror victims and are hostage to religious, sectarian violence unleashed as a consequence of the US invasion and the fall of Saddam Hussein's government.

Whereas violence and intractable conflict seem certain to remain a prominent and tragic part of the human condition, some conflicts have been successfully transformed for resolution. Many decades of struggle in South Africa ended with the building of new institutions that transferred government power to the black majority. Although all of the parties still need to agree to the overall political relations, decades-old sectarian violence in Northern Ireland has been stopped. Three decades of civil war in Angola finally ceased in 2002, moving toward political transition. The reconstruction of war-torn societies was accompanied by negotiated settlements of civil wars in El Salvador, Guatemala, and Mozambique in the early and mid-1990s. These examples suggest that conflict can be transformed to avoid further hostilities and continuing violence. On the other hand, the Israeli–Palestinian conflict has been rekindled following a seven-year period (1993–2000) of efforts to bring harmony between the two adversaries. What are the differences that distinguish these conflicts? This is one of the questions which this book plans to address.

In understanding conflict, it is imperative to examine the sources of discontent and animosity, to identify the phases of evolving relationships between adversaries, and to illuminate the escalation of their struggles and the eventual recession of violent cycles to the peaceful resolution of differences. Given the enormity and severity of the consequences of uncontrolled violence, serious attention needs to be devoted to the regulation and management of hostile relations, even if it may take longer to resolve deadly conflicts.

The methods of intervention in any type of violence have to be associated with understanding the very nature, causes, and dynamics of the conflict. This book is intended to advance our knowledge of the psychological and structural conditions for conflict that are embedded at various levels of social and political systems. It covers the decision-making processes in the social dynamics of human interaction which can be transformed. Our analysis needs to include the causes of violent conflict and the interconnectivity of diverse elements within and between conflict systems. With this purpose in mind, the chapters in this book illustrate how conflict emerges and escalates prior to an endeavour to regulate and overcome antagonistic relationships. At the same time, multiple types of conflict relationship at the inter-group, national, international, and global levels will be discussed in the context of past and current efforts to manage irreconcilable differences.

The nature of conflict

Conflict represents the persistent and pervasive nature of inter-group and international competition among disparate interests and values that underlies power dynamics. The comprehension of mass violence and war needs to be based on an understanding of institutional roles besides the psychological and behavioural elements that instigate aggression. The experience of conflict is so basic that its negative effects spread to many aspects of a community's life.

The sources of adversarial relationships are not limited to tangible economic interests or control over power, but also extend to value and identity differences. The antagonisms in question may arise from interpersonal tensions between government leaders, labour management issues comprising multinational corporations and manual workers, disagreements between states on foreign policy directions, or international quarrels over trade imbalances and disparities in decision-making power at the World Bank or other international organizations.

Since conflict is entailed in diverse types of social interactions, its concepts have been applied to a variety of situations. The potential for conflict exists where opposing interests, values, or needs tinge our relationships with others. The latent conditions of conflict eventually translate into multiple forms of enmity in the visible issues.

In general, conflict is most popularly described as 'a struggle over values and claims to scarce status, power and resources' (Boulding, 1962: 5). The efforts to attain desired objects become more intense in the absence of agreed rules prescribing their equitable allocation. People's expectations alter in response to a shift in their social and economic environment. If governing norms are too rigid to be adjusted to new demands and expectations, such inflexibility breeds resentment utilized for the mobilization of groups that are discontent with the status quo (Mack and Snyder, 1971). In conflict situations, the dynamics of actions and counteractions inevitably engage attempts to control the other's behaviour, often with the intent to injure or destroy. In addition, violence may follow an unconstrained attempt to dominate in a fight over power, prestige, and material interests.

The essential nature of a conflict situation is easily understood in terms of the difficulties involved in meeting everyone's aspirations simultaneously (Pruitt and Kim, 2004). Goals and activities become incompatible when one's own interests are threatened by the actions of another. Parties to conflict make attempts to prevent each other from achieving desired objectives, in part, owing to perceptions of divergent interests. Tensions essentially emerge due to the pursuit of different outcomes or disagreement on the means to attain the same end.

Thus, a conflict situation is represented by perceived goal incompatibilities and attempts to control each other's choices, which generate adverse feelings and behaviour toward each other. In the end, 'what is at stake is the relationship itself and how the relationship is defined' (Lulofs and Cahn, 2000: 4). If the sources of discontent are left unaddressed, the conflict has the potential to affect negatively an interdependent relationship that is mutually beneficial.

The relationships in conflict are often described in terms of an exercise of coercive power. In a generic sense, power provides the ability to 'compel others to do something' and is also the source of people's ability to exercise control over decision making on valuable positions, limited goods and services (Winter, 1973: 5). In an adversarial relationship, a coercive process is linked to one party's efforts to change the other's objectives and behaviour. Thus power becomes an important element in the struggle for winning a conflict, since it is essential to engendering a desired difference in the targeted person's emotions and behaviour.

The context of defining conflict

In ordinary parlance, 'conflict' has been broadly associated with tensions surrounding decisions on various choices, sometimes being manifested in confrontations between social forces (Dahrendorf, 1959). The nature of the contest can be illustrated in terms of how issues arising from a variety of competitive social relationships are defined and framed. We confront an unlimited array of issues that stem from diverse social settings. Differences in opinions, disagreement, and arguments are ubiquitous in every human relationship, whether organizational, communal, or international. Long-term grievances over economic and social inequities are derived from a failure to enhance the quality of life of a particular group (Azar, 1986).

In a broad sense, the concept of conflict has been stretched and moulded to describe any discord resulting from almost every aspect of social situations. The existential, penetrable nature of decision making over incompatible choices can impact politics down to such mundane choices as where to shop and eat. The term 'conflict' has been applied to quarrels within a family and workplace arguments as well as violent clashes between states. Thus it was declared long ago that 'the distinctions between conflict and non-conflict are fuzzy at best and at worst are not made at all' (Mack and Snyder, 1971: 3).

While practitioners have often used 'conflict' and 'dispute' synonymously, John W. Burton (1990, 1997) developed clearer distinctions. According to Burton, conflict is interpreted in the context of a serious nature of challenges to the existing norms, relationships, and rules of decision making. On the other hand, the term 'dispute' applies to management issues and the control of discontent relating to the implementation of specific policies. In so doing, it may respond to the unfairness of authoritative decisions without questioning the legitimacy of decision making rooted in dominant values and established institutional procedures.

Polite disagreement, quarrel, litigation, and war differ in terms of the intensity and scope of activities (Burton and Dukes, 1990). The sources of misunderstanding and misperception are as diverse as a lack of information, misinformation, inadequate knowledge, and different interpretations of data or legal principles. Contradictory interests, hostile sentiments, and irreconcilable values are signified by antagonistic attitudes and behaviour. Beyond these elements, a destructive type of conflict involves attempts to inflict physical harm on the other side.

The bulk of interstate relations at a management level, like domestic affairs in an ordinary political setting, reflect disagreements within the existing system in lieu of hostile behaviour. If it is embedded in long-term rivalry, a simple argument may turn into a deadly contest with increased stakes. A protracted period of struggle stemming from value differences, as well as incongruent political and economic interests, is more serious than dissimilarities of opinion, mere bickering, and quarrel in electoral politics. In this situation, simply walking away from escalation becomes more difficult especially in the event of poorly handled inter-group cleavages spilling over into organized, armed clashes.

In a broad context, conflict can be compared with an intense form of competition. It is inevitable, even without direct contact, as exemplified in the efforts to expand sales in a consumer market. In the natural world, competition is considered to be an underlying rule of the game for survival, regulated by the surrounding environment, between and within species in search for food, shelter, and other limited resources.

Thus competition between behavioural units is the most universal and basic form of interaction in the world of living things, which is full of many mutually incompatible positions, for example, in the quest for scarce food or prestigious jobs. If the struggle is waged more directly and consciously, it may be regarded as a form of 'conflict'. In fact, competition is not identical to conflict, because the purpose of competition is winning valuable or scarce objects, not the destruction or injury of opponents (Mack and Snyder, 1971).

In economic transactions and sports, competition is governed by an acknowledged process of decision making. Many forms of competitive interaction may become so highly regulated and institutionalized that the participants do not challenge the fairness of the rules that determine the outcome. Thus, disputants in a legal proceeding, partisans in a legislative body, or candidates in an electoral race are seeking irreconcilable goals by means of procedures that may be so well accepted by all of the participants that violence is eschewed and hostility remains minimal.

Many types of competition are resolved automatically through the impersonal forces of economic and social transactions. Even market mechanisms, however, do not operate in a vacuum without regard to pre-existing power relations and other types of arrangement that favour one over another. For example, by privileging certain communication skills, personal background, and social status, labour markets advantage one group of individuals over another. Owing to the inevitable interference of informal influence and recognition, sole reliance on market forces has not always guaranteed fairness, and has sometimes contradicted the general principles of equity and protection of public interests.

Regulations usually embody rules that bind acceptable means of contest to be adopted in pursuing contradictory goals by prescribing and proscribing conduct. In general, competitors are limited regarding what they can do to each other in the course of their efforts. Established procedures and rules may clarify the legitimate forms and degree of coercion, in addition to setting a limit on the circumstances under which a permissible level of force will even be tolerated.

The degree of institutionalization of competition differs according to how the rules have been internalized by the participants and have been supported by traditional norms or broadly accepted criteria. Thus the effectiveness in the control of conduct is affected by not only sanctions, available for the enforcement of rules, but also an internal sense of moral obligations.

Disputes can be provoked by broken agreements, unobserved norms, and unfair rules on access to resources. The established remedies may include group sanctions, arbitration, or court procedures. Disputes within an institutional framework can also be settled either by direct bargaining or facilitated by professionals (Burton, 1997).

International disputes can be handled by institutional procedures derived from environmental or trade treaties. For example, quarrels, stemming from unfair practice in the exchange of goods and services, have been mandated to the World Trade Organization's arbitration panels which interpret rules agreed upon by member states. The institutionalized rules reflect the need for the professional management of international disputes.

Fragile political and judicial institutions, in combination with ambiguities in rules, lead to unregulated competition and struggle. In this situation, conflicts outside judicial and bargaining processes emerge, along with declining central authorities. The requirements for new rules arise from modifications in technology and economic systems that create uncertainties. A lack of a world authority, in conjunction with a weak international legal system, has been one of the main obstacles to regulating the clashing interests and differences in values that are commonly manifested in an international conflict (Goodman, 2005; Waltz, 2007).

Given anarchy in an international system, many serious quarrels have often been handled through military force. The US invasion of Iraq in 2003 represents the ignorance of established international procedures such as votes at the UN Security Council following the UN inspection of Iraq for weapons of mass destruction. The use of force and torture can be asymmetric and unjust in places such as China-occupied Tibet, but the international community has not made more concerted efforts to mitigate that suffering. New types of violence (such as terrorism), which are increasingly prominent in the international scene, certainly require different approaches to our understanding of conflict that cannot be contained in normal interstate relations.

Socio-psychological dynamics

Diverse forms of competition between parties with incompatible goals can be explained, in part, by subjective character. However, any events also have to reflect an underlying objective situation that contains contentious values and power imbalances. Equally importantly, inequitable social and economic relations have to be felt by those who organize protest. Thus, 'material bases of social life as well as psychological aspects of social relationships' have the main impact on behavioural responses and interactions (Fisher, 1990: 31).

The subjective side of conflict, anchored in perceptions of each other's intentions and interpretations of behavioural responses, suggests that decision making is not always rational, far from the reflection of the real events in the external world. Poor communication, miscommunication, and the stereotyping of adversaries are often ascribed to the misperceptions and misrepresentation of evolving events. The degree to which subjective components differ from the objective reality can be an indicator of how realistic an actor's response to a given conflict situation might be.

Differences in perceived interests, values, and needs are perhaps the most basic elements in the motivations behind social conflict. Inter-group conflict often represents different ways of life and ideologies with implications for incongruent views about relationships with others. Feelings of injustice emerge from the suppression of inherent social needs and values that have existential meanings and which cannot be compromised. In discussion about substantive issues, however, the perceptional difference alone does not illustrate the existence of objective realities that are independent of the awareness of opposing parties.

Inter-group relations are constrained by a superimposed political structure in addition to their own internal dynamics. Thus the analysis of social conflict needs to focus on how group processes are linked to structural conditions such as oppressive social relations and exploitative economic systems. Diverse dimensions of conflict dynamics can be illuminated in terms of the nature of evolving power relations in favour of one party over another as well as psychological impediment. For example, the Chinese quest for superpower status and the US response reflect the objective reality of a rapid increase in Chinese military strength and economic wealth, accumulated as a result of the huge trade surplus with other parts of the world. At the same time, US-China relations face different expectations and psychological uncertainties about the future roles of China, and American acceptance of the ambitious new power that challenges Western democratic values and political interests.

The mixture of objective and subjective elements varies under different circumstances, which are influenced by the level of power asymmetry and other aspects of conflict relationships such as moral asymmetry. A general audience can accept the moral and political legitimacy of each partisan's claims differently. While one party may lack the objective physical capacity to change the other's behaviour, its moral legitimacy may draw public support that creates a new reality for the struggle waged by marginalized groups.

Even though China has far superior military and diplomatic power unmatched by the exiled government of Tibet, the latter's yearning for autonomy and freedom has been widely supported by many Western politicians and by the public, who are sympathetic to the Tibetan cause. In creating a new subjective reality, the Chinese government has completely rewritten existing Tibetan history with the intention of distorting the objective historical facts.

The relationships between subjective and objective elements in each party's decision making also change along with the evolution of conflict. Negative psychological processes, which obscure objective reality, are derived from the escalation of hostilities. Emotional aspects, including anger, hate, pain, and fear, intensify following material loss and physical destruction.

The de-escalation of adversarial interactions is accompanied by the objective realities of the conflict's devastating impact and ensuing efforts to assess the existing realities more seriously. While changes in enemy perceptions are necessary for reducing mutual enmities, it has to be embedded in alterations in certain realities, involving the removal of specific policies or visible actions (for example, economic sanctions or military strategies) that continue to cause harm to others.

The endeavours to change psychological relationships (reflecting hatred and resentment) will be fruitless as long as the objective realities of alienation and marginalization continue under oppressive political arrangements (Jeong, 2005). Understanding an adversarial relationship would have to go beyond the issues of misperceptions and emotional attributes of conflict, entailing decision-making power which dictates substantive outcomes.

The difficulties in the establishment of objective reality through the subjective understanding of the world have lent to an intersubjective frame of conflict analysis that allows the meanings of conflict to be constructed through social interaction. Perception and cognition are biased by our values and motivations, whereas communication is often charged with emotions and misinterpretations. Thus, 'the reality out of which we operate' has to emerge from our shared senses, which also reflect our subjective experience in an objective world (Fisher, 1990: 6).

Conflict situations

In conflict situations, two or more social entities are connected to at least one form of antagonistic interaction, through interference with one another's efforts to satisfy their needs and interests at the expense of those of the other. The perceived goal incompatibilities are likely to promote conditions for adversarial relationships, since the other entity is seen to be a barrier to achieving the goal. A manifest struggle can be waged through the obstruction of the other party's quest for valuable objects. The contradictory claims to scarce status, power, and resources are often represented in purposeful efforts made by actors to defeat, thwart, remove, or at least neutralize their rivals (Coser, 1964).

The contest is inevitable when the goals of opponents are mutually exclusive as a result of the negative impact of one side's choice on the other. Thus, a manifest conflict process involves direct and indirect efforts to undermine the adversaries' goal-seeking capability. The manifest struggle is contrasted with latent conflict situations in which groups may not be even aware of their opposing interests. Disharmonious interests between economic classes, for example, would not automatically translate into specific expressions of organized interests without mobilization efforts.

As discussed above, the most commonly accepted description of a conflict situation focuses not only on incompatible ends but also on irreconcilable relationships. Goal incompatibility, in itself, does not necessarily constitute antagonistic conflict situations, in that the parties might still find ways to live in peaceful coexistence (Bartos and Wehr, 2002). When one party attempts to control another in order to deal with the incompatibility, this can result in a process of inflicting psychological or physical harm. Such negative interactions based on hostile emotions can be fuelled by means that are not acceptable to the other side.

The emotional realities, embedded in interactional dynamics, can be defined by the underlying psychological patterns of a struggle. Hostility and other related feelings can be ascribed to the cognitive appraisal of threat to one's own interests and existence. The perceptions of threat, along with an affective reaction to the other's aggressive behaviour, activate intense feelings of anger, anxiety, and fear.

Incompatibilities in goals can be more easily managed or removed by the clarification of misunderstandings if the perceived difference is illusory, or is not based on real sources. If each party's intentions are not to obtain the same object desired by the other, an understanding can be reached to permit each party to accept the fact that they are not actually attempting to achieve the goal believed to be the same.

Different degrees and types of goal incompatibility shape the course of a conflict. The de-escalation of conflict may follow the abandonment of goals pursued earlier when the goals cease to be perceived as attractive. In particular, the appeal of goals is likely to be reduced by a rise in the costs involved in acquiring them.

Deep divisions can also be overcome through transformation of the structures of goal incompatibilities. The salience of goals may differ, depending on the level of the stakes and involvement of each party in their pursuit. There will no longer be a conflict if one party gives up the special interest the other desires. The partial attainment of goals through their subdivision may also give rise to some satisfaction. Disputants can jointly seek mutually desirable solutions by pursuing a superordinate goal. Integrative solutions based on mutual satisfaction strengthen collaborative relationships, maximizing long-term benefits.

Intractable conflict

Intractable conflicts are highly pervasive, encompassing many aspects of the relationship, often among multiple actors. They can take place between individuals, between ethnic groups, and between sovereign states. In contrast with easily manageable interest-based disputes, disagreement over religious or other types of value (with existential meanings) can evolve into threats to individual or collective identity. Large scale inter-group conflicts such as civil wars tend to add an enduring and intransigent character to the experience of total investment in the fight for survival.

Whereas intractable conflict may begin in much the same manner as mundane conflict, 'a distinct set of dynamics, circumstances, and issues' makes prolonged conflicts even more immune to resolution efforts (Coleman, 2000: 429). Their effects become widespread in almost every dimension of human life with the threat of annihilation accompanied by an entrenched and dangerous process of escalation. While there are objectively identifiable issues and external situations, the perceived intractability of a conflict is sustained by subjective processes of meaning making that contribute to inflexibility.

Partisans are not likely to change their positions on needs or values that are regarded as vital to their own core identities and survival. The questions of clashing religious, ethical, or personal beliefs are not easily compromised when challenges to them generate feelings of threat. Most importantly, however, the inevitability of a costly fight becomes acceptable due to systemic and psychological distortions within a group or country (Babbitt, 2006).

Repeated and concerted attempts to resolve deep-rooted, long drawn-out conflicts are resisted by the delegitimization of each other's security needs. The denial by one party of the humanity of the other is a basis for the justification of the continuing conflict. One's own beliefs on physical, territorial, cultural, and economic survival become justifications for every expression of conflict behaviour. Because of the emotional involvement and irreversibility, partisans have a strong desire for vengeance. Pessimism prevails in feelings of hopelessness about the potential for ending the vicious cycle of attacks and revenge.

Conflict is often negatively transformed through the ups and downs of a continuing fight. An unresolved conflict over a long period of time, for example, between the United States and Iran, between Israel and Syria, and between the Greeks and Turks in Cyprus, is likely to resurface repeatedly with intervals of dormancy and activity. A high level of intensity and destructiveness is maintained by a sustained period of escalation, before intense physical or psychological fighting eventually subsides. Temporary settlements may be reached at the end of an intense period, but each ending awaits another ebb and flow of confrontations and hostilities. The persistence through the repeated cycle over time is characterized by sporadic increases in occasional outbreaks of violence. These protracted conflicts have lasted for several generations in Northern Ireland, Arab–Israeli rivalry, and the contentious relations between North Korea and the USA.

The psychological states and experience of intractable conflict reflect chronic feelings of uncertainty, stress, and grief in company with a sense of hardship, lack of control, and helplessness, particularly in such places as Palestine and Chechnya. At the same time, psychological mechanisms are adapted to the challenges of intractable conflict, including the ability of endurance (Pruitt, 2005). Positive self-identity is boosted in a struggle with an enemy to strengthen determination and solidarity. Patriotism becomes a rallying point in withstanding enemy attacks and absorbing sacrifices. Threat is emphasized to cope with chronic stress and to mobilize the society to win.

External conflict distracts attention from internal problems, furnishes unity and coherence, and allows the development of a sense of purpose (Deutsch, 1994). On the other hand, a deep investment in the continuation of the conflict frequently stems from displacing the original sources of grievance into such non-rational psychological elements as scapegoating others for purposes of tension relief and the projection of disapproved aspects of oneself onto the adversaries. In many tribal communities that lost their land to invaders, scapegoating is sadly reflected in the self-infliction of wounds visible in alcoholism and family abuse that were previously unprecedented.

As reflected in inter-ethnic conflicts in the Balkans and Northern Ireland, some psycho-analysts argue that longevity of conflict is ascribed to the accumulation of animosities and other negative emotions that are often supported by collective memory (Volkan, 2006). In intractable conflict, collective emotional orientations determine the content and nature of social identity. Institutional or popular narratives, based on a shared account of the history, fulfil psychological needs through the glorification of past events. At the same time, a selective bias contributes to the dehumanization of adversaries.

Protracted civil wars in Africa tend to perpetuate a culture of violence and fear, which radicalizes militia groups and condones human rights violations. The new generations, who are growing up in an intractable conflict, have no conception of reality other than fighting and believe that it is normal to live in such a society. The bedrock of intense social violence is found where physical or emotional abuse, along with gross injustice, is routine.

Constructive versus destructive conflict

If conflict is considered, in itself, to be neither bad nor good, an important question is what conditions give rise to a constructive or destructive conflict process.

What are the criteria for being constructive or destructive? How does a conflict move in a destructive, rather than a constructive, direction? When can a conflict become more constructive? It is the context of a struggle and communication patterns that, in part, determine the nature of a conflict.

The constructive or destructive phenomena of conflict can be framed by the feasibility of transforming adversarial relationships, being enhanced by mutual understanding. Distinctions can be made as regards the processes facilitating or inhibiting communication. The consequences of the struggle can be judged in the context of achieving justice for the victims. The positive and negative aspects of conflict also need to be assessed in light of the means of waging conflict, violent versus non-violent, which have long-term consequences for future relations. The orientations of conflict, understood by each party, are likely to influence their choices of action such as the destruction of adversaries or the pursuit of mutually acceptable goals.

Functions of conflict may simply include the search for an outlet to discharge an aggressive instinct in enmity outside of the group. As the struggle becomes an objective, in itself, adversaries may feel that they simply have to fight, no matter about what. Thus conflict waged for internal psychological needs does not serve any purpose other than the release of tension, making it difficult to bring about a negotiated settlement. The failure to control negative emotions and feelings allows conflict to take its own course, independent of original causes and triggers.

The increasing alienation of disenchanted groups is prone to create clashing value systems and subcultures. The dysfunctions of social conflict, manifested, for instance, in the rise of ultra-nationalist movements in Europe, are revealed by the attack on the core values of Western democratic society, maladjustment, and disintegration. Unregulated conflict interferes with the normal operation of any organization or system, and reduces internal cohesion, impeding clear and effective communication. Resources are mobilized for destructive purposes, instead of productive social and economic activities.

By nature, a destructive conflict is sustained by escalatory spirals that produce self-perpetuating damages following a heavy reliance on threats and coercion. Violent behaviour, encouraged by a dehumanization process, is designed to cause harm to other conflict participants (Kellett and Dalton, 2001). A destructive course of hostile interactions has a very high potential for aimless violence, deception, and power manipulation. Excessive violence by militia groups in places such as Darfur in Sudan needs to be controlled by humanitarian intervention forces.

Although conflicts tend to have negative connotations, not every conflict is harmful if it ultimately produces a creative element for changing societies, while achieving the goals and aspirations of individuals and groups. If the outcome brings about positive changes, as demonstrated by not only apologies and compensation for the past abuse but also future prevention of victimization, that can be considered to be constructive. Non-violent conflict that is aimed at the transformation of oppressive relations is inherently good and serves as a vehicle of liberation, in contrast to the consequences of accepting the superficial harmony of the status quo.

In change oriented theories, conflict is viewed as an inevitable process of social progress. The costs and benefits of the conflict ought to be judged in the context of any given situation involving the availability of alternative means to violent resistance. Even though a positive social change, geared toward justice and equality, must be gained through struggle, the sole dependence on coercive force perpetuates a cycle of violence, making conflict resolution a more distant possibility. As illustrated by the example of terrorist acts, anyone who depends on violent means for short-term success loses moral credibility and authority, no matter how justifiable the sources of grievance might be.

A conflict becomes disparaging when it turns into a mere power struggle for unilateral gains. A positive outcome of conflict cannot be produced if the participants are dissatisfied in the process of settlement, retaining a sense of loss. When one party achieves a victory, that leaves a bitter legacy of defeat experienced by their adversaries. The decrease in discord would be assisted by the existence of a prior experience of cooperation besides efforts to explore a creative response to difficult issues. Obtaining a mutually satisfactory agreement relies on the circumstances for negotiation that allow partisans to maximize their joint outcomes.

Root causes of conflict

Most conflicts involve value differences and power disparities, whereas misperception and miscommunication play an important role in the evolution of adversarial relationships. Even though a conflict may originate from economic and other material sources, it can be quickly expanded to identity differences with escalation. In most complex conflicts, a variety of issues, such as the availability of resources and basic human needs, are interrelated with each other.

Substantive issues of conflict can be tied to a range of contested objects (namely, wealth, power, and prestige) and their conditions of availability. In addition, reasons for the struggle may be based on feelings of deprivation, injustice, inequity, and frustration beyond incompatible roles and positions. A challenge to the existing relations also arises when the expectations of various groups are not met in a given social structure.

Manifold socio-economic and cultural concerns are often mixed with political issues related to the status of minority groups (Ross, 2007). In Europe, the prohibition of Muslim women's headscarves has become a symbolic issue in national politics, because the matter raises questions about tolerance and diversity in a pluralistic society. The long animosity between Tutsis and Hutus since the independence of Rwanda is characterized by group competition traced back to the colonial period. The political and military elite of the Tutsis and Hutus have organized violent campaigns to dominate state institutions. In Sudan, Burundi and other ethnically divided African countries, the discontent of marginalized ethnic or racial groups resulted in several decades of civil wars. Political violence, as happened with the Muslim youth riot in France in October and November of 2005, can be attributed to a systemic failure to incorporate marginalized groups.

Deterrence strategies, based on threats and punishment, are unsuccessful, or inoperative, when the accumulation of deep resentment by the oppressed groups seeks an outlet for violence (Burton, 2001). Fear does not always suppress human behaviour. Many conflicts of injustice are rooted in a history of colonialism, ethnocentrism, racism, sexism, or human rights abuses.

As each group wants to maximize its influence in a tense stalemate, a struggle for dominance is not easily amenable to quick resolution. In a situation featuring the severe imbalance of power, the more powerful are inclined to exploit or abuse the less powerful. Salient inter-group distinctions serve as a means of maintaining or strengthening one's predominant power base. In an ethnic or racial conflict, hierarchical relations have been established by a denial of access to decision making and the rejection of power sharing political institutions. Along with these circumstances, the deprivation of cultural autonomy and economic opportunities may instigate an uprising. The imposition of policies on the prevention of ethnic language education in Kosovo was one of the most contentious issues felt by Albanian inhabitants prior to their insurgent movements of the mid-1990s.

Inequitable access to economic and social opportunities is often associated with a lack of political participation. The dissolution of the federal government in the former Yugoslavia has followed economic collapse in the midst of rising levels of hostilities among multi-ethnic groups and nationalities. The primary issues of decades old conflict in Northern Ireland have revolved around the Catholics' desire to be united with Southern Ireland and the Protestants' insistence on staying within the UK. This struggle reflects, in part, a history of political dominance, economic inequality, and disparity in access to education, health care, housing, and jobs.

Levels of analysis

The complexity of conflict differs, depending on whether it focuses on interpersonal, inter-group, and international relations or global agendas. The sources and situations of conflict reflect issues at different levels of relationships. A deep rift, rooted in organizational structures, differs from mere emotional, personality conflict. The internal split, derived from competition among multiple factions, has an impact on capabilities to fight with external enemies.

The recognition of divisions within a multi-ethnic and multiracial society interferes with various types of decision making in politics and social life such as the selection of friends. In establishing their relationships with others, people tend to perceive themselves in terms of racial, ethnic, religious, or other social categories. Reflecting the antagonism among members of diverse communities, elections in Bosnia-Herzegovina have further deepened political divisions with voting patterns roughly along ethnic lines.

These categorizations have complicated human relations at various levels. While the political elite may pursue territorial ambitions and compete for economic resources, excessive nationalistic aspirations have led to the denial of self-determination for minorities. The treatment of Muslims in American society may mirror a larger public perception in the aftermath of the terrorist attacks.

In more repressive societies, an individual level conflict may be traced back to structural causes of injustice. For example, a quarrel between Tibetan and Chinese youths in a train can be seen not only in terms of personal dispute, but also in the overall context of the Chinese occupation and domination of Tibet. The police may easily accuse the Tibetan youth of subversive activity if he engages in arguments with a member of the dominant Han nationality. Thus, ethnic and racial conflicts have implications for the conditions of individual well-being.

While the state is the most important unit in international relations, ethnic, religious, and other identity based groups have played an important role in determining contemporary conflict issues across or within state territorial borders. An identity group in multi-ethnic states makes an essential demand for autonomy. In the aftermath of two World Wars and colonial struggles, many groups have been put under the control of new sovereign state power that does not afford political and economic opportunities for minorities. The minority rights of Kurds scattered across several different Middle Eastern countries have been suppressed in Turkey, Iran, and Syria. The status of Kashmir has been a source of long contention among many factional groups that have different affiliations with India and Pakistan. Tibet and Aceh were annexed by China and Indonesia, respectively, without the consent of the inhabitants. The recognition of group-level rights has become essential to the solution of many contentious contemporary conflicts.

The outcomes of conflict at a global level often reflect power asymmetry among multiple actors, including tribal, indigenous populations, advocacy groups, and multinational corporations in such issue areas as rainforest destruction, overfishing, and many other important issues that will determine the future of human civilization (Leatherman and Webber, 2006). Many non-state actors such as environmental and religious groups operate not just at local but also global levels. In dealing with global issues, opposing positions may emerge between blocs of countries across different issue areas. On global warming, in concord with China and India, the Bush Administration opposed the European initiatives to implement an international treaty on the control of greenhouse gas emission levels by each country. Japan, Norway, and Iceland defied an international ban on whaling despite opposition from other Western countries, which gave voice to the public outcry, responding to protests of anti-whaling citizen groups.

Hostilities at a given level can affect the dynamics of conflict relationships at other levels in complex ways. When President Bush called Kim Jong-Il, the North Korean leader, a 'pygmy', it did not help to manage the issue of nuclear weapons programmes pursued by Pyongyang. In its negotiations with the American government, the North Korean leadership has continued to complain that it was not treated equally and respectfully, justifying its position in not giving in to demands of nuclear disarmament. The accusations of alleged Pakistani support for the ousted Taliban forces by President Hamid Karzai of Afghanistan have been enmeshed in his acrimonious relationship with Pakistan's President Musharraf, hampering US war efforts against al-Queda.

According to Immanuel Kant's moral theory, human behaviour should not be treated differently at personal, communal, national, and international levels. The behaviour of individuals seeking recognition in society is no different from that of identity groups whose political status and legitimacy is denied. The need for development and autonomy of the individual is often explained by the same motivation of an identity group seeking human security. The suppression of individual esteem and group autonomy has generated a demand for human rights protection and self-determination. In the aftermath of some recent civil wars, government leaders (for example, Slobodan Milošević in former Yugoslavia and Charles Taylor in Liberia), responsible for atrocities and massacres, were brought to the international criminal court, even though they claimed that these acts were committed by their subordinates.

Overview

Every conflict involves political, ethical, and psychological dimensions. Identity and power differentials underlie the social, organizational dynamics of conflict. The motivations for waging conflict range from the pursuit of narrow interests by sectarian groups to the promotion of justice. The sources of conflict in many non-Western societies are rooted in imbalance in economic and political systems that encompass disparity in the distribution of wealth, legislative and administrative power among ethnic, religious groups. The global context of conflict spawns opposition to discriminatory treatment and protests against war or environmental destruction.

In general, conflicts can be categorized in terms of types of actor and adversarial action, ranging from war to non-violent struggles. International conflict is not necessarily restricted to hostile interstate relationships or ethnic warfare. The response to terrorism, for example, has global implications that require analysis of complex relationships between the emerging political forces in the Islamic world and the legacy of Western domination in the Middle East.

Interaction patterns in conflict situations can be ascribed, in part, to the attitudes and behaviours of the parties. In addition to the psychological basis of animosity, we need to examine relationships between parties, not only symmetric but also asymmetric, on both political and moral dimensions. The process of actualization of latent sources of conflict has an impact on the formation of issues beyond the selection of responses, whether violent or nonviolent. In addition, many conflicts reflect characteristics of different issue areas: ethnic, racial, religious, labour, environmental, etc.

This volume focuses on the causes, processes, and conditions of conflict as well as the behavioural patterns involved in antagonistic interactions between adversaries. More specifically, it explains the escalation, entrapment, de-escalation, and termination of conflict. In so doing, it sheds light on diverse phenomena, ranging from group dynamics to the structural transformation of an adversarial social system. The establishment of a new relationship would not naturally follow an official agreement reached at formal negotiation settings without healing past grievances.

Whereas this introductory chapter has reviewed basic concepts and principles, the next chapter illustrates the analytical frameworks and elements that are entailed in understanding conflict. In Chapter 3, various sources of conflict are attributed to dysfunctional psychological mechanisms, social systems, and the role of identity and power in the creation of social boundaries and hierarchies. Chapter 4 examines conflict situations in light of socio-psychological aspects of competitive behaviour and the role of cognitive and institutional processes in decision making.

Chapter 5 assesses a conflict process in the context of the relations both between and within parties as well as the external constraints on inter-group interaction. The complexity of conflict relationships is discussed in Chapter 6, providing a typology of different patterns of interlinkage between actors, issues, and time. In addition to deepening our understanding of an action-reaction model, Chapter 7 covers organizational, behavioural variables involved in conflict dynamics.

In explaining escalation, Chapter 8 reviews conflict spiral models that feature the psycho-political dynamics to dominate each other. Chapter 9 looks at de-escalation in terms of diminishing hostilities and other conditions for bringing about conciliation. Specific strategies and modes of de-escalatory action are discussed in Chapter 10. After reviewing the types of conflict outcome, Chapter 11 focuses on the implications of various methods of ending struggle.

Conflict Analysis Framework

2

Multidimensional frameworks of analysis are necessary to examine conflicts comprising diverse types of parties and issues. Reflecting differing degrees of complexity, each conflict is most likely to have a varied temporal process and outcomes. The profile of conflict situations emerges from investigating the context and dynamics of adversarial relationships. In addition, a conflict 'tree' can be used to shed light on the root causes, manifested tensions, and their effects.

Mapping methods provide a system for illustrating the scope of a conflict by assessing the goals of the parties, the type of their relationship, and the issues in contention. Identifying the parties to the conflict is an essential step prior to understanding their positions, interests, and capacities as well as the level of external support. The evolution of relationships between parties and their social context can be examined in terms of short-term and long-term dynamics. A timeline tends to be formulated on the basis of how the main parties see the significance of each event, especially in a long-running conflict.

The processes for conflict management or resolution can be clarified by exploring strategies that respond to the origins of contention, for instance, related to security, political, economic, and social issues (Sandole, 2006). The analysis of linkages between micro-level activities and macro-level forces covers the main obstacles working against a peaceful solution and the internal and external factors behind prolonging the conflict. Overall, mapping entails essential information that is fundamental in planning a constructive response, including the control of violence (Wehr, 1979). An important purpose of conflict mapping is to help opposing parties distinguish their existing positions from their true interests and needs, while clarifying a variety of options for settling the costly struggle.

Focus and elements of analysis

Each analytical step needs to enclose a set of guiding questions towards enhancing our understanding of the hidden and manifest issues embedded in a given conflict. The predominant trends in the specific areas of conflict assist in the examination of the potential for runaway scenarios of hostile interaction. Even though each conflict situation may be unique, indicators can be developed to illuminate relationship dynamics in a variety of contexts. In addition, a particular flash point can be revealed by a timeline which focuses on the evolution of relationships between actors.

Indicators are needed to reduce a complex reality to a few concrete dimensions and to denote valuable pointers against which to monitor any changes. Each party most often has its own perceptions of adversaries' goals, attitudes, and behaviour that differ from those of the adversaries themselves. In the exchange of each other's experiences and perceptions, separate cognitive maps of the same situation represent different viewpoints (Fisher, et al., 2000). Thus, it is imperative to have a mix of perception based indicators (embodying the meaning of conflict as held by the parties themselves) and objective indicators (corresponding to existing realities as defined by outsiders).

It is not only types of party, goal, issue, and strategy that characterize the nature of conflict, but also the modes of process and outcomes of struggles. As is illustrated by Figure 2.1, mapping methods can be formulated to identify and assess key conflict actors, particularly from the following perspectives of 1) interests, values, and underlying needs related to motives; 2) goals (represented by purposes and aspirations); 3) issues (derived from concerns about

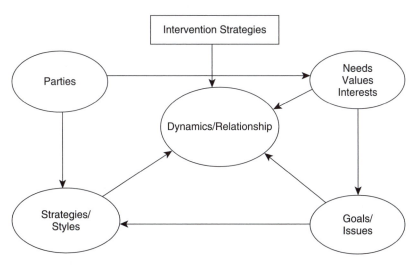

Figure 2.1   Conflict mapping

well-being). These factors play an important role in not only shaping conflict strategies but also moulding dynamics linked to mutual relationships. The mapping should permit interveners to identify specific behaviours which ignite confrontation and tend to perpetuate the escalation of conflict.

The groups involved in conflict can be categorized in terms of dissimilar levels of commitment to the struggle and different abilities to mobilize resources as well as their attitudes toward each other (associated with feelings of 'like' and 'dislike'). Issues characterizing conflict may originate from incompatible values, interests, and needs. The salience of goals (such as survival) and related issues (for example, the attainment of scarce resources) constrain the range of choices. The different degrees of goal incompatibilities have an impact on the levels of difficulty encountered in reaching a negotiated settlement. Adjustments in strategies and orientations toward struggle are likely to be revealed by changes in the goals that are, in part, derived from the costs of conflict and the prospects of winning. Each party's perceptions of the salience of their own and the other party's goals will impact the degree of willingness to accept compromise.

Relationship dynamics based on each adversary's identity, esteem, and sense of reality explain the levels of a conflict's pervasiveness and duration. The relationships between the parties are, to a great extent, shaped by the strategies of struggle and the nature of contentious issues. In coping with conflict, each partisan may choose avoidance, yielding to, and contending with the other side's demands as well as accommodation. These behavioural styles evolve during the progression of conflict along with changes in the stakes and the availability of alternative means to adversarial struggles provided by mediation or other types of intervention. In formulating strategies to prevent escalation, third party intervention needs to shed light on the destructive behaviour that propels an undesirable course of events (Isenhart and Spangle, 2000).

Parties

In actor analysis, mapping can focus on individuals or groups that are in a position to alter conflict dynamics in one way or another. Efforts should be made to figure out those who might be affected by the outcome of a particular conflict, as well as those who are currently concerned about the situation, but have not yet become vocal. The modifications of power alignments between primary contestants are visualized, in part, on the basis of availability of potential allies (and their possible entry points for action). Each partisan has a different capacity to pursue their salient goals, articulate issues, and express interests, as derived from different values and needs.

Organized movements such as Hamas and Hezbollah have developed not only structures of armed resistance but also parallel political representation. At the initial and even escalation stages of conflict, parties may not be willing to recognize their adversaries as a legitimate group with whom to negotiate.

The Irish Republican Army (IRA) and the Palestine Liberation Organization (PLO) were regarded as terrorist groups, and banned from any official contact by both the British and US governments, prior to initiating discussion about peace agreements.

The main contenders are persons, groups, or institutions that are engaged in adversarial activities and have a main stake in a conflict outcome. They directly oppose one another in pursuit of respective goals. Various features of conflict groups can be illuminated by membership types, prevailing attitudes toward existing policy or relationships, the legitimacy of their goals and means for struggle, and types of mobilizational resource. Ideologically based or more value oriented groups do not eagerly search for areas of compromise in order to promote their moral causes or political convictions such as the legality of abortion.

In protracted conflict situations, contestants have direct allies or sympathizers at varying points in time. The ally's support increases the total resources available to their primary actors. The expectations and mobilization efforts of the original contestants can change with the support of new allies. The interests of allies, drawn into the fray, are not always the same as those of the original parties. While activists get involved in promoting a social cause and see a conflict's larger social context, advocates are more oriented towards protecting the interests of victimized groups with a focus on a fair process (Blalock, 1989).

Intermediaries can be mediators, arbitrators, and others who are in a position to facilitate a settlement or resolution process. Impartial third parties attempt to explore the areas of mutual interest among all of the parties. In conflicts of any complexity and duration, third parties may simply not be able to remain neutral mediators (Kleiboer, 1996). Others may play critical roles in replenishing the resources needed for settlement or in limiting the use of extreme means through their efforts to control violence. In an atrocious conflict, external intervention may be required to regulate the intensity of the armed struggle prior to initiating any process of settlement unless the primary contestants put self-limits on the conduct of their behaviour. There are, then, different circumstances and conditions under which third party intervention contributes to the mitigation of conflict.

Conflict processes and outcomes affect diverse actors in a direct or indirect manner (Hocker and Wilmot, 1978). Veto groups (such as insurgent groups opposed to political stability in Iraq) may not have decision-making power, but do have a capacity to block or sabotage a political process. Even if they are negatively affected, many vulnerable persons or groups, for example, inhabitants in the Amazon rainforests affected by oil drilling, do not have an ability to prevent the intruder's actions.

While existing groups may initiate conflict, new actors may emerge as a result of the conflict itself. Involuntary groupings are mainly determined by inherited characteristics (based on not only such physical types as race, sex, and age but also kinship and ethnicity) over which members do not have any control. Party boundaries may not be clearly demarcated, as is illustrated by the fact that members of conflict groups are often recruited from a wide spectrum of social categories and classes. In unorganized political violence such as riots and armed rebellions, parties often have illusive representation.

Parties differ with regard to the level of their engagement in conflict events given their diverse capacities to make decisions and act. The increased number of constituencies and their divergent interests generate intransigence in decision making. The heterogeneity of group membership creates difficulties in reaching consensus on the means, even if they may agree on the general objectives of their movements and specific goals.

The ability of a party to be effectively engaged in a conflict is connected to the degree of internal cohesiveness and the extent of coordination among member activities (McGrath and Argote, 2001). In terms of internal decision making, loosely organized racial and gender groups are less effective in the development of effective strategies for struggle than are tightly organized sectarian groups. In particular, the strengths of voluntary associations fluctuate, as their members' commitment and loyalty are not consistent with a weak internal bond.

In a nutshell, the differences among actors can be identified by their goals, attitudes toward particular issues, motivations to realize their interests, and capacities to manage relationships with other actors. Each party's main goals may suggest its expectations of conflict outcomes. The level of the party's expectations is certainly affected by its ability to mobilize the most important types of resources for the struggle.

Goals

In conflict situations, 'goals' can be defined as desirable future conditions that originally motivate the partisans to contest with each other. While tangible goals may include territorial, political, and economic advantages, less tangible goals involve prestige, honour, and respect. The pursuit of these goals entails costs, unless they are gained without any resistance. The subjective importance of goals determines a party's willingness to pay a high price for the conflict. Given the ephemeral nature of conflict, the significance of goals can change with increasing costs and decreasing utility to achieve them. As the more or less acknowledged objectives of parties are revealed, goals translate into specific demands being made by one party or the other.

The process of goal formulation is not straightforward or rational, especially when both sides are not easily able to identify their true motivations and interests in the struggle. In order to search for areas of compromise, essential and non-essential goals need to be separated. Goal incompatibility is created when conflicting parties exclusively seek the same thing. In general, parties may end up settling with something different or unexpected, due to the scarcity of material objects or difficulties in obtaining the conditions desired. The availability of substitute goals diminishes persistence in the endeavour to fulfil original aspirations. Each party can have a multiplicity of goals with differing preferences. The existence of heterogeneous factions within a party and their diverse interests may generate the relative mixes of goal preferences.

The divisions between allies and adversaries, along with their opposing goals, better illustrate the nature of conflict. Long-term dissatisfaction with efforts towards particular goals results in the harbouring of negative sentiments toward opponents. The demand expressed may reflect long-term discontent that follows deprivation and frustration, based on the denial or loss of substantive rewards (Gurr, 1970). The growth of in-group identity and solidarity can bolster determination to pursue previously ignored matters more aggressively. The existence of other important concerns, along with limited time and resources, can repress the pursuit of new goals. Changes in goal hierarchies are, however, often accompanied by new attitudes and behaviours.

Issues

Each issue can be regarded as a point of disagreement to be resolved, thus revealing what the conflict is about. Issues may revolve around specific concerns that are associated with interests and values, or around the general relationship founded on long-standing grievances. New complaints can also emerge from mistreatment of each other in the course of a conflict. The complexity of the conflict will be increased if there are large numbers of issues with different significance to the multiple parties in contention.

Different layers of concerns can be divided into main issues and sub-issues that are analogous to the relationship between the trunk and branches of a tree. Some issues may reflect the roots of the conflict, while others might reflect symptoms, being manifested in behaviour. Highly specific positions are separated from those that are more ambiguous or symbolic. The matters of contention can be identified and grouped according to factual differences (clarified by objective criteria), interests (related to the distribution of positions, money, and resources), value differences (with stakes in prestige and meaning of life), and emotional disturbance (touching upon relationships).

Issues need to be examined beyond the surface phenomena, since the contention is likely to be attributed to more than one source. Specific issues, such as police brutality against minority youth, can escalate into a national struggle surrounding core identity and self-esteem. The issues of police cruelty are a specific manifestation of the larger substantive matter of how each society treats their minority population.

The same issues may be articulated at different levels, involving deeper relational implications. At a local level, demand for ethnic autonomy might be expressed in terms of maintaining cultural traditions, but the main stake at the national level might be a lack of power sharing arrangements in a government decision-making process. Contested issues are rarely singular or straightforward, in that even the same concerns may not be experienced similarly. The agreement on the issues is not likely to emerge if parties disagree on the causes of contention or interpret the other's concerns and motives differently from how they are actually felt. Multiple interpretations of issues may be overcome by efforts to search for a common understanding of the conflict.

Such issues as recognition, respect, justice, and security are less tangible than those that stem from economic, material concerns. Relational issues in identity-based conflicts are frequently entangled with territorial or other tangible issues (Bartos and Wehr, 2002). A pervasive quality of many ethnic struggles entails deep symbolic meanings that are interconnected with political domination. The tangible issues that trigger hostilities in ethnically divided communities (for example, land, money, and water rights) are inclined to contain the symbolic meanings that are constructed and assigned to past episodes of conflict. Hence, tangible issues might be transformed to advocate abstract nationalistic ideologies.

The objective structure of the issues may differ in every conflict. Some issues are distributive, meaning that the rewards are difficult to divide and therefore are 'zero sum' in nature. Accordingly, one party's gains will inevitably be a loss for the other party. In contrast, other issues are considered integrative, with a satisfactory combination of gains available to all involved. Non-negotiable issues become reconciled by the exploration of conditions for mutual coexistence. Seemingly intractable issues can be negotiated upon the transformation of existing relationships and institutions.

Interests

'Interests' refer to the political, economic, occupational, and social aspirations of individuals and groups. These aspirations are what the parties are motivated to achieve. Parochial, narrow group interests are not the same as public concerns related to the protection of the environment and economic justice. Groups may agree to choose to benefit only their own narrow interests, while hurting the public good such as the destruction of habitats for endangered species.

Contradictory interests may be generated by competitive social situations that involve a high win–lose component. If each party has desires without perceptible limits, their behaviour will be directed toward the maximization of gain at the expense of an adversary. Pursuing material interests, status, power, or privilege at the sacrifice of others is one of the clearest forms of substantive conflict. When competing motives are involved in acquiring scarce resources, such as a limited piece of land or positions, the main question is how to make decisions on who gets what. In terms of conflict management, economic interests can be more responsive to compromise through negotiation than are value-based conflicts.

As related to material goods or role occupancy, interests (associated with specific, tangible wants) are, in general, transitory, altering with circumstances. The pursuit of desirable objects can be given up, especially if they are not an inherent part of the individual, as are essential human needs or intrinsic values. Whereas interests may become involved in formulating policies and tactics in a quest for the satisfaction of needs and values, negotiable interests are distinguished from conditions for decent human living such as autonomy and freedom that are not to be traded.

Value differences

Values are anchored to shared concepts of desired ends and the means to reach them. A scale of beliefs is adopted to define a range of acceptable and unacceptable behaviours with the creation of rules that constitute the basis for mutual expectations. These norms guide individuals in an unfamiliar territory of social life, serving as 'signposts' (Brown, 1988). Our belief systems influence the way in which we interpret the behaviour of others and situations.

Value differences reveal a variance in preference for, or principles attached to, a major cleavage in ideology or a way of life. Values often provide a rationalization for standards and methods of resource allocation. In addition, shared beliefs underlie an orientation of society, legitimizing or de-legitimizing certain group behaviour. Moreover, a psychological construct can be created to make judgements about appropriate relationships between individuals, groups, and the outside world. In essence, individuals may use normative standards to elevate positive self-interests but to negate the other's.

While values are often defined in terms of beliefs and perspectives that we have about ourselves and other people, these thoughts do not exist in a social vacuum. Various characteristics of particular social communities are immersed in cultures and identities that are illustrated by linguistic, religious, class, ethnic, or other distinctiveness. These unique features, in part, influence predispositions that affect the way we decide to behave toward others. In fact, our behaviour hinges on the manner in which we reorganize the internal mental representation of our relationships with an external world. Ideology based views about the world and its order impinge upon not only the pursuit of substantive goals but also choices of tactics such as the embracement or rejection of violence.

Efforts to convert and suppress other values might be part of a struggle in conflict. In oppressed situations, cultural values held by marginalized groups bestow a tool to protest the injustice of an imposed system (Freire, 1998). In their endeavour to convince government elites to see the injustice of militarism, peace movements have pursued the conversion of decision makers' views through civil disobedience or other forms of non-violence. As demonstrated by the history of civil rights movements, public attitudes can be altered in the span of a generation or two, following economic and social integration through such policies as the prohibition of segregation. At the end of a conflict, persons of different convictions may even be assimilated into a single value system, which is likely to absorb some features of all.

Some value conflicts have been provoked by the rejection and prohibition of minority cultures and their social practices. The employment of separate customs, lifestyles, dress, religion, and language as bases for discrimination is frequently justified by law, resulting in strengthened solidarity among minority groups. In human history, wars have been fought to preserve religious identity and practice as well as the freedom to teach ethnic languages at school in minority regions. Leadership emerges to defend cultural autonomy and mobilize an ethnic community for political purposes.

Besides national or ethnic identities, globalization has produced diverse life style patterns associated with a new social status and has brought sensitivity to migration of populations, policies on AIDS, and so forth in political mobilization (Leatherman and Webber, 2006). Intractable dimensions of conflicts, for instance, relating to the abortion rights issue, are often embedded within a larger set of religious beliefs, gender orientations, and national politics that intersect with ethical principles, philosophical world views, or cultural traditions. The total ban on abortion in Nicaragua, even in circumstances under which the mother's life is being threatened, has generated a global outcry. Deeper divisions within and across national boundaries have been exposed by an offensive attempt to portray abortion as genocide by new EU parliamentary members from such conservative Catholic countries as Poland. This kind of challenge to cherished norms and values by newcomers has become an obstacle to maintaining harmony within the expanded EU.

Human needs

Compared with values acquired through socialization, human needs reflect universal motivations. Being intrinsic to biological and physical survival, as well as self-esteem and autonomy, basic needs are considered to be universal and primordial, and perhaps even genetic. The denial of identity, security, and recognition is a critical and fundamental concern for most intractable conflicts in places such as Northern Ireland, Palestine, Chechnya, Nepal, Tibet, and the Muslim regions of China. Thus the suppression of a desire for self-fulfilment and human development provides a socio-political context of intractable conflict. Human needs, not subject to elite control, are an essential element in the analysis of behaviour and decision making (Burton, 2001). Such commonly sought needs as security, personal safety, and development cannot be altered or undermined by authoritarian orders.

The inherent drive for survival and well-being cannot be manipulated or eliminated by coercive forces or other deterrence methods of controlling behaviour. A negotiated outcome, leaving the underlying needs unfulfilled, might lead to a short-term settlement, but it rarely contributes to long-term resolution.

According to John W. Burton (1990), Herbert Kelman (2002), and other prominent scholars in conflict resolution, human needs theory serves as a framework to analyse the root causes of conflict. The pursuit of individual needs is the reason behind the formation of identity groups in search of dignity and security.

The very existence of people is threatened under circumstances of oppression, discrimination, and isolation. The process of conflict resolution should bring about social, economic, and political changes that cater to human needs. Consequently, institutions should be adapted to the satisfaction of essential human requirements (Rubenstein, 2001). From a human needs perspective, conflict resolution will not be achieved without responding to gross inequalities and high levels of alienation. Conflict transformation follows transition from a system of traditional institutional power, maintained by elite-dominated norms and interests, to a system of human needs.

Strategies, tactics, and culture

In coping with conflict, people employ particular styles, strategies, and tactics. In general, a 'strategy' serves as an overall plan for responding to a given situation. On the other hand, a 'tactic' is regarded as 'a specific observable action that moves a conflict in a particular direction in line with the strategy' (Lulofs and Cahn, 2000: 100). The adoption of particular strategies is influenced by different styles and attitudes toward conflict.

The strategies of suppression are likely to invite such tactics as threats, harassment, and the actual physical control of opponents. In making a demand, meanwhile, the weaker side may use non-violent resistance based on civilian direct action, most notably, sabotage and hunger strike. Any efforts to prohibit a non-violent struggle may eventually encourage the eruption of violent resistance.

Confrontation strategies can take mild or intense forms, comprising formal complaints and protests, economic boycott, the agitation of violence, and support for internal opposition within an adversarial side. International crisis behaviour involves psychological threats, military posturing, and retaliation through direct military actions. Indirect threats may depend on such diplomatic actions as the disapproval of policies, calls for the international investigation of treaty violations, demands for compensation, and the rebuke of an opponent's decision. Stronger non-military sanctions range from cutting off diplomatic and economic relations to denying the government's legitimacy.

Preferred conflict behaviour may vary among cultural perspectives and value systems that affect human action and communication. A high-context culture is geared towards appreciating the meanings embedded in the interpretation of social relationships, emphasizing concerns for others' feelings and face-saving tactics, rather than direct arguments. As is often represented by practices in the corporate world or a legal contract system, a low-context culture prefers explicit rules and explanations. It is contrasted with the high-context culture that mirrors intimate relations of traditional communal or tribal societies.

As a culture-dependent construct, conflict is featured by communication patterns, adaptable to diverse social functions. In responding to how conflict should be managed, cultural values, expectations, and attitudes can guide a communication process. In a setting of high context culture, preventive strategies are utilized prior to the surfacing of conflict. On the contrary, overt argumentations and confrontations are embraced in Western societies characterized by a low context culture. In fact, an aggressive verbal language embodies the expression of explicit warnings and threats. Open confrontation, based on the pursuit of exclusive, individual interests, can be distinguished from the emotional appeal of a group bond. The nature of conflict in a low cultural context is perceived to be instrumental in a battle for a larger slice of the pie. On the other hand, a high cultural context focuses on expressive relationship issues (Ting-Toomey, 1985).

Conflict-coping styles and orientations

Partisans are inclined to choose conflict avoiding, contending, yielding, or accommodating styles. Behavioural orientations to conflict can be defined as a preferred mode of managing adversarial situations, reflecting, in part, the way in which people think and feel about their relationships with others. The adoption of a particular style and its changes over the course of conflict have different behavioural implications for adversaries. One party's style choice may induce the other's behaviour to become either more aggressive or more compromising.

Conflict-coping styles are represented, in part, in communication patterns. For instance, aggressive communication patterns, based on verbal intimidation and assault, are a manifestation of a contending conflict style. Accommodation styles are more easily observed in non-assertive communication geared toward empathic listening. In addition, cultural interpretation and gender orientations are likely to have an impact on conflict styles. Feminine values tend to support accommodating styles with more of an emphasis on mutual understanding and compromising attitudes than masculine values associated with competition and hierarchy.

Avoidance

The avoidance style is oriented toward inaction or an ignorance of uncomfortable issues by being non-committal. The suppression or postponement of conflict produces less direct interaction with adversaries. A low level of interaction results from a decreased commitment to conflict. Those who get nervous about a conflict may want to believe that it will go away if they pretend that there is no problem. Withdrawal from confrontation may be motivated not only by a desire not to risk the relationship but also by a fear of the conflict's effects on one's own well-being. Parties may feel that the cost of the contest is too high emotionally and materially when they have a low investment in the outcome. If parties have a negative perception about conflict and feel that the fight is not worth the effort, little energy will be extended towards overcoming challenges that arise from dealing with people who differ in terms of lifestyle, ideas, and values. In essence, conflict avoidance stems from reduced goal utility and a low likelihood of meeting expectations as well as the high costs involved.

In an overwhelming power imbalance, a weaker party tends to be hesitant to initiate confrontation. People can be passive or unassertive when they lack the power necessary to face their adversary. A prolonged, inappropriate avoidance of conflict is also often perpetuated by the inflexibility of a stronger party. In a dominant relationship, discussion about issues is suppressed so long as the weaker party remains subordinate. The mere containment or repression of demand is considered to be a destructive way of responding to conflict, especially when the denial of unacceptable hierarchies is no longer feasible.

Sometimes, avoidance is favoured as a strategy to 'buy time' prior to developing responses to conflict. One party may choose to wait for the opportune moment to confront its adversaries. Postponement is also inevitable or advantageous if power relations can, in the future, be rebalanced in one's own favour as regards economic and military strength.

If conciliation is a desirable condition for the resolution of differences, the passage of sufficient time may present an opportunity to ease hostilities and anger with a 'cooling down' effect. In the event that the parties embrace strategies not to work through uncomfortable confrontations, joint avoidance might be the norm of conflict management. By diminishing dependence on each other, parties lower the influence of the other in their decision making.

Yet more rigid exchange patterns of fighting and threats may be expected following the initiation of a long-awaited conflict. The conflict might eventually get out of control and need to be tackled. Avoidance strategies can be re-evaluated by means of reordering overall preferences in goal hierarchies. Challenging others would beget a better result if rules and procedures of conflict management were established to guarantee a fair process for all sides.

Contending

A contending approach focuses on scoring a victory, defeating the other party by attempting to prove how wrong they are. A struggle to gain advantage in the relationship is geared toward weakening a protagonist's position, because the other's vulnerability would mean one's own greater strength. In international politics, some parties more readily choose contentious styles, in tandem with bluff tactics, to boost the image of being tough. The use of coercive tactics by one side may encourage the other to take up equally threatening approaches. On the other hand, contest may be inhibited by such perceived costs as the risk of alienating and antagonizing others as well as the loss of support among moderate constituents concerned about the initiation of a conflict spiral.

In most situations, all other conditions being equal, contest is inevitable when one party tries to settle differences on its own terms without the consideration of the other's interests. The unilateral pursuit of one's own interests, in association with attempts to force one's decision on others, generates competitive, adversarial relationships. Contending parties insist on an opponent's concession and stick to positional commitments that indicate a refusal to move from a particular stance (Carnevale and Leung, 2001). In the win–lose approach of a zero-sum game wherein one seeks gain at another's expense, efforts to prevail lead to aggression and a struggle for domination.

In power imbalanced relationships, the stronger side more easily employs a contentious style towards overwhelming the opponent's apparent resistance to yielding. In win–lose settlements, the defeated party piles up grievances and holds grudges, waiting for an opportunity to retaliate. Conflict is likely to be protracted if one party relies solely on confrontational strategies and if the other party has both the capacity and determination to counter them.

In tandem with contentious approaches to conflict, realists in international politics have long argued that methods of deterrence are needed to control aggressive behaviour through the fear of retaliation. The pursuit of stability has relied on mutual threats in a balance of power system where the military and economic strengths are, more or less, evenly distributed between opposing blocs of countries. Once both parties adhere to a contentious style, however, a head-on collision is expected. This is most likely to happen under perceived conditions of equal power relations. When parties have fewer shared interests, they would probably be more committed to obtaining their exclusive goals without regard to the other side's well-being. Pressure and intimidation tactics have been a popular means in maximizing both the psychological and physical effects of contending approaches.

Yielding

In yielding, one party offers unilateral concessions by taking the other's perspectives or interests more seriously than one's own; it is the fastest way to settle differences. Yielding can take place in a variety of intimate settings, ranging from interpersonal bonds such as friendship and love to kinship relationships. A common group identity engenders a concern with the welfare of others. As a matter of fact, an intrinsic interest in the happiness and success of others makes concessions easier.

In other settings, yielding might reflect instrumental concerns as a strategy of advancing one's own interests. Unilateral concessions can be made with the expectations of reciprocity or as part of efforts to garner even bigger concessions from the other side in the future. Yielding is likely to be seen as investment for inducing or convincing the other side to collaborate. Appeasing, meanwhile, excludes any threat of force and bestows only positive inducements.

Appeasing the other's demand denotes lowering one's own aspirations, scaling down original demands or goals (Pruitt and Kim, 2004). Acquiescence, or giving in to the other's claim, may sometimes be based on the illusion of harmony and an attempt to avoid ill feelings. In the event of strong resistance from an opponent, appeasement can help to defuse an imminent crisis of war, but conciliation alone may not limit the continuously excessive demand. Parties may resist yielding in case they anticipate that even partial concessions send signals of weakness. The success of yielding depends on an accurate assessment of an adversary's motives and attitudes.

Accommodation

Accommodating styles are more visible when all sides search for shared interests in locating options that gratify mutual goals (Hocker and Wilmot, 1978). Integrative bargaining strategies can be pursued when everyone recognizes that their interdependence is mutually beneficial. Each participant initially aims to influence the outcome to their own advantage, but they may soon realize the infeasibility of obtaining unilateral gains in the absence of collaboration with the other. In promoting a joint aim of settlement, a deal can be reached through negotiation with modification of strategies of maximizing individual benefits. Parties may cooperate to establish agreeable facts by exploring a fair assessment method of each other's claims. Whereas persuasion is necessary to convince the opponent, compromise of one's own interests can be made in line with an adversary's concessions.

Through accommodation, all sides should be able to put away their exclusive concerns in order to please each other. Most importantly, accommodating moves are also preferred to avoid violent confrontations. In a compromise situation, neither party totally wins or loses as a result of the trade-off of concessions in favour of what each considers the most important. In reality, however, because all parties are unable to get exactly everything they want, some parties may feel that they got less than deserved. In this situation, the exchange of offers and concessions may leave lingering feelings among those whose vital needs have not been met. On the occasion that some may feel so uncomfortable with conflict, however, they may want to reach for whatever 'quick fix' solution is available to them, as though putting a plaster on a wound.

A collaborative-integrative strategy looks for a win–win outcome, being enhanced by shared information about each other's priorities. It is contrasted with a competitive-distributive strategy which generates a clear win–lose outcome. Common ground can be discovered by means of a search for an alternative that suits both sides (Miall, et al., 1999). In this way, mutual satisfaction comes from joint gains and trust relationships. Empathy is geared toward an understanding of the other side's position and a positive regard for the partner. Problem-solving attitudes rely on respect not only for one's own interests and needs but also for others in an effort to seek mutual goal compatibilities.

Decisions on choice of strategies

The choice of conflict strategy and style (avoiding, contending, yielding, and accommodating) is likely to be affected by actor motivations and situations. It is especially determined by power relations and the salience of issues from the perspective of each party as well as their will and commitment to conflict. In workplace disputes, all other conditions such as personality differences being equal, managers are most likely to prefer different styles in handling interpersonal conflict with superiors (avoidance or yielding), with subordinates (contending), and with peers (accommodating). Similarly, in conflict with a weaker state, a stronger state is likely to favour contentious military strategies without fear of retaliation. Weak states, meanwhile, are more likely to adopt an avoidance or yielding strategy in order to minimize the risk of devastating loss.

The selection of particular conflict styles and strategies is most likely based on what is gained and what price is paid as well as the availability of an alternative course of action. Yielding is likely to take place under the circumstances of time pressure—for example, close to a deadline to meet a court filing or following an ultimatum of war—or in a situation of high-cost engagement without an alternative option of avoidance. The degree of flexibility in one party's bargaining stance can be associated with the level of their dependence on the other side's cooperation for meeting essential goals. A more conciliatory bargaining stance, involving fewer threats of punishment, stems from a considerable degree of dependence that benefits the party. A high level of interdependence dampens contentious styles, in that a joint gain can arise from mutual accommodation rather than stubbornness. Thus mutual dependence as well as shared values decreases the prospect for 'push–shove' conflict spirals.

Bargaining stances are likely to be softened to lower the risk of an accelerating conflict spiral accompanied by 'push–push' dynamics. The choice of strategies behind seeking or giving up exclusive gains for the benefit of others also hinges on relational dimensions that reflect not only power but also affectionate emotions such as trust, caring, and intimacy, for example, between parents and children. Care for the relationship shuns the adoption of contentious styles, involving instead the suppression of one's own needs and interests.

Conditions for conflict

In order to understand given conflict dynamics, it is necessary to identify the existing potential that aggravates hostile interactions. Integrated analysis of multi-sectoral activities is important in effectively responding to the confluence of different conflict causes and dynamics. It is also essential to establish linkages between types of conflict relationship and behaviour. Various sociopsychological characteristics of a given system influence the effectiveness of potential strategies for preventing or curtailing uncontrolled violence. Under certain structural conditions, intervention would not be able to bring cooling down effects to escalating conflicts immediately.

The prelude to conflict is accompanied by the translation of latent conditions, such as discontent stemming from social injustice and growing inequity, into social mobilization which demands changes in the status quo. Triggers, including the violation of a cease-fire, often facilitate the outbreak of new fighting or refuel old conflicts in a tense political crisis. Triggering events, for instance, street demonstrations in the midst of skyrocketing food prices, ignite explosive situations in a 'latent' conflict phase. In particular, political instability is also created by many unpredictable events, including but not being limited to the assassination of state heads or opposition leaders, violent revolts, sudden economic crisis, or military defeat. It is notable that the same types of mass behaviour do not always catalyse a chain effect culminating in violence or war without ripe social and psychological conditions for explosion.

The existence of differences in values, norms, status, and class divisions serves as a precondition for social conflict (Kriesberg, 1998). The loss of substantive rewards and the denial of legitimate group status stimulate frustration and deprivation towards social mobilization. Immediate changes in a public mood function as proximate causes for the sudden eruption of mass revolt or militant action. Even though they are situational, the manifestations of hostilities are apparently symptomatic of a deeper problem, contributing to a climate that is conducive to violent conflict or its further escalation.

The necessary conditions for conflict are often structural. The collapse of the former Yugoslavia has been attributed to economic deterioration and political disintegration, in the midst of the failure of old federal structures and norms to integrate diverse groups. The sufficient cause can be psychological and organizational ability to mobilize groups.[1] The endorsement of ethno-nationalism by political leaders reinforces exclusive ideology and propaganda. In the absence of any restraining forces, this process effectively translates a tense social environment or economic collapse into an opportunity for rapid mass upheaval or armed struggle.

The short-term dysfunction of the political and economic system does not necessarily provoke violent conflict if there is a strong political institution supported by the population. Social uprisings and street violence in stable Western democracies have not generated a rift in the existing political order due to the existence of strong consensus on the values and institutions among the citizens. As we have seen in the division of Czechoslovakia into two states in the early 1990s, opposing groups do not need to get engaged in a destructive process of antagonism even during the transition period if there is a stable leadership committed to peace.

Thus emerging conflict can be controlled by inhibiting conditions that involve either an existing system's strong capability to absorb socio-political stress and crisis, or the weak capability of disenchanted groups to challenge the existing structure's normative and coercive apparatus. Even though there may be a significant level of discontent among the population, dissenting groups and organizations may be incapable of mass mobilization as a result of internet surveillance and other tight communication controls. Opposition struggles may also be ineffective due to ruthless repression by the ruling elite, as exemplified by Burma, Eritrea, China, and Saudi Arabia. Each regime has different levels of vulnerability and institutional ability to minimize pressure for change (Stetter, 2007). As observed in the collapse of Indonesia's Suharto regime in 1998, following the Asian financial crisis, sudden changes in the economic situations may weaken a regime's ability to control its population.

The phases of conflict

In general, an entire cycle of conflict proceeds, over time, through a series of recognizable stages, comprising initiation, escalation, de-escalation, and cessation (Kriesberg, 1998; Mitchell, 1981). Even if every conflict has its own dynamics, there is a common, though not always predictable, process, following precipitating events that signal the surfacing of a conflict. If a successful resolution is not reached, leaving a bad emotional residue, the ending may serve as a temporary stop gap for a new cycle of conflict to begin in the future. In order to understand a given context of conflict steps, it is necessary to identify the patterns of interaction between adversaries at different stages of the struggle.

Once conflict is initiated, it is exposed to various types of transformation, along with a proliferation of issues and an increase in the intensity of struggles. The number of participants multiplies when specific issues become generalized to the level of an existential struggle, entailing identity and autonomy. The war with the remnant of the Taliban and Osama bin Laden's group in Afghanistan, following the attacks of 11 September 2001, has quickly been expanded to a fight between the Western alliance and a range of radical Islamic groups around the world.

Analysis of a conflict process can explain the development of relationships at different phases following changes in each party's perceptions of the other's intentions and goals. The modes of inter-group relations have a significant impact on escalation and resolution. Whereas enmity is a consequence of a hostile interaction during escalation, it needs to be overcome to facilitate a movement toward de-escalation and resolution. Therefore, activities of conflict are organically related to each other in terms of their synergy.

In the evolution of conflict, interaction patterns become more complex, involving multiple parties and a large number of issues. The intensity of conflict is determined by the extent of destructiveness in a deadlocked struggle.

In general, bipolarization in the relationship tends to bring about a conflict of greater intensity and the simplification of each party's image with dehumanization. Inter-group polarization, meanwhile, is bound to consolidate positions of hawkish leaders with an emphasis on internal cohesion and unity.

Various stages demonstrate typical behavioural patterns and psychological conditions (Jones and Hughes, 2003). Dynamics of unrestrained escalation and polarization carry participants away from cooperative efforts by means of run-away responses to hostilities. Increasingly malign motives are reinforced within each party by stereotypes. In particular, opponents are perceived as a negative mirror image of oneself.

A conflict vacillates between constructive and destructive phases. The process of escalation turns a low-intensity conflict into a high-intensity struggle. Each party tries to outdo the other's behaviour in a vicious circle of hostile action and negative reaction. A retaliatory spiral is inevitable in a competitive escalation cycle. In a conflict spiral, every exchange gets increasingly intense, corresponding to each other's actions. In seeking revenge, each party punishes the other for actions regarded as aversive. A blood feud is intensified by retaliation after retaliation. This process is predominated by 'the feelings of being trapped in a set of circumstances beyond one's control' (Lulofs and Cahn, 2000: 77).

Unless one or both of the main adversaries are completely destroyed or vanish after intense fights, escalation is eventually predestined to subside, due to the difficulties in maintaining a costly struggle over a sustained period. In particular, a conflict is not likely to last when each party feels that the outcomes are too low to meet their expectations. A continuing conflict demands too much sacrifice with not only time consuming but also emotionally charged struggles. If conflict is drawn out without a settlement in sight, the losses are likely to exceed the gains. In a stalemate situation, then, conflict can be frozen following exhaustive fights without the obtainment of original objectives.

In reality, it is difficult to achieve conflict resolution that fully addresses all of the contentious issues. Yet the danger of leaving unresolved conflicts in the dark is that they can grow into large and unmanageable catastrophic situations such as the Rwandan genocide in 1994. A conflict that could have been resolved initially becomes destructive if it is lent to uncontrolled emotions and behaviour. It takes much more effort to bring about the constructive transformation of a conflict once a vicious cycle of violence has been set in motion (Mitchell, 2001).

Various stages of interaction are more easily recognized in a conflict which has progressed over a longer period. With changes in settlement situations, some conflicts might be reinitiated. A continuing cycle of civil wars in Angola during the mid-1990s was attributed to a failure to implement the internationally brokered arrangements that were to end armed hostilities. A conflict becomes cyclical as each wave of episodes generates similar dynamics of interaction with predictable patterns of behaviour. Such adversarial relationships can be altered not only via their own internal dynamics but also through external pressure or intervention.

A conflict context

The context of a conflict can be illustrated in light of historical events or incidents within which it is embedded. One conflict is connected to another by means of geographic boundary, political structure, or diplomatic relations. For instance, the Vietnamese invasion of Cambodia in January 1979 dragged China, the USA and the Soviet Union into regional power games. The history of a conflict, and its physical and organizational settings, constitute the context of an ongoing episode. At any rate, conflict does not emerge in a vacuum. The relationship between parties can also be affected by types of communication network and organizational links.

Often the dynamics of one conflict originate from the course of events in another with converging issues and parties. The difficulties experienced in resolving conflicts between Israel and Palestine have been partly created as a consequence of their interlinkage to other conflicts in the Middle East. By defining a setting in which conflict relationships evolve, external events determine the scope and character of the struggle. In order to be able to manage one conflict proactively, it is important to recognize the effect of others that are ongoing at the same time and which may be linked.

There are many different types of linkage; one conflict may be nested within another (Dugan, 1996). Disputes over specific, functional issues (such as rules on the passage of humanitarian assistance or the interpretation of cease-fire violations) can be embroiled in a long-running conflict. In handling the current relationship effectively, the first step is to acknowledge the history of the underlying conflict. It is this history that often explains why people feel as they do and which can give hints about possible remedies for the current situation. A history of past events must be taken seriously, then, to assess not only their impact on the development of an ongoing conflict, but also on possible approaches for conflict management or resolution.

Conflict intervention

The control of violent escalation is a main focus of conflict intervention and management, prior to seizing an opportunity for resolution. A proper policy of conflict prevention entails not only the constant monitoring of potential flashpoints but also immediate actions to remove the conditions that facilitate the outbreak of violence. The minimalist aim of conflict prevention is at least to block a crisis from spilling into an openly violent conflict.

The conditions for third-party intervention are, in general, hampered by the availability of little time for a negotiated settlement. In contemplating intervention, we cannot wait for mature conditions to arise, especially when quick intervention in a highly authoritative style is demanded in situations where many civilian populations face being killed or being forced to flee, as is exemplified by the 2006 humanitarian crisis in Sudan.

Explicit models and techniques for intervention have been designed for identifying the roles of various actors and stakeholders not only at the international level but also at the local. The best known examples of intervention in the middle of military conflicts include the dispatch of humanitarian forces to Somalia in 1994 and NATO air strikes in Bosnia-Herzegovina in 1996 (Talentino, 2005). In these incidents, the use of coercive force was fully justified to compensate for the insufficient local capacity to contain armed groups. In the case of Macedonia in the late 1990s, preventive diplomacy combined with a small contingent of UN peacekeeping force effectively stimulated dialogue among the various political forces and ethnic communities. Indeed, a negotiated settlement was eventually reached following the efforts to contain the emergence of the Albanian insurgency and avert its spill-over. Most successful prevention is geared toward developing synergies between immediate actions and long-term policy change.

Different levels of intervention by regional powers can be utilized in support of creation of peace zones and facilitation of dialogue by community leaders and tribal elders in an effort to minimize the negative potential for violent conflict. Synergies at a local level may have regional and national significance in nurturing a supportive environment of conflict transformation. Intervention in power imbalanced situations—as exemplified by the NATO intervention in Bosnia-Herzegovina to cease Serb militia massacres and subsequent US support for strengthening the armament of the Muslim group—has sometimes been oriented toward changing the balance of forces against the continuation of violent conflict. Ultimately, strategies for reducing the negative forces linked to violence need to focus on identifying elements that transform the motives behind a perpetuation of conflict. The exploration of options needs to consider not only the capacities of the parties but also the specific conditions of conflict dynamics at any given time.

The context of an entire peace-making enterprise is clarified by mapping relationships and issues (Saunders, 1999). A series of informal, non-governmental contacts were made in an attempt to reduce tension between American and Russian societies at the height of the Cold War period. The process was designed to enhance mutual understanding through joint efforts to develop a conflict map of the adversarial relationships. In addition, scholar-practitioners have applied interactive, collaborative methods of conflict resolution to cultivate opportunities for facilitative dialogue in many ethnic conflict settings (Kelman, 1972; Mitchell, 2001).

The principles of conflict resolution

While history, perceptions, and identity are inherently present in conflict formation, they can also be utilized in managing conflict and contributing to a sustainable peace. Some of the most powerful tools for peace building entail acknowledging past harm, developing empathy toward the other's suffering, and remedying the necessity to allay the fear of victims. Perceptions of collective victimization such as the Holocaust go deeper in the history of Jews, for instance, and feed present patriotism and unity in Israel with unyielding support from abroad.

In essence, conflict management is designed to control violent and costly struggle in order to minimize the negative impacts of unrestrained forces. On the other hand, this process may be seen simply as an attempt to maintain the status quo and perpetuate the existing state of affairs. The United Nations has maintained its peace keeping missions in Cyprus for the last several decades, but, so far, it has not been successful in producing an agreement that is satisfactory to all of the parties.

The initiatives toward conflict resolution are hindered by the refusal to recognize the legitimacy and rights of groups that have been marginalized by discriminatory social structures and norms. In addition, a lack of agreements on suitable processes for resolution has been an obstacle to discussion about substantive issues. The initial stage of discussion relating to disarming North Korean nuclear power capabilities in 2003 and 2004 faced gridlock due to the opposition of the Bush administration to bilateral talks with their foe. The North Korean government resisted the US administration's persistence with multilateral talks as a forum to exert undue pressure on them for unilateral concessions.

The promotion of harmonious relationships in the wider social environment is often viewed as the goal of conflict resolution. Yet, the outcomes of agreements would not be sustainable if settlement process were not to address injustice and other types of structural violence that oppress human conditions. The ignorance of long-term, underlying issues needs to be tackled by overcoming power asymmetry with the empowerment of marginalized parties.

Conflict analysis should reach, beyond the treatment of symptoms such as control of individual behaviour, to highlight their root causes. Introducing a new social and political formula that meets the essential security needs of all sides can change the status quo. Lasting peace is most likely to be achieved by eliminating those conditions that have led to violence in the first place. Reconciliation remains an essential step for ultimate transformation of relationships, as 'some conflicts leave residues' of animosities (Lulofs and Cahn, 2000: 316).

Notes

1 A 'sufficient cause' means that, every time a certain event happens, a particular outcome is expected to follow. There are often multiple causes for one incident. Swimming after heavy drinking serves as a sufficient condition for drowning, for example, but the swimmer's death might also be attributed to other sufficient causes such as heart attack or poor swimming skills.

A 'necessary cause' for a specific event indicates that certain conditions should pre-exist for the occurrence even though nothing can happen without the involvement of a sufficient cause. Gravity, for example, is the necessary cause of a box falling to the floor, but gravity, in itself, does not generate the movement, in that the box has to be dropped in the first place.

Part II
Sources and Situations

3

Sources of Conflict

Managing and preventing conflict begins with understanding the sources of social struggles. We can explain the basis of conflict and related behaviour in terms of human motivation, patterns of social interaction, and institutions. Many consider conflict to be irrational and undesirable, yet we nonetheless need to examine various factors beyond misperceptions, anger and frustration, and other psychological variables. Proper communication among adversaries—designed to remove misunderstanding—is not sufficient to resolve the differences without tackling root causes. In many instances, beneath deep hostilities and antagonism lie power imbalances and economic disparities that generate grievances. This chapter reviews various types of structural and psychological theories which illustrate the basis of destructive conflict.

Realistic versus non-realisitic conflict

Realistic sources of conflict include material scarcity, limited positions and other objective situations which produce differences in interests and competing aspirations. The pursuit of specific goals is based on the consideration of costs and benefits as well as beliefs about the likelihood of obtaining them. On the other hand, non-realistic conflict is mostly attributed to the expression of anger, anxiety and shame tied to personal or group level stress. Incompatibilities may exist due to misunderstandings derived from miscommunication of intentions. But antagonistic relationships are not simply ascribed to communicative behaviour, given the roles of power, economic and social competition, and identity in controlling group dynamics.

In ordinary circumstances, antagonistic behaviour is mixed with non-realistic elements of acting out frustration in tandem with the exacerbation of grievances and other negative emotional energy. Even though a conflict may start with objective differences, these may be inappropriately expressed. In some situations, aggressive action is directed, in a pathological manner, toward bystanders or socially marginalized groups for the purpose of a release of tension. Hostility and frustration can be displaced onto any convenient person or group that may not even resemble the original source of frustration. Such a substitute group is selected when it is difficult to take an action against the identified causes or when the actual basis of the hostility is not known.

Intense struggles over differences in political, economic interests are perpetuated by individual predispositions to violence (Wright and Taylor, 2003). Sometimes, the rationalization of human aggression has even depended on the construction of a comprehensive ideology. Intentions and actions to destroy rivals are, in part, associated with the fear or envy of other groups. The aggressiveness of group members is often supported by sinister motives. The malign character of opponents may have been fabricated to release individual frustrations in aggressions against another group. Massacres and genocide acts, destroying all, or part, of a category of ethnic, racial, religious, or other groups, permit violence that exceeds the bounds of morality or law.

The roots of conflict

Various approaches to the analysis of a violent conflict have focused on how we interpret the social, psychological, and biological conditions of human behaviour. The sources of conflict have been relegated to either larger social structures (shaped by institutional relationships and value differences) or an internal psychological environment. At an institutional, collective level, conflict is embedded in socio-economic conditions that put different groups in opposing positions. Psychological research traditions have pointed out aggregate, societal level frustrations arising from group interaction. On the other hand, those who shed light on the qualities of human nature suggest that, regardless of social structures, violence is endemic and universal.

Factors at the macro, societal level are concerned with the way the existing order is legitimized and institutionalized, even though it does not accommodate the needs of ordinary people. The sources of competition have been ascribed to social conditioning, historical processes, or even economic greed. Indeed, authority relations and political hierarchies explain the nature of a group status in a given social structure. Macro conflict originates, to a great extent, from a lack of equitable allocation of resources and an unequal access to power.

According to various psychoanalysts, individuals may be predisposed to the incitement of violence via instinctive impulse associated with unfulfilled psychological needs. Intrapersonal tensions and other psychic variables have been ascribed to violence at all levels, namely, interpersonal, inter-group, inter-societal, and international. In this tradition, an inner stimulation explains a desire to control other groups (Scharff et al., 2007). In describing a person's behaviour, an internal psychological environment has been linked to unlocking inhibitory mechanisms of aggressive instinctual drives or frustrations.

Theories on personality disorder and psychological imbalance focus on the role of unconscious forces in destructive conflict. Psychic factors have been employed to illustrate group experiences and behaviour toward others especially in such cases as genocide killings committed by the Serbs and Croats in Bosnia-Herzegovina and by the Hutus in Rwanda. At the same time, a permissible political environment has to exist to tolerate mass killing and other atrocious behaviour that are not acceptable in an ordinary social setting. Overall, substantive descriptions of particular events and contextual explanations of human behaviour need to be offered in terms of not only frustration but also the pursuit of self-interest and strategic considerations.

Human nature and determinism

Despite the evolution of human society, all civilizations and cultures have been full of experiences of uprisings, riots, coups, terrorism, and revolution. Even though scientific knowledge has increased with various types of technological advance, the extent of human collective violence today has grown worse since ancient times. Normal and common psychological processes in many conflict settings consist of negative feelings and distorted thinking in support of hatred and aggression. Harmful emotional processes, combined with the availability of weapons and other lethal means, often more easily incite aggression and violence.

With a focus on the propensity of human beings linked to violence, a long philosophical and religious tradition has placed instinctive impulses, independent of experience, as a source of destructive behaviour. In the broad socio-biological conception, aggression is genetically programmed in the nervous system, whether it is manifested in a quest for national territory or personal wealth. Aggressive behavioural characteristics of the human species are explained by the primitive urges to fight and dominate—not necessarily in reaction to some external event. This organic mechanism of survival and adaptation is extrapolated from evolutionary history by analogy to animal behaviour in nature (Lorenz, 1966).

In pessimistic views, a violent conflict may be inescapable in human relationships due to unconscious motivations alone (as asserted by the psychodynamic theorists) or in combination with competition for limited supplies of basic necessities. Albert Einstein's letter written to Sigmund Freud, prior to World War II, illuminates the continuing debate about human nature and aggression. In response to Einstein's questions about reasons for an easy arousal of hatred, Freud (1933a) traced the roots of violence to the death instinct's operation for destruction. The drive for self-annihilation is deflected outward, for self-preservation purposes, to impel the destruction of external targets. The only way to control a fatal human instinct is to enforce mutual obligations against the perpetual danger of an instinctual manifestation in aggressive behaviour.

It will be a never-ending debate whether aggression is innately based on a human instinct, or is related to a physiological predisposition for species survival, or is nurtured in a social context. In motivational theories, aggression stems from a blocked energy of frustration produced in a diverse social, psychological environment. If aggression is considered to be a reaction to an external stimulus, the activation of an internal physiological mechanism can be, in part, attributed to a social environment.

Aggression—defined as a deliberate attempt at psychological and physical destruction—is instrumental if motivated for external rewards or specific gains as opposed to a strong emotional arousal to injure others. Instrumental aggression, instigated by political or economic benefits, is learned independently of frustration. On the other hand, endogenously motivated aggression is spontaneously generated and is not subject to removal by social reforms (Berkowitz, 1990).

In a traditional instinct doctrine represented by Austrian psychiatrist Freud and ethologist Konrad Lorenz, human suffering is traced not to deficiencies in social institutions but to intractable human nature. Therefore, destructive impulses need to be restrained and diverted away from expression in war. The biological origins of aggression, meanwhile, are certainly contrasted with social and educational learning contexts. Imperialist policies on war and conquests have been intellectually rationalized by 'stages of evolution', presented in the form of 'social Darwinism'. Hereditary or genetic determinism has been promoted to justify ethnic, racial, religious, cultural superiority, for example, in India's caste system. The 'survival of the fittest' principle has legitimized hierarchical relations on the basis of differences in social status and class.

Internal psychology and Freud

In psychiatric traditions, internal unconscious states shape assumptions about the motivations and judgements of human behaviour. Internal tensions and pressures are built up to release destructive energy. Extreme forms of human aggression have been explained by the Freudian doctrines of a struggle between the subconscious pleasure-seeking 'id' and the conscience-based 'superego', with the intermediary role of rational principles of 'ego' (responding to external reality).

In Freud's view of psychosexual development, the biologically rooted, infantile 'id' generates aggressive impulses by pushing our basic instinctive drives, for instance, toward sex and food, demanding immediate satisfaction. The fully unconscious 'id', ruled by the pleasure–pain principle, is directly opposed to the super-ego, that is, the conscience serving as the internal moral judge. The role of 'ego' is to find a balance between primitive drives of 'id' and 'superego' that cultivates a sense of morality. The uncontrolled 'id' instigates behaviour that conflicts with society's norms, internal feelings of guilt, anxiety, and inferiority (Freud, 1933b).[1]

In Freudian theories, the death instinct discharges aggression as an end in itself rather than a means to an end, revealing the ubiquitous human compulsion. Indeed, violence is most likely to be observed in the efforts to fulfil individual instinctual needs. The death instinct is presumably driven to remove all tension through inward aggression directed toward self. To prohibit self-destruction such as suicide, the drive is channelled away from the self toward others. As a consequence, overt aggression is the re-direction of internal aggressive drives.

Any unfulfilled energy may be discharged via a wide variety of substitutive activities or be displaced toward the marginalized social groups. An instinctual impulse of human behaviour has been applied not only to the decision-making style of top political elite but also to the malevolence of an aggressive mass culture. Psychic energy and other basic psychological drives need to be constrained to control a lust for hatred and destruction.

The intervention of social institutions such as family and religion is necessary to reduce the negative interplay of instinct. According to the Dalai Lama (1997), human sentiment translates into a range of positive emotions, such as compassion, beyond the negative emotions associated with destructive impulses. Requirements for love and social support can channel destructive energy flows into positive ones.

Collective memory

As a psychological defence, deep commitments to cultural groups can be developed to buffer unconscious death-related anxieties. Intra-psychic, unconscious fantasies and anxieties have been linked to aggression by chosen trauma and resistance against peaceful adaptations. The sources of oppositional group identities include the hidden psychological 'transcripts' and symbolic sites that explain atrocities and glories of past wars (Volkan, 2006). In preparing for the Six Day War of 1967, for example, Israeli sentiment was ascribed more to a deep-rooted trauma born of past Jewish suffering, especially having been drenched in the Holocaust memory, than a reaction to an imminent Arab threat (Segev, 2007).

According to some analysts, the ethnic warfare in the former Yugoslavia was fuelled by ethnic ideology rooted in a 'powerful reservoir of traumatic memory', associated with World War II atrocities in the Balkans (Agger, 2001). The suppression of public discussion about the carnage during the Tito period did not prohibit the replay of a 'hidden transcript' of past memories attached to all of the pain, sorrow, guilt, and shame since the start of the 1991 civil war. Nationalist propaganda served as a vehicle for releasing poisonous emotions at local community and societal levels in ethnic cleansing. It has been suggested that psycho-political trauma can be reduced by societal healing, inter-communal dialogue, and truth and reconciliation commissions.

Frustration and aggression

In contrast with Freud and Lorenz, psychiatrist John Dollard and his colleagues (1939) attributed aggression to frustration that is not necessarily related to human instinct or nature. Frustration, as a psychological state, results from interference with an individual's pursuit of a desired object. Hindering goal-seeking behaviour, for example, related to reducing hunger and thirst, elicits an attack on the blocking source or its surrogate (Conteh-Morgan, 2003; Goldstein, 2002). Thus, failure to obtain food, territory, or even economic recession exposes the predisposition to, and readiness for, violent behaviour.

The nature of frustration reflects the type of goals and means that are available to the groups. The more unrealistic it is to achieve a desired end state, the deeper frustration might be felt. A lack of alternative means to obtain the blocked goals induces a stronger urge to act. The level of intensity and frequency of blocking is positively correlated to the depth of frustration.

In order to avoid self-defeat, aggression is not easily directed toward the original target of frustration which has superior power. Even though frustration may be suppressed in tandem with withdrawal, avoidance, submission and even acceptance, it is often concentrated on other sources. Therefore, aggression may be displaced on inappropriate targets in a response to the fruitless efforts to eliminate the sources of frustration which often happen to be those in power positions (Dollard et al., 1939). In this case, aggression is aimed at self-enhancement by scapegoating members of social outgroups viewed as devalued.

Mass pathology or a collective madness, accompanied by wider social, economic, and political 'frustrations', has drawn intense concerns about a prejudice against minority groups blamed, as scapegoats, for societal ills. As frustration is expressed in a distorted form, a group of persons may find joy and excitement in attacking another group, especially in the absence of any fear of retaliation. This is well illustrated by the Kosovo Albanians' attack on gypsies after the withdrawal of Yugoslav federal troops in 1999; and Iraqis victimizing Palestinian refugees who were favoured under Saddam Hussein's regime.

Theories on aggression, whether being stimulated by the internal human psyche or externally, propose that, in order to control the conversion of frustration into aggression, destructive impulses need to be channelled into sports and other non-lethal forms of engagement. At the same time, there is a growing understanding that frustration does not automatically translate into violence. In fact, people respond differently to discontent in diverse emotional states of anger arousal and do not select the same methods for discharging frustration. Experiences, rather than genetic constitution, hold sway over the amount and direction of aggression (Brown, 1988).

Some even argue that how to manage frustration is a learned behaviour based on personal experience, mirroring a way of interacting with others. It has also been suggested that aggressive behaviour is obtained by imitating an influential role model. Indeed, aggression is supported and even encouraged, in some cultures, through national media, entertainment, or education. As seen in the ethnic civil wars in the Balkans, aggression may even be glorified for the attainment of victory.

Emotional experience

The substance and fabric of protracted conflicts are not adequately explained in the context of rational choice models of costs and benefits which focus on tangible calculations. Economic rationality oriented toward the pursuit of self-interests is not apt to elucidate retributive action, based on indignation and righteousness. A boiling emotional core, replete with humiliation and rage, is involved in malignant social processes. At the same time, deep feelings of pride and a quest for dignity provide solidarity with a group (Scheff and Retzinger, 1991). Extreme reactions are, in part, related to such emotional states as despair, disempowerment, helplessness, and a desire for revenge. Human suffering, sorrow, and pain are largely characteristic of struggle.

The psychology of humiliation highlights the most potent, pervasive human emotions behind intense struggles, producing rifts in people's lives. According to Algerian psychiatrist Frantz Fanon (2004), brutal suppression is not capable of breaking the will of the oppressed. Moreover, the use of violence by the colonized frees them from their inferiority complex and despair. He continues to suggest that by using violence, the oppressed feel fearless, restoring their self-respect. This understanding has been applied to such cases as Hamas' and Hezbollah's struggles under oppression and attacks by the Israeli military as well as resistance against past colonial occupation in Vietnam and Algeria.

It is important to note that emotional experiences are shaped by cultural norms and other social contexts. Given that social experiences are permeated with meanings, our feelings of hate and rage are socially formulated in shaping relationships. In considering their different roles under diverse circumstances, raw emotions are formed and acted upon in a dissimilar fashion. Their type and depth explicate the staying power of the emotions involved in sustaining a conflict.

Relative deprivation

The failure of political systems to consistently meet people's social and material expectations can translate into a negative mood that instigates political action. A continued improvement in life conditions may eventually begin to decline, involving growing unemployment, declining material production, and disproportionate tax burdens. Despite deteriorating conditions, expectations based on wants and aspirations tend to remain steady. People's expectations are not easily suppressed or contained for a long time, and this leads to their frustration. Thus, a shift from social and economic progress to a state of recession is encountered with a high level of uncertainty and anxiety. Relative deprivation arises from a gap between people's expectations and their actual obtainment especially commensurate to capabilities.

According to the 'J-curve' of Davies (1962), expectations go up linearly at the same rate, even in the event of decreased satisfaction at an actual level. Widespread popular discontent stems from a sharp reversal of material satisfaction, combined with a long period of rising expectations. Thus a violent reaction to an abrupt downturn is most likely to be accompanied by a sustained period of economic and social progress. During the Russian Revolution of 1917 and the Egyptian Revolution of 1952, for example, economic improvement and rising expectations were followed by a sharp and sudden deterioration of life (Davies, 1962).

As seen above, imbalanced changes in expectations and fulfilment produce a wide level of dissatisfaction. The feelings of frustration come from a growing divergence between anticipated and manifest reality. Greater instability is produced by the simultaneous occurrence of a substantial increase in expectations and rapid declines in actual fulfilment. In another pattern, a long improvement creates conditions for the expectation of continued progress that exceeds unchanged capabilities.

Most significantly, structural inflexibility is, to a great extent, accountable for the reluctance of institutions to accommodate new demands. The rise of popular protest is likely to result from the combination of unfulfilled expectations and perceptions of unfair treatment, as represented by the demand of African-Americans, in the 1960s, for greater opportunities to garner upward social mobility and political participation (Gurr, 1970). As happened in the wake of the collapse of Communist governments in Eastern Europe during the late 1980s, demonstration effects also elicit acute feelings of discrepancy between expectations and gratification.

The decline relative to other referent groups, in particular, engenders deeper resentments, in conjunction with an existing sense of unjust disparity. These feelings of frustration only deepen when one group witnesses a gradual decline or loss despite another's continuing gains. Discontent is also likely to be bred when one group perceives that it has made a much smaller gain than a rival group (Besancon, 2005).

Violence is an instrumental means of expressing chronic feelings of anger that are spawned by perceptions of the differentials between reality and expectations. The magnitude of violence is associated with different degrees of deprivation, namely, mild, moderate, or intense, as well as its duration. Feelings of deprivation derived from unfulfilled aspirations for achievable or desirable outcomes are likely to be translated into violence through mobilization capabilities. In the end, a balance of coercion between a government and dissident groups determines the nature of violence occurring (Gurr, 1970).

Overall, a persistent sense of inequality, when combined with the availability of a means of destruction, composes one of the conditions for the initiation of violence. Reward systems and social stratifications (seen to be unfair) cause social stress and group conflicts. The disadvantages of income and opportunities for occupational advancement have an impact on the perceived limitations of what individuals are able to achieve within a given system. Frustration is set off by a disparity between the formal status and actual achievement, in tandem with a felt inability to control one's decision and action.

The role of comparative disadvantage in the instigation of conflict is mitigated if negative changes in material expectations might be compensated by the availability of opportunities in other areas such as educational achievement. Most importantly, the critics argue that relative deprivation does not count different levels of individual perceptions about group fortunes. In particular, people may have different, desired standards for comparison, and do not necessarily experience the same level of dissatisfaction with their current status (Barkan and Snowden, 2000). For instance, even such seemingly objective deprivation criteria as unemployment rates do not always indicate the intensity of subjective feelings. A low level of social esteem and prestige may contribute to a lack of intense feelings about deprivation needed for collective action.

Human needs

The sources of intractable social conflict originate in a set of unsatisfied existential and other deep-seated needs. Human needs are ontological and essential elements for our subsistence, even though differences in culture and education might lead to diverse interpretations and salience. The theories of inter-group conflict situations, as driven by unmet needs, have been applied to the analysis of many protracted struggles around the world where the demand for autonomy or independence is prevalent (Mitchell, 2001). In addition, the oppression of basic needs, not only physical but also psychological (self-esteem, recognition, and respect), has fuelled ethnic and other identity-based conflict. Thus the motivational aspects of social action are relegated to the relentless pursuit of non-negotiable conditions for human existence.

The unyielding drive to fulfil individual and group needs has explained human behaviour and social interaction. Essential needs for survival entail security and safety (from fear and anxiety), belongingness and love, recognition and acceptance by others, dignity and feelings of personal fulfilment (Galtung, 1990). Psychologist Abraham Maslow (1971) argues that different needs can be attained separately by suggesting a needs pyramid in which basic items related to safety and security (such as food, water, and shelter) have to be met first, being followed eventually by self-esteem.

It is generally accepted, however, that, even though material needs must be met, most intractable sources of conflict are ascribed to perceived threats to identity and security. The denial of these ontological conditions, as well as unmet physical needs, is attributed to the suppression of human fulfilment. Wherever possible, physical and political restraints need to be eliminated to develop the capacity to exercise choice in all aspects of life (Bay, 1990). The fair allocation of resources among all members of a community is needed in order to guarantee choices and access to social and economic opportunities. For John W. Burton and other conflict resolution theorists, primary attention was paid to identity, a sense of self in relation to the outside world, along with the need for recognition of each group's language, traditions, and religion. Territorial divisions, return of refugees, allocation of water, and many other issues in the Israeli–Palestinian conflict are ultimately linked to identity and security needs that are yet to be addressed and satisfied on all levels.

Laws and social norms are institutionalized to socialize individuals into conformative behaviours, more specifically, to constrain and manipulate individual behaviour within societal requirements. Ontological human needs are set in sharp contrast with traditional state norms. The state legitimacy is challenged when traditional authority norms do not respond to the inherent needs of persons. When human needs cannot be attained within the boundaries of existing social relations and institutions, individuals and identity groups seek means outside of official realms (Burton, 2001). A lack of institutional responses to essential needs, or even the denial of development requirements, generates a conflict. Thus, a human needs framework shifts its unit of analysis from states to identity groups. Behavioural considerations in the principle of inherent human needs stress that law and order cannot be sustained, only on the basis of fear and threats, without satisfying essential human ontological conditions.

Functional and dysfunctional conflict

Theories based on the traditions of Karl Marx support the idea that a change in human relations inevitably comes out of social conflict. In Marxist analysis, economic forces, especially the forces of production, constitute an essential element in setting the stage for class and other social conflicts. In functionalist views built on Max Weber's perspectives, however, stability and order are explained by complex interrelationships among primary economic and social institutions. For Weber, the functions of a society can be adjusted to underlying conflict situations.

In contrast with coercive views of conflict in Marxist traditions, the consensus-equilibrium perspective of society regards conflict as dysfunctional, especially in considering that it creates tension, disturbances, and strain within a 'harmonious' system. The established roles, functions, and norms serve as a medium in support of order (Parsons, 1951). Even if difficulties arise in the process of interaction among different components, the functions performed by each segment of society provide adjustment for the integral system. Values legitimize a balance secured by political functions.

Basic cleavages over the distribution of political and economic power focus on the very nature of division of labour and social differentiation. In this situation, social coherence needs to be achieved by rebalancing different forces of the system in efforts to explore new arrangements that are acceptable to diverse groups in a changing environment. Internal cohesion is created by the institutionalization of conflict regulation mechanisms so that a conflict does not become dysfunctional or pathological (Dahrendorf, 1959). 'Safety valve' functions have been designed to reduce social stress with system-adaptive consequences.

Social change

From a Marxist perspective, individuals in a particular category are inevitably engaged in a common struggle against those who belong to an opposing one. In essence, group divisions always have an economic base, for it is the material conditions of life that are crucial for understanding social relationships. According to Karl Marx, it is not individual attributes or interests, but rather the interplay of broad social forces, that bring about change. A key to understanding social struggles is to examine class structures based on the economic division of labour. The nature of group relations is characterized by economic stratifications maintained by either hidden or overt forms of coercion (Tormey and Townshend, 2006). Since incompatible political interests determined by class relations drive conflict, a consensus-based society can, for the Marxist, be achieved only by a classless society.

Marxist analysis attributes structural change not to a sermon on a desire for harmony or goodwill but to political revolution. Individual interests and consciousness are shaped by relative positions in a social hierarchy that are, in turn, relegated to his or her economic status. The interests of a worker demanding equitable payment are contrasted with those of a manager who wants to pay less. In a capitalist society, legal and political institutions, meanwhile, correspond to the mode of an economic system that protects private ownership and business interests (Marx and Engels, 1947).

Economic motivation locates every group in society, namely, buyers and sellers, management and unions, in a constant state of opposite interests. In the end, the competition in a capitalist economy is expected to produce a further concentration of capital into fewer hands. The unfair advantages for bigger industrial enterprises are certain to wipe out smaller businesses. Thus the system allows one group to enjoy an advantageous political and economic status at the sacrifice of others. According to the Marxist thesis, a fundamental transformation in the system is inevitable when the control of the main economic means by a few brings about further inequality and more discontent.

As a permanent feature of a society, a structural conflict is more generally described beyond class relations (Dahrendorf, 1959). Various social cleavages provide the basis for conflict; this does not refer just to those formed by antagonistic economic interests. Differences in power are structurally based, reflecting the way in which society is arranged. Economic considerations are important only if they have significance for political struggles. Power differentials are reflected not only by the entire society, but also in its social organizations. It is not wealth or property but power that is more directly related to the forces of change.

Different interests are formed on the basis of structural divisions of domination and subordination (Dahrendorf, 1959). In essence, conflict is a dialectical process that propels the transformation of society by incorporating opposing elements. Old social institutions are reconstructed with the ascendance of a new elite. The support or rejection of the status quo centres on the question of whether to challenge an existing social and economic hierarchy based on wealth, race, and ethnicity. The awareness of opposing interests is needed for forming self-conscious conflict groups that are able to pursue collective action. Shared interests have to be more explicitly expressed prior to the development of these groups.

Conflict imbedded in social structures

When structures fashion a situation of competition for power and status, conflict becomes cyclical, inherent, and endemic in social relations. The fragmentation and polarization of all interests reflect structural divisions, rooted in different social categories such as religion, language, and ethno-political affiliations. Interests are divided and cross-pressured by multiple group memberships based on professional associations, sports leagues, social clubs, and economic institutions. This cross-pressure undercuts the potential for social cleavages to be translated into permanently opposing categories. The coexistence of a variety of contrasting interests contributes to the segmentation of individual interests that could have otherwise been concentrated on a superordinate issue.

Involvement in multiple relationships minimizes the possibility for the development of superordinate conflicts fought around a monolithic issue. Engagement in one big battle over particular interests can be averted by the existence of various groups that pursue segmented and mutually contradicting interests. Religious and social groups may moderate or contain violence by emphasizing psychological comfort and social harmony. If intersecting, multi-fold groups get involved in many conflict structures, diverse interests balance out differences in continuous interactions. Despite their domination in one arena, a group might be put in a subordinate position in another area. Once values and interests begin to coalesce into one societal cleavage, the division of groups and individuals into opposing clusters is likely to generate intense struggle.

When opposing interests are pushed in diverse directions under cross pressures, many local disputes are isolated to a small set of issues. Even if multiple relationships and interactions are not likely to assure the end of some violence, many conflicts can remain segregated events at the margins. A violent strike at a single car manufacturing plant, for example, will not spread across entire industries and engulf the whole country to bring about a government downfall.

The absence of pluralistic groups weakens and eliminates cross pressures by consistently placing identical groups of people in the same dominant and subordinate relationships, thus firmly dividing the society. All important social issues become a matter of control by one group, as is illustrated by the domination of an authoritarian government. However, the government would eventually face a crisis, since it could not totally control every aspect of society through coercion for a sustained period.

Once conflict involves the power elite versus the rest of society and also once all issues are related to a matter of grievances against those in power, then the magnitude of violence overwhelms various sectors of a society. Even a minor matter may touch upon the exercise of a government's power and therefore might contribute to violent escalation. In this situation, a strike at a steel mill (owned and run by the government), as was exemplified by the Solidarity movement in Poland during the early 1980s, becomes a crisis of legitimacy for the government elite if that strike is not controlled by force.

Identity formation

In mobilizing one group against another, identity plays an important role by maintaining boundary functions. Identity is related to the norms, beliefs, practices, and traditions that influence one group's interaction with the surrounding environment. Identity formation relies on 'categorization that perceptually homogenizes ingroups vis-à-vis outgroups' (Hogg, 2001). Threats to identity augment the potential for destructive conflict in conjunction with the fortification of rigidified group boundaries. The perceptions of self supply the lens through which one views others. In conflict situations, a positive self-identification stems, to a large degree, from a favourable comparison of an 'in-group' with 'out-groups' (Operario and Fiske, 1999). Stronger, exclusive identity increases the chances for an in-group to defame, and justify discrimination against, an out-group with the development of stereotypes.

Identity is ascribed to the establishment of a relationship beyond a mere psychological state. Different types of identity can be put on a relational canvas that is both subjective and objective, for example, African-American versus black American, reflecting on situational salience. Invigorating a particular type of identity (ethnic, racial, and gender) entails not only an active role of individual actors but also situational interactions (Tajfel and Turner, 1986). The significance of identity is not the same at different stages of individual engagement with a social conflict.

In the constructionist perspective, group boundaries are shaped by a social context; the process of articulating identity with perceptual filters, such as strong feelings of a common fate, takes precedence over an objective, absolute category. A group identity serves as a cultural resource and, being reinforced by emotional attachment, remains a site for mobilizing forces. The dominant themes of a culture can be transmitted into the hearts and minds of people, supplying a powerful political weapon. Various family, primary education, and other socialization patterns contribute to the regeneration of old symbols and myths.

Cultural imperatives are borne out of a language that plays a formative role in the emergence of nationalist ideologies. Being ubiquitous in a culture, ethno-linguistic habits support the maintenance of interethnic boundaries (Gudykunst et al., 1989). Many marginalized groups have attempted to revitalize beleaguered, traditional languages in a formal public domain. Language policies based on linguistic discrimination can fortify the exclusion of others from political office and economic improvement. Internal strife in Sri Lanka originates in the government's efforts to marginalize Tamils by precluding their ethnic language from an official status in the late 1950s. By creating powerful boundaries, the linguistic and communication divisions may intensify cross-national competition in a multilingual society such as India.

The social construction of identity is often related not only to the promotion of a separate parochial distinctiveness but also to the formation of a larger community, as seen in discussion about the entry of Turkey in the EU and the reformulated role of racial identity in South African politics. Turkey's Islamic identity is regarded as an obstacle to its assimilation into the EU, the members of which share Christian heritage. The black leadership does not want to emphasize the white–black difference in its governance of South Africa after taking power contrary to its struggle against the white minority government during the apartheid period. Because identity is not immutable, its forms, nature, and significance differ at a particular historical moment.

Any form of peaceful coexistence relies on the construction of superordinate values in conjunction with the toleration of differences among separate group identities. Thus, inclusive categories can coexist with lower level identities (Bizman and Yinon, 2004). At the same time, the perceptions of past experiences and future expectations can be modified through a cooperative interaction designed to reduce inter-group bias. Major conflicts in multicultural societies are rooted in a lack of respect for divergence with an emphasis on a dominant group's value preferences. Multiple dimensions of a marginalized group's identity, represented by such social and cultural traits as language and religion, strengthen internal unity and motives for empowerment.

Through re-categorization, members of different groups are conceived of as part of inclusive categories. Degrading group boundaries comes from expanded interactions along with the discovery of common characteristics (Dovidio et al., 2005). Therefore, identity transformation derives from increased positive contacts with others and perceptual changes. In such countries as Switzerland, coexistence among multiple identity groups has been promoted by mutual respect for each others' unique histories and cultural traditions as well as through economic interdependence.

Politicization of identity

Incompatible value preferences or principles may touch upon various elements of culture and politics. An identity base has socio-political ramifications when positive and negative value systems are placed on skin colour, religion, gender, language, or occupation in justifying group relations. In many divided societies, highly subjective political evaluations often merge into objective categories that are employed to bestow or withhold a privileged status or wealth. Identity politics are not an isolated group phenomenon, not being divorced from the mobilization of racial or ethnic categories in an intense struggle. Since 2000, Zimbabwean President Mugabe has used the confiscation of white-owned farms as an attempt to dilute mass opposition to his autocratic rule.

The purpose of social categorization may include one group's attempt to fabricate a higher moral ground in maintaining domination over another. The competition for higher social status often generates a political struggle. The illegitimate superiority of one group over another sows the seeds of potential conflicts with the disproportionate distribution of wealth and power. Not only emotional significance, attached to group membership, but also the primitive impulses, based on dislikes and enmities, are implicated in degrading the portraits of those in competition for power. In fact, dominant groups endeavour to preserve their social and communicative distinctiveness by undercutting the subordinate group's status (Bourdieu, 1991).

Identity is adaptable to either the intensification of conflict or the management of hostilities. In many multi-ethnic societies, a mutually competitive orientation is associated with perceived out-group hostility that, in turn, promotes ethnocentric attitudes. National identity can easily turn into a negative tool for intentional manipulation. The rise of hyper-nationalist movements has been responsible for genocide or 'ethnic cleansing' (Jones, 2006).

Repeated experience leads to the solidification of beliefs and perceptions of self and others. Each event may be built upon the mobilization of groups and societies that define themselves according to their opposition to the negative other. Identity plays a crucial role in forming pervasive narratives to present an account of a particular group's history and its rights and claims. In the justification of a conflict, one party dominates the other, presenting little ground for trust or cooperation.

Nationalism and the state

Nationalism hinges on a primordial human attachment to an imagined community linked to a historic homeland and a common fate (Anderson, 1991).

Solidarity stems from a bond that is manufactured by shared culture, memories, common ancestry, and ideological preferences.[2] A nation, as a behavioural entity, seeks political and social goals, whereas nationalism develops a sentiment of loyalty (Connor, 2002). In its anti-colonial opposition to France and Britain, Arab nationalism constituted a common ideology for many groups stretched from Morocco to the Arabian Peninsula with an emphasis on their common linguistic, cultural, and historical heritage. Its origin is traced back to a demand for greater autonomy made within the Ottoman Empire in 1913.[3] Nationalist sentiments became more prominent in the wake of substituting the Ottoman authority's brutal repression with the British and French colonial division of the eastern Arab lands. In the post-colonial period, pan-Arabic nationalism had to compete with religious sects, tribes and other subnational loyalties, and was further weakened due to rivalry between Egypt and Syria in the early 1960s.

Individuals are psychologically more strongly attached to a 'nation' than a 'state', which is represented by a government or other bureaucratic entities. When a state comprises a single nation, almost everyone is supposed to accept and support the state legitimacy. A nation state is regarded as the primary home of the population's political identity and loyalty. In multi-ethnic states, the persistence of subregional identities often clashes with the demand for a loyalty to a state, as is illustrated by the primary allegiance of the Welsh to Wales rather than to Great Britain, the Walloons in more close association with Wallonia than with Belgium, or the Québécois with Quebec rather than with Canada.

In considering that there are very few ethnically pure states, the divisions of 'minority versus majority' have been inevitable. Indeed, artificial political and territorial boundaries were crafted in the birth of many modern post-colonial states such as India, Pakistan, Sudan and Burundi. There are now groups of people who are scattered across newly established international borders (Calvert and Allcock, 2004). Historical claims to statehood have been a source of many clashes between the elite in control of government institutions and ethnic groups. Minority groups in Kashmir, Chechnya, and most of the former Yugoslav republics have challenged the central authorities. In a crisis involving a whole society, for instance, Rwanda, Serbia, and Croatia, the full range of media technologies has been re-moulded as a propaganda tool to instigate mass murder.

Yugoslavia's disintegration into now six separate states has produced a source of more instability due to a lack of agreements on boundaries among diverse national groups that were previously integrated under a federal system. In Kosovo and Bosnia-Herzegovina, diverse ethnic group members remain in their enclaves with little contact with other groups. Similarly, 15 new states were born out of the Soviet Union, establishing new divisions and tensions within each. Most ethnic minorities have been negatively affected by the nationalistic rule of the new state elite. The isolation or segregation of minority ethnic groups spread across various geographical units exposes vulnerability to systematic or random violence.

In order to construct social bases of support for central authority, the elite of newly founded states try to undermine identification with, and loyalty to, traditional social systems embedded in communal life. The periods of state formation instability often end up with autocratic governments of one type or another, for example, in Kazakhstan, Turkmenistan, Tajikistan, and Uzbekistan, eventually provoking rebellious movements. In particular, the civil war in Tajikistan of 1992–97, which was responsible for the death of between 50,000 and 100,000 people, is ascribed to the disenfranchisement of ethnic groups from the Garm and Gorno-Badakhshan regions by the newly formed central government.

The exclusionary acts of leaders representing the dominant group are more likely to enrage a minority population. The pursuit of self-defined interests can be justified by a separate ethno-national community on the basis of disadvantages vis-à-vis other groups. Further grievances follow when the perceived distribution of rights and privileges is not considered to be legitimate. In a quest for autonomy, ethno-national groups search for security, but several ethnic communities may express a desire to control the same territory in which there is a mixed population (Stetter, 2007). In addition, minority group leaders may want independence, while the existing authority wants to keep up territorial control. Serbia, for instance, wants to maintain its rule over Kosovo, while Albanians seek independence with the future status of the Serb enclaves left in a grey area.

Given its tendency to turn into hatred of others, hyper-nationalism gets out of hand, frequently sparking the most brutal form of violence. The intense emotional feelings are mobilized for the internal justification of atrocities. In particular, people can be encouraged to treat abusively the 'others' who refuse to be assimilated into the 'homeland' or 'motherland'. In inciting an interstate war, as exhibited especially by Germany and Japan during World War II, political leaders utilize unmet nationalist aspirations for territorial expansion. Violent conflicts, since the beginning of the twentieth century, have accounted for well over a hundred million lives, and many of these conflicts are attributed to hyper-nationalism.

A contemporary state system

While adversarial relationships between states are ascribed to the competitive pursuit of economic or military interests in a power politics model, the explanation of many contemporary conflicts arises from the desire of ethnic or nationalist groups to secede. Geopolitical and geo-economic significance, for example, attached to competition over vast oil reserves, has encouraged the meddling of major powers in ethnically diverse parts of the world. Religious and linguistic differences often surface as a visible division overlaid in ethnic animosities and territorial disputes.

Geographical and historical rivalry, for example, between India and Pakistan, has been fabricated by colonial rules and in a post-colonial quest for independence. Along with the establishment of new states, there has been more political violence of different scales, ranging from adverse regime changes and revolutionary insurgencies to ethnic wars and genocides. Political and economic integration through modernization has increased the stake in the control of central state institutions, subsequently with the outcome of comparative disadvantages and inequality for diverse minority groups (Ellis, 2006).

Ethnic conflicts often transcend material grievances to entail religious and other types of demand relating to autonomy and freedom. The state is often ripped apart by inter-communal violence, as demonstrated by the struggles of Muslims against other Muslims in Iraq and warfare between Muslims and non-Muslims in Sudan. The Taliban government of 1992–2001 in Afghanistan imposed extreme Islamic rules based on the strict interpretation of Shariah. Ethno-religious conflicts are locked into deeper communal divisions expressed in violence between Hindus and Muslims in India, between Christian Armenians and Muslims in Azerbaijan, and between Roman Catholic Croats and Muslim Bosnians in Bosnia-Herzegovina.

Government discrimination against minorities

Significant changes in the global system of states were accompanied by the decolonization of European-controlled territories in Africa and Asia, in particular, between 1950 and 1975. The number of independent states more than doubled from 79 independent countries in 1950 to 161 in 2003, increasing the potential number of ethnic conflicts (Marshall and Gurr, 2005). Ethnic group affiliation is directly related to political mobilization and competition for state power in Ethiopia. Ethnic and racial discrimination, for instance, against the Roma of Bulgaria and against indigenous tribes in Brazil, illustrates prevailing patterns of societal composition and contention in each society.

The extreme end of ethnic diversity includes India, China, Burma, Ethiopia, Uganda, Pakistan, Indonesia, and independent states carved out of former Soviet republics, as opposed to the ethnic homogeneity of Korea, Japan, Sweden, and Denmark. The dissolution of the Soviet Union on December 31, 1991 created new divisions within each of the former Republics by putting one ethnic group in charge of a newly independent state. The rights of many Russian speaking and other minority populations in the newly formed states have been severely restricted by a suddenly emerging ruling elite. Whereas the independence of Bangladesh in 1972 turned repressed ethnic Bengalis in Pakistan into the ruling majority, the new state's attempt to control minority ethnic groups produced tension with tribal groups located in the Chittagong Hill Tracts.

While some ethno-national groups are small and geographically dispersed, such groups as the Kurds have a strong support base with geographic concentration. The Druze, whose traditional religion began as an offshoot of Islam, are scattered across Lebanon, Syria, and Israel. The Druze have been officially recognized as a separate religious community with their own court system. In many instances, governmental policies substantially restrict minority groups' cultural practice and political choice. Especially, continuing repression limits group mobilization in support for autonomy, as is best represented by Tibetans and Uyghurs in the Western part of China. The most severe repressions of ethnic minorities are also found in Burma, Sudan, and former Soviet republics such as Uzbekistan.

When one group is dominant and sets the political agenda, its claims are made at the expense of others' rights. Political or economic discrimination against constituent ethnic groups by state elite lies at the heart of an ethnic conflict. In fact, a wide variation in the number and sizes of minorities oppressed by state entities characterize conflict dynamics in multi-ethnic societies (Hechter and Borland, 2001). In countries such as China, the well-being of ethnic minority groups has been further undermined by rapid economic change, environmental exploitation, and the transfer of the dominant Han nationality to previously autonomous ethnic regions. Indigenous peoples in Latin America are disadvantaged economically, even though there are some hopeful signs in Bolivia, where social activist President Evo Morales has been attempting to empower economically impoverished, highland, indigenous people despite resistance of powerful, lowland, oligarchic political and economic interests. There is a high likelihood of ethnic discontent in countries where groups are under-represented in government decision making.

Changes in the status of minority groups have rarely been easy except in the break-up of multi-ethnic federal states. Secessionist movements can be peaceful in such instances as the division of Czechoslovakia into two states. Even successful secession by a province, region, or a sub-state area from an existing state may generate disagreements over borders, for example, between Ethiopia and Eritrea.

Ethnic or religious separatist movements, organized, for instance, by the Karen and Arakan of Burma, the Mindano of the Philippines, the Aceh of Indonesia, and the Patani of Thailand, have formed military resistance (Minahan, 2002). The oil-rich and mainly Muslim republic of Chechnya failed to split away from Russia, continuing to absorb military oppression. Secessionist wars can spill over international borders. In blocking Kurdish nationalist movements scattered in Turkey, Iraq, and Iran, Turkish military campaigns targeted Kurdish fighters with incursions into Northern Iraq since the 1990s. This cross-border spillover is also visible in the Democratic Republic of Congo, Rwanda, and Burundi, where ethnic groups span state borders.

When the political autonomy of national minorities is curbed, an adjacent kindred state may get directly involved in the conflict. The suppression of Hungarians in Slovakia and the treatment of Russians in Estonia, Lithuania, and Ukraine have produced simmering tensions between the minority group's host countries and the adjacent states. Trans-state conflict would similarly be inevitable if a nationalist group in a sub-state region were to join a neighbouring state that shares the same religion, language, and other aspects of cultural traditions. Even though remedies need to be made with institutional changes, a concern over sovereignty and territorial integrity has undermined secession movements by treating the demands of self-determination as domestic issues.

Terrorism

Non-combatant, civilian populations have become a target of indiscriminate violence executed in a systematic and deliberate manner as collateral damage. Whereas a one-sided imposition of violent force upon a victim is immoral, deadly terror and intimidation tactics are 'the continuation of war by other means' (Clausewitz, 1984). Acts of terrorism are regarded as a subset of politically motivated violence. The marginalized may attempt to use terrorism to amplify a small amount of violent power, calculated as leverage to bring about psychological effects on a much stronger enemy.

As more than guerrilla warfare, terrorism is conducted by faceless enemies with irregular tactics. Its controversial character is well reflected in a popular phrase 'one person's freedom fighter is another's terrorist'. As a political form of violence, terrorism often targets the prevailing symbols of authority structures in order to draw attention to a political agenda (Richardson, 2006). A surprise attack can be launched to seize a momentary, situational, or imagined advantage in an asymmetrical power relationship before the target musters adequate protection.

As a means of repressive policies, authorities may also use cruel, inhumane methods against constituents in an effort to coerce order best illustrated by Idi Amin who ruled Uganda between 1971 and 1979. Large-scale attacks on Christian, black Africans by Muslim Arab militias have been endorsed and even supported by the military government in Sudan. The acts taken by governments have aims to terrorize populations within their own or other states. Restrictions on access to food, water, and other basic needs, as well as the use of lethal force, target civilian populations, as in Russia's indiscriminate attacks on civilian areas of Chechnya and Israeli attacks against Palestinian residential areas. In these cases, fear is imposed as a powerful instrument of statecraft (O'Kane, 1996)

Psychological effects are more important than the attack's physical destruction in judging the impact of terrorism on the population. The perceptual response to the terrorist act obtains peculiar social prominence in the collective consciousness projected, in large part, by surprise, indiscriminate violence beyond ethical boundaries (Soeters, 2005). An extraordinary terrorist act captures our imagination more effectively as a special form of political violence. In fact, an act of terrorism stands in contrast against normal social expectations and contexts.

Therefore, terrorism depends on a highly personalized use of violence with a more immediate impact on a perceptual level. Psychopathic violence is tactically and logistically differentiated from more complex forms of militant action. The actor may rationally calculate violent acts for an emotional effect. Terrorist attacks may have been adopted to support sustained, armed insurrection, as seen in the example of Chechen fighters struggling against the Russian government. Terrorism has been combined with guerrilla warfare by Iraqi insurgents acting against the US occupation.

The events of 11 September 2001, motivated by a fundamentalist religious faith, were plotted to produce large effects, with more than three thousand deaths. A dramatic show of destruction was orchestrated to garner huge public attention. Islamist extremists, mostly of North African origin, conducted a series of coordinated bombings against the commuter train system of Madrid on the morning of 11 March 2004, which killed almost two hundred people and wounded over two thousand. On 7 July 2005, a series of suicide bombing attacks on London's public transport system, undertaken by four British nationals of Pakistani descent, cost over fifty lives along with about seven hundred injuries. These were followed by four attempted bombings in the British capital on 21 July. In protest against Jordan's pro-Western stance, suicide bombers organized attacks on three hotels in the capital Amman on 9 November 2005. While the 11 September 2001 attacks reflect, in part, the Arabic world's sentiment about US policy toward the Middle East, the bombings in London and Madrid were motivated by resentment of the UK and Spanish governments' support of the Iraqi war.

The general lawlessness, accompanied by the brutal communal warfare in Sierra Leone, Liberia, and the northeast provinces of the Democratic Republic of Congo, caused systematic victimization of civilians. In the north of Uganda, the rebels of the Lord's Resistance Army preyed mostly on children. In Iraq, mainly urban insurgency and sectarian fighting have led to attacks by disenfranchised religious groups, accounting for high numbers of civilian casualties. The direct and indirect effects of combat operations have brought about severe disruptions in essential services and other devastating impacts on civilians. In unruly civil war situations, warlords have taken advantage of disorder and have used horrific acts against defenceless victims purely in the pursuit of satisfying their own greed and power.

Notes

1 In resolving this, 'ego' depends on such defence mechanisms as rationalization, denial, displacement, and fantasy.

2 The Communist parties, led by Greeks in Cyprus and Sikhs in the Punjab, played a crucial role in their early struggle for asserting national rights.

3 As nationalism can go beyond religious differences, one of the early foundations for Arab nationalist movements was developed by Syrian Christian intellectuals.

Conflict Situations and Behaviour

4

Inter-group behaviour can be examined from the perspective of multilayered social and psychological structures. Whereas the functions of political, economic, cultural, and historical processes help in understanding the macro-social context of a conflict, biased expectations and enemy images generate misperception and suspicion. Objective conflict conditions are not necessarily commonly understood by all parties, given the involvement of various degrees of unrealistic components in a continuing process of social interaction. In a socio-psychological approach, considerable subjectivity inevitably filters the experience of conflict situations and value judgements about outcomes (Fisher, 1990). A comprehensive, yet restrictive, theory is essential to the analysis of a scope of realistic and non-realistic sources of conflict.

The first part of this chapter explains complex patterns of social interaction shaped and re-shaped by individual actor choices. Overall, 'conflict is acted out in the behaviour of individuals' and groups of individuals (Tillett and French, 2006: 200). The structure of interaction in most conflict relationships is closely interwoven with both competition and cooperation. Game theories—represented by the pursuit of self-interest and its impact on a collectively determined outcome—and other decision-making theories have been applied to the analysis of antagonistic actions. Inter-group theories, combined with the analysis of leadership images and perceptions of enemies, can be applied to the initiation of an international conflict.

In illuminating a conflict situation, psychological mechanisms are related to the justification of one group's actions toward another. The key socio-psychological aspects of human behaviour would not be illustrated without a focus on cognition, affect, motivational elements and their organizational contexts. Enemy images, stereotypes, and perceptions of threat are used for further developing a sense of differentiation between 'us' and 'them' and promoting in-group solidarity. The second half of this chapter also sheds light on how parties assign different meanings to adversarial relationships through cognitive filters and sensory information.

Socio-psychological approaches to conflict

In an adversarial relationship, competitive orientations and group hostilities involving perceptions of threat intensify a desire for control over resources or territorial claims (Cashman and Robinson, 2007). Whereas objective criteria—such as real differences in interests, values, needs, or power—drive inter-group conflict, the active construction and representations of the existing reality entail cognitive processes. In developing conflicting behaviour, social, economic, and political interests are twisted with a psychological response to a hostile environment. Perceptual biases arise from the effects of social categorization in which group differences create divisions among people (Hogg, 2001). Socio-psychological processes play an important role in influencing the intensity of a conflict, even though structural constraints, for instance, emanating from limited capabilities to fight, confine the parameters of behaviour.

Behavioural patterns are activated by particular situations and roles. A social and psychological context defines the nature of struggles originating from competition for positions and status. The tactics of coercion, threat, or deception are employed to maintain domination and increase power differentials. At the same time, an unrealistic ingredient of misperception and miscommunication is implicated even in many pure types of interest-based conflict. Hostilities, even coming from one source such as territorial disputes, may then entail national pride and other issues (Fisher, 1990). The 1981 Falklands War between Britain and Argentina indicates that, in fact, territorial control can carry far less economic or other practical value than symbolic significance attached to 'power status', 'sovereignty', or 'national ambitions'. Adversarial relationships are fuelled not only by a mixture of economic disparities, value incompatibility, or power differences, but also by emotional ingredients.

If groups are differentiated in a competitive social context, the categorization of individuals into groups is most likely to generate a certain amount of bias in favour of one's in-group members with a high likelihood of discrimination against out-groups (Ellis, 2006). Increased hardening of in-group and out-group categories stems from stereotypical enemy images and a reduced ability to empathize with those who do not share the same interests or values. A hostile act may evoke a magnified response with the involvement of deprivational factors, escalating to an open, destructive struggle.

A contentious, win–lose competition between two collective entities is illustrated by a tendency toward zero-sum thinking in combination with increased mistrust of the motives of the other side. Fears, whether grounded on true facts or in imagination, often serve to feed and freeze the stereotyped images of adversaries. In international conflicts, perceived threats are often caused by misinterpretation of intentions and actions (Jervis, 1976). This is further exacerbated by the nature of crisis decision making which causes stress to the political elite. The risk-taking propensities of decision makers can be ascribed to psychological stress and other emotional states.

Cooperative and competitive relationships

Various forms of perception, attitude, and communication can explain cooperative versus competitive social interaction. Cooperative social interaction focuses on the perceptions of similarity in tandem with the development of trust and open communication. A perceived similarity in beliefs and attitudes stimulates the pursuit of common interests. Competitive interaction, meanwhile, generates suspicious and hostile attitudes that are reinforced by limited or misleading communication.

Whereas mutual opposition may arise from the perception of scarcity, the necessity for cooperation is derived from interdependence that induces each party to explore strategies of maximizing joint gains (McCarty and Meirowitz, 2007). The existence of competing interests does not necessarily promote adversarial relationships if the legitimacy of each other's interests is recognized in a search for an equally satisfactory solution. In the absence of the ability to dominate an adversary, the utilities attached to attaining one's own specific goals, especially in an interdependent relationship, are better served by a willingness to cooperate.

Since the foundational work by John von Neumann and Oskar Morgenstern (1944), various outcomes of conflict and cooperative situations have long been explained by game theories which represent the multiple choices available to actors and their consequences. The structure of interdependent interests produces either a pure competitive conflict known as a 'zero-sum game' or a variable-sum outcome. In a zero-sum game, one side's gain is automatically considered to be the other's loss, representing a situation in which any rewards are always attained at the opponent's expense. A positive sum or win–win situation produces a mutually beneficial result, while in a negative sum situation, the contestants experience mutual loss. In a non-zero-sum game, mutual outcomes, mathematically calculated, can have net results greater or less than zero. Thus, a gain by one does not necessarily correspond with another's loss.

The main focus in game theory is the outcome of interactions between two or more players, each seeking their own best interests. Individual strategies can be cast in a wide spectrum of competitive-cooperative relationships. Rational choice theory highlights individualistic decision making, motivated by the desire to maximize 'expected utility' and minimize loss. A particular set of preferences within a fixed array of possible choices shapes the expectations of actors about the outcome in a search for the greatest benefits. Most importantly, variance in collective decision outcomes is determined by the mutual effects of individual preference (Walt, 2000).

Each side is compelled to decide whether to cooperate for, or defect from, a shared cause of joint interests. Decision-making behaviour in game theory exhibits the consideration of the outcomes of a highly conflicting situation (Rapoport, 1966). When opposing interests put two players in a pure competitive situation, irreconcilable elements of goals are fused into win–lose struggles. As pure contest or harmony does not exist in world affairs over a sustained period, mixed motives reflect a situation in which cooperative and competitive interests are interwoven (Schelling, 1960).

In the selection of actors' strategies, pay-off matrices are predetermined by a set of inviolate rules. The outcome expectations of actors are reflected in making certain choices. Players do not radically deviate from predictable courses of action, in that their choices are limited by pay-off matrices. Game theories assume, therefore, that the patterns of actors' behaviour and strategies are explained by the available choices.

By choosing different strategic positions, one party unilaterally attempts to change or restrict the choice of the other. In a sequence of decisions, each party's moves based on feasible choices are controlled by a competitive situation. Each decision maker attempts to minimize losses and maximize gains under the constraints of given situations (Rapoport, 1990). In game theories, the emotional or other irrational psychological characteristics of decision makers are not regarded as significant in determining the outcome. When each opponent's interests are diametrically opposed, the best solution is to choose the option that gives the most to be assured. In the end, all two-person games suggest an equilibrium point at which the best interests of all of the parties are balanced.

Mixed motives

In a mixed-motive game, the two players produce not only win–lose but also win–win and lose–lose outcomes by selecting competing or cooperative options. The 'prisoner's dilemma' game presents four possible outcomes in a two-by-two matrix of cooperation and defection. This expected pay-off is illustrated by a frequently cited story of two suspected criminals facing jail terms with the outcomes determined by their different choices (Blalock, 1989). Each of the two prisoners, arrested by police for a bank robbery, is asked to plead guilty to the charge. Mutual confession would lead each of them to spend five years in jail. In the event that one pleads guilty as part of a plea bargain and the other does not, the confessor will go free while the silent suspect ends up being locked up in jail for 40 years. If both refuse to confess, neither can be convicted of the bank robbery due to a lack of evidence. However, each will still be convicted of a violation of lesser charges such as illegal possession of assault weapons, and receive a year's jail term.

The confession by one and refusal by the other will bring about the stiffest jail term for the prisoner who declines to confess, while granting a 'free life' for the confessor. Without knowing the other's decision, the most preferable choice for each is to admit to the robbery in order to avoid a 40-year prison term. The worst scenario following a confession will be a five-year jail term. In the best scenario resulting from the other's silence, the confession brings the outcome of a 'free life'.

Presuming that both parties are not able to communicate with each other, the rational behaviour for each prisoner is to mistrust the other and plead guilty. The temptation to defect is strong, given the perceived costs of being a 'sucker' as well as the maximum interests gained by the other's one-sided cooperation. Defection incurs smaller losses than unconditional cooperation, which will lead to a big loss in the likely event of the other's betrayal.

In the prisoner's dilemma, however, the pursuit of exclusive individual interests ends in deadlock. By cooperating with each other to remain silent, both criminals might have a jail term reduced to a year instead of the five years resulting from simultaneous defection. Therefore, a less optimal outcome is produced by mutual defection. Joint cooperation yields a far better result than the pursuit of exclusive individual interests. As a consequence, defection by both sides is an individually rational choice, but it is not the most optimal outcome collectively. Despite the joint benefit of mutual cooperation, each party tends to be content with the course of defection in the absence of a trust relationship.

In a nutshell, the outcome in an interdependent relationship is contingent upon the course of action generated by the different choices of players. If one player defects from cooperation with the other staying on course, the defector enjoys the maximum gain in the pay-off matrix. In a continuing game, the cooperating party will soon switch to a mode of defection for retaliation (Axelrod, 1984). Defection of the other party is almost certain when one player's move is motivated by maximizing their own gains at the expense of others. After experiencing the worst outcome, the cooperative party will retaliate by switching to defecting responses in the very next move. In interdependent conflict situations, cooperation yields a positive-sum game of mutual gains, but the unconditional yielding of one party permits the other to exploit their good will (Sterling-Folker, 2006). In the 'prisoner's dilemma', overall, contending strategies of mutual defection produce a sub-optimal situation.

A tit-for-tat strategy

A 'tit-for-tat' strategy is regarded as effective in generating reciprocal moves toward cooperation. When games are played more than once, each move becomes one of many sequential responses to the other's previous move. Repetitive rounds of interactions can be expected eventually to produce a pattern of cooperation through self-policing mechanisms. One party's cooperation on the first move can be pushed back by the other party's betrayal. The first to violate the cooperative game will be relentlessly punished by the opponent, reducing incentives for cheating. In an indeterminate number of repeated games, both players ultimately attempt to induce each other to reciprocal acts of reward. If the other party returns a favour with a cooperative response, the initiator reciprocates in kind, as long as the other party stays on the course of collaborative acts. Thus, whether positive or negative, a tit-for-tat strategy relies on reciprocating each other's actions.

Actors are less motivated toward cooperation in a one-time transaction which rewards cheaters with the betrayal of trust, causing a devastating outcome to the collaborator. Repeated interactions provide an opportunity to learn that mutual defection produces a less desirable outcome than mutual cooperation. On average, the best results, yielding a large total benefit, are obtained by a tit-for-tat pattern of nearly identical responses (Axelrod, 1984). The retaliation against the other's competitive actions prevents further attempts at exploitation; cooperation can be resumed if the adversaries abandon a strategy of unilateral gains after the punishment.

Whereas general outcomes are dominated by competition, the norm of reciprocity shapes behaviour. Whoever cheats first will be retaliated against by the other's cheating in the next round. Therefore, each party feels inhibited from making unilateral gains as a consequence of retribution. The patterns of a stable cooperation will be developed if future encounters between the same players prohibit the defection that is likely to be more costly in the long run. In the end, all of the parties are expected to reach an understanding that mutual cooperation yields a higher average reward and minimizes loss.

By generating the fear of retaliation, a tit-for-tat strategy is adopted as a form of deterrence. A temptation to attain unilateral gains is curtailed by one party's reprisal against another's defection. Thus a punitive conflict situation is created by the actual employment of each party's potential power for retribution. One's threat of retaliation should be reasonably persuasive to assure the other adhering to the cooperative rules.

In mixed-motive situations, a competitive orientation is modified to protect mutual interests by averting destructive dynamics in which an uncontrolled competition engenders an escalating spiral of ultimately punitive interactions. In a malignant social process, each party cannot easily retreat despite the fear of unacceptable psychological and material loss as well as the prospect of costly and dangerous outcomes.

The pursuit of a win–win strategy may entail the risk of catastrophic abuse by hard-line antagonists whose single desire is to overpower the other party. Even if its gains can be short-lived, a hard-line approach promotes bullying tactics. In a tit-for-tat situation, conditional cooperation limits any exposure to risks of deception while exploring mutual gains (Osborne, 2004).

By learning the values and skills of cooperation, each party should become aware that the future is important in relation to the present. One sided gain can be achieved by exploitation, but it does not yield benefit in the long run. In fact, short-term gains are overshadowed by long-term costs. The conditional forms of trust are more likely to produce a predictable pattern of behaviour that protects mutual interests, often supported by a faith in the other party's current leadership or a powerful third-party guarantee.

The existence of commonly accepted communal norms of reciprocal cooperation permits punishment for cheating on a partner. It can be administered not merely by the victims but also 'by onlookers refusing to deal with someone who has just established a reputation for being untrustworthy' (Binmore, 2007: 12). Whereas conditional cooperation is regarded as most visible in international relations, the rules predetermining the pay-off matrix of 'cooperation' and 'defection' are not constant, depending on the issue areas and patterns of power relations between interacting parties.

Security dilemma

In security dilemmas representing one of the essential characteristics of international politics, an independent action taken by one state to increase its security leads other states to feel more insecure. In their nuclear arms competition before the late 1980s, neither Washington nor Moscow trusted each other. Each strived to be assured of sufficient nuclear arsenals in the case of a first-strike action by the other, fuelling motives for continuing weapons escalation. In the security dilemma trap, each party obtains poor outcomes because of a lack of cooperation combined with an attempt to maximize competitive self-interest. One state may want to build its strength out of feelings of threat, but, in turn, it prompts the other to build its own strength. Consequently, these competitive, independent military build-ups make both parties feel more insecure. Ironically, the reactions of each party are not considered to be irrational, for acting in response to the threat, perceived in the increased military strength of the other, is actually deemed to be necessary or desirable.

Indeed, states do not easily agree to cooperate even if doing so would serve their best interests in a 'prisoner's dilemma' situation. As illustrated by an arms race, the adversaries do not agree to cooperate given that one's own initiatives for reduced arms (seen as a cooperative move) can lead to the worst outcome (of unilateral disarmament) in the event of the other's refusal of a reciprocal move (interpreted as a 'defection'). An attempt by one party to maximize its own advantages through military build-up puts competitors in a vulnerable position if they do not continue to counter the threat. However, such competitive arms accumulation will lead to high economic costs and the danger of war. This outcome is not preferable, compared with mutual restraint which controls the endless military competition.

In competition for arms build-up, therefore, each country's attempts to advance its unilateral security will produce poor outcomes. Despite preference for an outcome of winning, or at least an avoidance of loss, the situation easily ends up absorbing high costs without achieving superiority (Walt, 2000). A compromise, then, could be the most optimal solution especially under circumstances in which winning is unlikely to happen. Cooperation towards restricting arms yields low tensions without permitting the other's superiority or the devotion of huge military spending.

In order to circumvent the situation inherent in the 'prisoner's dilemma', both protagonists have to coordinate their actions to reciprocate each other's initiatives of arms control. Without full trust or good faith, antagonists can still be engaged in coordination and avoid the risk of being exploited by having a means of verifying each other's cooperation. Especially, tricking the other into taking unilateral and unreciprocated cooperative action is not easy if each side retains the capability to switch back to competitive moves in the event of the other's cheating.

Irrevocable commitments

The game of 'chicken' represents the situation of being locked into a contest of wills in which neither side is willing to be the first to concede. Its analogy is drawn from an episode of gang members seeking leadership among their peers. Driving cars at high speed on a direct collision course has served as a method of testing 'bravery'. The first driver to turn aside to avert a head-on collision is regarded as the 'chicken', losing prestige and being humiliated. On the other hand, the unwavering rival earns applause and fame. Thus the winner is determined by who is willing to take more risk. However, suppose that both sides were determined to seek a win, such a situation would almost certainly guarantee death for both players.

In the 'chicken' situation, the most desired outcome for each side is its own win without the other's fight, whereas mutual avoidance of collision can result from compromise. If both swerve at the same time, neither wins, but both survive. By veering off course simultaneously, each saves their lives by an act of cooperation. Despite the potential benefit of being reckless, the danger of staying on the steady course is a zero chance of survival if the other side also adopts the risk of gambling. Under these circumstances, the other's win is certainly better than a fight that will produce mutual loss.

In a game of chicken where the competitors lose by engagement, mutual avoidance creates a tolerable outcome even without a search for positive common interests. In general, however, the temptation to win a total victory can incentivize a party to be competitive and unyielding. Even if the mutual destruction of collision is the least desirable outcome for both parties, each would be more inclined to remain firm in order to prohibit the other's victory. Eventually, the two drivers speeding toward each other in a deadlocked game may wait too long for the other to have time to veer off.

In the 1938 Munich crisis, Adolf Hitler gambled on the weak resolve of the British and French, believing that the two European powers were too afraid of fighting another war. The successful showdown made Hitler become too confident in using bristling tactics of threat again in combination with armed actions. Despite their desire to avoid war, this time, the Western democratic powers were determined to deny Germany another gain. It set off World War II, when Hitler invaded Poland in September 1939 after disregarding Germany's earlier agreement not to make any further territorial claims.

A major war might bring about the worst catastrophic outcome, yet the coordination, necessary to avoid an unintended, disastrous clash, would be difficult in the 'chicken' situation. In particular, one party may want to frighten the other into concessions when it believes itself to be in a strong position. At the initial stage of such a situation, each party tends to be motivated to be tough and intransigent in order to scare the other into submission rather than choosing to fight. A strong commitment to belligerence produces an advantageous outcome only if the other side is willing to give way. Otherwise, a collision course of destructive total war is inevitable.

During the Cold War rivalry, attempts by the United States and the Soviet Union to outmanoeuvre each other led to the Berlin blockade of 1948 and the Cuban Missile Crisis of 1962. In retaliation against Western moves to consolidate German territories (occupied after World War II) despite opposition, Soviet leader Joseph Stalin cut off railroad and other means of land access to West Berlin in the summer of 1948. British and US authorities airlifted supplies to the enclave for a year under the direct and implicit threat of use of force. A major war was averted, in that the Soviet leadership did not challenge Western allies' air supplies over the land blockade. Even though the Kremlin withdrew its blockade in the end, its initial decision could have easily provoked hostile military encounters.

Since each side's attempt to win over the other in a 'chicken' situation would result in the worst outcome of a collision, both sides favoured a compromise based on mutual concession rather than a major war. Both superpowers voluntarily stepped back from several crises by communicating a desire to limit escalatory confrontation. Yet each side had initially attempted to induce the other to give in by signalling and demonstrating its own inflexibility and by refusing to make any concessions. A firm posture was adopted to force the other to lose its nerve and concede until the last possible moment.

In a 'chicken' situation, each side feels an incentive to take coercive actions pre-emptively in an attempt to frighten the other side into capitulation. The opponent faces a choice of either submission or an unwanted fight. By initiating a competitive action first, therefore, one party presents the other with an unpalatable choice (Patchen, 1988). The discovery of the Cuban sites for Soviet missile construction in October 1962 provoked the initial American action to avoid strategic defeat of allowing a permanent enemy missile base near a US territory. The American government decision to inspect and abduct Soviet vessels approaching Cuba was designed to force Moscow to give up its missile build-up in Cuba, limiting the Soviet choice to either accepting the humiliating retreat or provoking a war.

In this case, the Soviet leadership fortunately conceded to the American demand, within two weeks, to dismantle a nuclear missile site in return for a US guarantee not to attack the Castro regime. In general, competition and coercion in a 'chicken' situation may get easily out of control if each side's escalatory use of threat is based on the anticipation that the other will eventually be intimidated to avert a fight. Threat may continue to escalate to the point that it is too late to back down. A catastrophic outcome is most likely when risk taking has been chosen as a deliberate strategy beyond the control of chance factors. Each will lose considerably more by favouring a 'chicken' game in this circumstance than under a more regulated conflict situation.

By taking a highly risky choice, protagonists may try to induce the other party to back off. A commitment to a particular line of action by one party can be challenged by the other to violate a trip-wire mechanism for the final step in instigating violence. If a fight is deemed inescapable given the other's intent, one party may even be tempted to contemplate initial military superiority by hitting first. A conflict results in a disastrous outcome, especially when one antagonist seeks the advantage of a pre-emptive attack. Being confronted with losses, in particular, policy makers are more likely to show risk taking behaviour than when they pursue a favourable new status quo (McDermott, 2001).

If one party is perceived to be irrational and unpredictable, and if it has the reputation of being willing to take considerable risks beyond its own control, the other party is more motivated to evade conflict. Some actors are more willing to take a calculated risk and appear to be irrational. In reaction to financial sanctions and other threats by the Bush administration, for example, North Korea conducted missile tests in the summer of 2006 and declared its nuclear power status a few months later, with the underground detonation of atomic devices, despite UN Security Council warnings. A party committed to a highly risky course of action may take the advantage of a more predictable, cautious rival. Some leaders expose their constituents to extreme risks by bluffing the other party into giving ground. Taking on much more powerful opponents against all odds is irrational, but it might be a strategy employed for internal domestic political purposes, as seen in Argentina's attacks on the British-controlled Falkland Islands in 1982.

The existence of attractive compromise solutions would make the futility of a deadlock or fight more apparent. The value of complete victory associated with unbearable sacrifice is reduced by incentives for conciliatory behaviour and disincentives for competitive struggle. A bigger prospective gain from cooperation, relative to the potential advantages of competitive struggle, increases the likelihood of a conciliatory response. In the continuing show of resolve by each adversary in a 'chicken' situation, the value of a compromise or even loss increases, compared with a win or deadlock leading to mutual annihilation.

In a situation where each side attempts to continue to apply pressure, believing that an opponent's timely submission will preclude a catastrophe, knowledge about the limits of the other's concessions helps to set a restriction on coercive action prior to a collision point of pushing for the choice of war. In US–Soviet relations, the adversaries decided to take control over the use of force in regional conflicts, along with regular communication lines, so that a crisis would not escalate into a major war.

The perceptions of power relations produce different expectations about possible outcomes. If one party feels more vulnerable to the use of force by its adversary, it is more likely to submit to the influence of threat. In order to avoid the 'chicken' situation, competition in equal power relations needs to be regulated by the development of rules that minimize actions based on threats and force. In an equal power relationship, an escalating spiral of mutual aggression is inevitably accompanied by a reciprocal exchange of threat or force.

Features of decision making

Conflict situations can be exacerbated by faulty decision making ascribed to leaders' risk taking personalities and their misjudgements. Rival states seek to undermine each other's efforts to prevail in the competitive relationships of world politics (Byrne, 2003). While each party is eager to control the other's behaviour through the manipulation of their expectations and perceptions, this attempt may have a reverse impact on the individual leaders' calculations, provoking deadly conflicts.

Psychological processes involved in major conflicts represent not only paranoid fear and the absence of empathy but also selective inattention to the adversaries' positive gestures. In addition to relational mistrust, self-image concerns as well as emotional arousal reinforce highly contentious behaviour. In the midst of fear of the ultimate tragedy, volatile psychological attributes range from prejudiced interpretation of the other's action and statements to overconfidence in one's own capacity. Each side tends to disregard an adversary's strong underlying sense of insecurity and fear of destruction. The patterns of misperception are shaped by a distorted cognitive process as well as stereotyping. These perceptual biases, along with other irrational decision making characteristics, impinge upon interaction between the antagonists.

In particular, cognitive bias in the interpretation of substantive issues narrows options. It has been suggested by many psychologists that expectations about the other's behaviour and traits are formed even prior to real encounters. Thus, stereotypes, associated with group differences, predispose a misinterpretation of an antagonist's behaviour and attitudes (Abrams, 2005; Försterling, 2001). Rigid, over-generalized enemy images and a lack of balanced perspectives are most likely to hamper rational responses to complex conflict situations.

Attributional distortion and stereotypes

In general, hidden assumptions and bias are implied in the behavioural outcomes of one's own group members as well as the behaviour by another group. For example, the plight of a homeless person is often automatically attributed to such internal features as a lack of motivation rather than economic recession and absence of social networks (Bordens and Horowitz, 2002). Similarly, inter-group conflicts, for example, between Hindus and Muslims in India, tend to become pervasive due to an attribution bias.

Social stereotypes and related dispositional attributes are activated to explain out-group members' undesirable actions even when those actions are related to common behavioural patterns held by most people under the same circumstances (Wright and Taylor, 2003). The Soviet Union's pursuit of nuclear parity with the United States in the 1970s and 1980s was attributed, by many American political leaders, to aggressor characteristics of the Communist leadership (such as ruthless preparation for war and insensitivity to the human cost) rather than being locked into the arms competition.

In attribution theory, the causes of behaviour are relegated either to an actor's basic disposition or external circumstances. These attributional factors are selectively applied in the distorted interpretation of both in-group and out-group members' behavioural characteristics. Virtuous behaviour by an out-group member is seen more in terms of situational causes than the actor's inner qualities or good intentions, thus taking away credit. The wrongdoing of out-group members is, however, linked to the group's innate nature or ability, largely neglecting the information indicating the circumstantial effects. In fact, an adversary's undesirable behaviour is often over-attributed to group characteristics, but is under-attributed to difficulties in the environment.

These perceptions are flipped in relation to in-group members. When in-group members do something wrong, their errors are justified via situational explanation with the denial of group qualities. Meanwhile, inner nature is emphasized in highlighting one's own admirable behaviour.

Inter-group biases in the above causal attributions are supported by emotional reactions toward in-group and out-group members. The internal characterization of socially desirable behaviour by one's own group, combined with an external attribution for negative behaviours, is likely to stabilize positive expectations for in-group members. Indeed, attributing the success of one's own group member to internal characteristics maximizes self-esteem and pride. In general, unfavourable stereotypes about opponents are sustained by the external attribution of positive out-group behaviour, along with the internal attribution of their negative behavioural outcomes (Försterling, 2001).

The mere perception of being a member of two distinct groups is sufficient enough to develop an orientation toward a favourable evaluation of in-group members' behaviour in comparison with others. By discounting the values and motivations behind the actions of their opponents, in-group members treat out-group members in a manner that is consistent with their expectations rather than actual traits. Increased solidarity and pride in one's own group further strengthen biases that overvalue in-group performance and undervalue out-group achievement (Turner, 1981).

Once formed, these expectations about 'the other' are likely to persist in conjunction with a tendency to interpret behaviour in a consistent manner (Hogg, 2001). The distrusted party's actions deserve little benefit of the doubt and are looked upon as threatening. These preconceptions rooted in false expectations get stronger with the repetitive patterns of observation. Even conciliatory behaviour is either disregarded as deceptive, or based on ingenuous motives. Negative views about the other reinforce one's own fear and suspicion, and are eventually confirmed by the other party's hostile response.

Inter-group communication is misperceived and misinterpreted through a negative stereotype anchored in a black-and-white enemy image. A stereotype supports a set of generalized beliefs about the attributes of people in different social categories connected, for example, to race, ethnicity or nationality (Dovidio et al., 2005; Rabbie, 1993).[1] In many Western societies, Muslim women are often subject to prejudices derived from their clothing or social customs. The distortion of communication comes from the tendencies to form expectations founded on stereotypes. By depending on stereotypical characteristics of their adversaries, in-group members look for certain types of out-group behaviour, perceive what they are looking for, and reproduce distance between groups.

Adopted as the justification of a personal belief or group attitude, stereotyping has not only cognitive, but also social functions. Stereotypes are simple and overgeneralized, anchored in depersonalized views of the other and often accepted without question (Schneider, 2004; Wright and Taylor, 2003). The social functions of stereotyping consist of the sustenance of positive in-group evaluation in support of increased internal cohesion. Dominant groups justify existing inter-group relations in terms of their comparative prestige. Overall, cognitive distortions hamper problem-solving ability in the absence of challenges to the stereotypes and misperceptions.

Images

In a deeply divided conflict, moral self-images are contrasted with negative enemy images attributed to evil motives. The 'evil' image of an opponent stems from a desire to attach the distinctive vices to the 'outside' group in comparison with the virtues of one's own group. A selective perception process can even strengthen this attributional distortion associated with negative evaluations of adversaries. The distortions of reality tend to be fed by a diabolical enemy image of adversaries. Even if the behaviour of others is not necessarily related to any evidence of hostile intentions, enemy images are often socially reconstructed as a result of competitive interactions.

Images are a powerful ingredient of perceiving the intentions and actions of others in the trajectory of a conflict. In pursuing confrontational policies, President George Bush has seen Iraq, Iran, and North Korea through the lens of an 'axis of evil'. Those perceived to be evil are likely to be viewed as having a hostile intent and making dangerous plans (Patchen, 1988). A war with a 'diabolical enemy' generates more rigid positions, supporting zero-sum thinking that leads to a mentality of securing overwhelming victory or facing defeat. Thus difficulties in changing enemy images perpetuate the conflict by fuelling goals that punish or destroy the opponent.

As a mental picture of the social and political environment, an image contains our judgements (good, bad, or neutral) and attitudes. The leaders often have beliefs that predispose them to recognize other countries with either peaceful or aggressive motives (Fisher, 1990). Beliefs about other governments are further distorted in ideological conflicts, as was expressed in US President Ronald Reagan's early 1980 speech that equated the Soviet Union to the 'evil empire'. In a hostile relationship, another actor's motives are also likely to be inferred from their past behaviour, construed to be deceptive. Varying degrees of biased inter-group perceptions and attributions are more likely to be engaged in assessing an ongoing conflict. Inter-group bias can lend ethnocentric valuations and stereotypic lenses to understanding a conflict episode.

Psychological aspects of social life are embedded in the interpretations we attach to the various features of an interactive situation (Brewer, 2003). The primary socialization process within an ethnic group and culture provides different meanings and priorities for the perceived dimensions of a social setting. Individuals and groups tend to sustain images of an enemy even without solid, confirming facts. Emotional responses to enemy images may reinforce a social learning process that contributes to the development of distorted cognitive constructs of adversaries.

In conflict situations, each side's views about the other are diametrically opposed in a mirror image. Each party associates violence and aggression with an adversary, while believing that peace, virtue, and justice are attached to their own. A 'good versus evil' dialectic of mirror images is reversely applied to the perceptions of opponents (Bronfenbrenner, 1961). The transfer of one's own vile self-images to an enemy is common in explicating unacceptable behaviour. The formation of a moral self-image is interdependent on the existence of threatening and aggressive enemy images. The negative effects of mirror imaging reinforce the tendency to observe the other as an aggressor that is not to be trusted, advancing policies on the verge of madness.

Interstate and ethnic conflicts reflect a hostile imagery along with competing interests. While empathy is rarely considered important in the conduct of international relations, images rooted in inter-group differences are significant contributors to violent conflict. Different interests are felt more acutely when they involve hostile images of the other side. Reciprocal cognitive distortion based on misperceptions leads not only to unrealistic images but also irrational behaviour.

The psychology of dehumanization

Severe actions against one's opponents are often rationalized by a dehumanization process that views enemies as unprotected by social norms from aggression. The images of enemies being evil produce increased violence, murder, torture, rape, and even mass-scale genocide. Any harm to enemies who are seen as a threat to one's well-being or values is considered to be warranted even with moral justification. This tendency has been observed in violent behaviour beyond differences in political and cultural settings.

According to some of the best known classical research on group processes, in-group democracy does not necessarily imply the application of democratic rules or human values toward out-groups (Sherif and Sherif, 1953). The aerial bombings of Dresden in February 1945 by the British and US air forces killed tens of thousands of refugees. Even though the top politicians and military commanders knew of little strategic value in firebombing, a sense of retribution justified the immoral acts. The August 1945 atomic bombings of Hiroshima and Nagasaki, under order of US President Harry S. Truman, brought casualties of as many as 214,000 civilians, the majority of whom were the elderly, women, and children. These incidents demonstrate that the political and military elites of democratic states do not necessarily abide by humanitarian principles in their war campaigns against enemy civilians.

Psychological distance justifies treatment not acceptable for those included in one's own community. With moral exclusion, enemy members are not recognized as part of a shared human community. From a perpetrator's viewpoint, the violation of generally accepted norms of behaviour seems reasonable, or even necessary, putting basic needs and rights of enemies outside the scope of justice. The stigmatization of groups as being morally inferior makes the persecution of antagonists psychologically permissible and even satisfactory.

In paving the way for intolerance and even the encouragement of atrocities, dehumanization restricts the usual moral inhibitions against the act of killing. The distinctive human qualities, shared by many individuals, are removed from the victims. Restraints against malicious acts are not applied to one's enemy, regarded as subhuman, inferior, and dangerous. De-individuation treats people as members of a category to which negative traits are attributed rather than as individuals who care for each other's well-being. Exclusion from the scope of morality can be rooted in ethnic, cultural, and ideological differences. In particular, 'ethnic groups low on the social distance scale may serve as ... objects for displaced aggression' (Sherif and Sherif, 1953: 117).

Violence, which was morally unthinkable before, is now out of control, along with the formation of diabolic enemy images further promoted by dehumanization (Audergon, 2005). Tutsis, in the eyes of Hutus, and Muslims, in the eyes of Serbs, are subject to feelings of intense hatred and alienation. Individuals are often instigated to participate in atrocious acts by demonizing language.

By portraying the victims as a grave threat that harbours hostile intentions, perpetrators may even institute policies in support of indiscriminatory attacks on enemies. As is well documented in recent civil war atrocities, for example, in Cambodia, Sudan, Guatemala, and Colombia, obedience by government and paramilitary soldiers permits sanctioned massacres in a pathological environment.

Emotions and self-justification

In a negative attribution cycle, distorted images of opponents may reflect the efforts to hide fear, shame, and vulnerability. High levels of hatred are often justified by the aims of defeating, punishing, or humiliating the adversary (Tillett and French, 2006). In most major conflicts, including the superpower arms race during the Cold War period, exaggerated fear and suspicion have motivated hostile behaviour with the development of an irrational 'overkill' capacity. Whereas war-preventing fear is the basis for reasonable deterrence, the 'macho pride' of being superior and tough drives motivations toward aggression. Macho pride results from yearning for a masculine, domineering image of one's own group. The perceptions, manipulated by ill motives as well as the emotions of anger and hate, engender hostile behaviour, distorting cognitive functioning (Fisher, 1990; Jones, 2001).

The prospect of taking certain actions can be emotionally more satisfactory for decision makers. Judgements about 'right' or 'wrong', 'courageous' or 'cowardly' stem from moral significance and ideologies as well as concerns with self-image. Not only 'courageous' self-images but also 'patriotic' values in support of the strong military often favour the use of coercive methods. National leaders may feel that it is right, and 'even a moral or religious duty, to use coercive methods in order to "win" against adversaries' (Patchen, 1988: 125). The shared moral principles, ideology, and self-image call for the automatic use of force in confronting a diabolic enemy. President Bush has, for example, legitimized the abuse of terrorist suspects at secret military prisons on the basis of 'the protection of democracy' and 'freedom'.

Cognitive consistency

Individuals have different ways to perceive themselves, their relationship to others and events which affect them. Their perceptions 'may or may not relate closely to "reality" or to the world as perceived' by others (Tillett and French, 2006: 202). New information is interpreted according to our accumulated experience which forms a set of expectations and beliefs. By simply ignoring or distorting contradictory facts, powerful images and expectations prompt conclusions prior to adequate information processing. In interpreting and retaining information, cognitive consistency moulds sensory data into pre-existing beliefs. The cognitive limits of rationality reflect the decision maker's tendency to simplify his or her understanding of a complex conflict situation.

Given that people tend to react to the world according to their own perceptions, subjective understanding can be a more crucial element in shaping conflict behaviour than the objectified knowledge of reality. Decision making is not predominantly a rational process, due to the fact that selection among choices is not always based on the full knowledge of alternatives. The information in support of existing beliefs is overrated, while any factual data challenging pre-existing expectations are undervalued. This cognitive limit lessens the effectiveness of decision making, consequently contributing to a piecemeal approach to problem solving.

In organizing incoming sensory data, information is selected and represented to provide cognitive consistency. This process interferes in the acquisition of information by precluding certain types of data. In addition, the meanings of critical information tend to be twisted to deny, or explain away, contradictory realities. The imposition of a cognitive order, however, hampers a thorough assessment of the situation by excluding information that is not compatible with an already assimilated body of knowledge and understanding (Nossal, 1984). The principle of consistency is adopted to rationalize the continuity of our behaviour or policy despite a systematic information-processing bias.

The process of perception is adapted to support the attitudes and beliefs that have been functional in maintaining expectations that meet psychological or organizational needs. The existence of inconsistency between one's own standards and behavioural outcomes generates an unpleasant psychological state, motivating people to reduce the dissonance. If group members are confronted with the undesirable consequences of their actions, for example, atrocious ethnic violence, they may want to diffuse their feelings of responsibility for negative outcomes (Cooper et al., 2001). The discrepancy between different, often contradicting, images of the world constitutes cognitive dissonance. Because the perception of inconsistency, associated with cognitive dissonance, is psychologically uncomfortable, people look for ways to block information that is not congruent with their beliefs.

A selective perception is oriented toward the reduction of cognitive complexity that causes decision makers excessive fatigue. Critical facts may not be taken seriously by a way of selective inattention, denial, or almost any other psychological tactic that diminishes stress caused by ambiguity, information overload, and time pressure. Logical contradictions are neglected by the necessity of psychological harmony.

After his military occupation of Kuwait in 1990, Saddam Hussein took a surprisingly uncompromising position and refused to yield to international pressure to evacuate his troops. He was hesitant to believe that the American government would carry out its threat despite continuing US military build-up, including the mobilization of more than 500,000 troops and other signs indicating American readiness to attack. Hussein's misjudgement is, to a large extent, ascribed to his low cognitive complexity in assessing the inevitability of withdrawal from Kuwait (Conway III et al., 2001).

A total disregard for information that is inconsistent with dominant frames of a belief system leads to the ignorance of any fallacies associated with one's own preferred actions. Cognitive errors explain inadequate decision making along with the selection of information in support of a particular position. Irrational consistency, supported by cognitive distortion, leads to favouring a particular policy with the distortion of any information that does not conform to the existing beliefs.

The decision maker lacking cognitive complexity complacently chooses to continue whatever he or she has been doing, ignoring counterfactual data, in spite of warning signals. By contrast, leaders with a higher level of cognitive sophistication are more oriented toward risk-aversion. Their responses to crises tend to be more cautious than those of leaders with a low complexity level. Even facing the impending crisis of a system collapse toward the late 1980s, Mikhail Gorbachev, the last President of the Soviet Union, refused to deploy military forces to quell rising levels of demonstrations and revolts that would have been quickly crushed under his predecessors.

By closing our minds to different points of view, the pursuit of consistency produces an irrational response to conflict situations. This tendency is even strengthened by belief systems or ideologies that encourage one-directional thinking (Ting-Toomey, 1985). The persistent denial of new information undermines our ability to respond effectively to complex conflict settings and learn from the environment. A variety of options are not fully considered in the event of limited time and pre-existing value judgements about appropriate actions.

Selective perceptions

The course of conflict is affected by decisions based on not only a limited ability to consider various options but also the misrepresentation or distortion of data. Perceptional and cognitive errors are inclined to interfere in an understanding of incompatible structures of adversarial relationships. Expectations, rooted in desired beliefs, impinge on the interpretation of new events.[2]

Decision makers are likely to pay most attention to any information that confirms their worst fears and fantasies (Brockner and Rubin, 1985). Prior to its 1979 invasion of Afghanistan, the Soviet leadership believed that political instability on its southern border would jeopardize its security. Intelligence information was distorted to discount an input which suggests protracted resistance from the Afghans, feeding a perceptual error of excessive military confidence (Fisher, 1990). Such selective perception comes from a failure to examine a variety of possible perspectives.

The fallibility of human perception is characterized by a degree of selectivity and distortion of information through a filtering process designed to eliminate the confusing complexity of sensory data. Impressions, once formed, strongly manipulate the evaluation of new information as part of the 'halo effect'.[3] Ideas that are not part of core belief systems are selected out with the rejection of non-conformist thinking and the rationalization of distortion. Ordinary decision makers assimilate incoming information into existing beliefs on the basis of what they expect to see. Pre-existing beliefs perpetuate present perceptions under the influence of widely accepted images of 'good' and 'evil'. Misperception, then, creates its own reality over time, even if it is drawn from subconscious motives.

A specific closure based on desired values is presumed to produce a tendency to freeze one's views selectively. Being confident of their views, decision makers inappropriately exclude alternatives through premature closure. The perceptions of a hostile, escalatory intent become stronger when the other side is seen as a single, unified entity which can act decisively, rather than being split into competing factions with different aims. Even though Muslim societies are profoundly divided, many of President Bush's policies about terrorism have been driven by a fatally flawed perception of Islam as violent and monolithic. While Christian and other religious values have also been utilized to promote extremist goals, the cause of violence has been associated, at least, implicitly with misconceived ideas of Islam, rather than resentment stemming from Western domination over the Islamic world. Perceptual and cognitive biases clearly hamper efforts to control conflict.

Schema and information processing

Relevant information needs to be called up to make a relatively reliable assessment about what to expect from others and how to respond to social situations. Cognitive generalizations founded on past experiences provide guidelines for quick and effortless judgements. Memories of a sequence of events are actively reconstructed into general, abstracted knowledge. A need to impose order on a complex social reality is fulfilled by the maintenance of existing knowledge structures. Reduced ambiguity in decision making stems from labelling information for the organization of an internally coherent knowledge system.

The management of a complex environment depends on pre-structures and categories that assist in the interpretation of experiences (Casmir, 1985). In organizing information for interactions, a 'schema', defined by cognitive structures, guides how to take in, evoke, and make references about a wide range of social stimuli or raw data. For example, a schema about a baby crying may include an empty stomach, dirty diapers, or a lack of attention (Bordens and Horowitz, 2002; Goldstein, 2002). Cognitive structures offer frameworks within which to assimilate information obtained from vast, complex, and volatile situations that are replete with contradictory meanings. In particular, a social schema constitutes 'a semantic network of associated meanings (or implications) emanating from a particular core belief' (Klar et al., 1988: 73).

Searching for schema-relevant information diminishes processing time by enabling the perceiver to fill in missing gaps in the sensory data. Generic knowledge, organized on the basis of a segment of past experience, helps to reduce stress and information overload by providing shortcuts to decisions (Nishida, 2005). A potential response is likely to arise according to the way an experience is encoded as benign or malignant. The construction and use of social categories have an impact on processing, organizing, and restoring information in the memory, and making judgements. While categorization 'renders the world more predictable and thus allows us to plan effective action', information loss is inevitable in encoding, representation, and selective attention (Hogg, 2001: 58). Thus, schematic processing may produce biased knowledge as a consequence of relying on illusory assumptions, faulty inferences, and incomplete information.

The recognition of goal incompatibility brings about the activation of a conflict schema. In considering that events can be perceived from memory traces of past occasions, a basic sense of conflict reflects images proceeding from previous responses to similar incidents. Information about conflict is accepted or rejected, depending on whether it fits one's own schema (Bordens and Horowitz, 2002). Analogical reasoning encourages the categorization of new situations on the basis of familiar earlier events. The support for the withdrawal from war in Iraq has been rationalized by reference to 'another Vietnam'.

The most popular, all-purpose historic axiom is the 'Munich Analogy' derived from the British/French failure to deter Hitler's aggression with concessions prior to World War II (Goemans, 2000). This analogy served as a justification for advocating a tougher, military action in a range of crises from the Korean War (1950) to the Iraqi occupation of Kuwait (1991). Diplomatic solutions have often been denounced or discredited as appeasement of aggressors, in spite of wide contextual differences, by hard line political leaders.

Policy makers have a limited capacity to process information, being prone to stick with simplified images (Tetlock and McGuire, 1985). Consistent, causal explanations are often imposed even if not fully supported by the information. American government officials have been publicly lambasting Iran for every unfavourable incident, ranging from a threat to the Lebanese government allied with Western countries and support for radical factions in Palestine, to arming Iraqi Shiite militias with deadly weapons. A behaviour that cannot be explained is attributed to factors known to perceivers. A set of basic, often unexamined, assumptions steers information processing toward an incorrect inference. The self-preserving biases of a cognitive system are decisively tied to 'distortion of information or ignorance of feedbacks' (Vertzberger, 1990: 130).

Whereas a schema is specific to what is perceived and modified by experience, it can 'serve as a starting point for future experiences, perceptions, and interpretations' (Casmir, 1985: 56). Competing sources of ambiguous information can be ignored or undervalued to support existing decisions. Prior to the Yom Kippur War in 1973, Israelis believed in their sufficient deterrence power and were insensitive to the possibility of the Arab decision on initiating a new war. In particular, the Israeli views were shaped by their understanding of the Arab states' political and military weakness. It was attributed to the Soviet refusal to supply offensive military hardware, Arab inferiority in the air, and a low level of domestic popularity of Egyptian leaders. Meanwhile, the Israeli security officials ignored the Arabic states' growing sense of impatience with a continuing diplomatic stalemate (Vertzberger, 1990).

Past success results in the insensitivity of policy makers to the requirement for change in the current situation. The same strategy is often favoured during the next episode of the conflict, ignoring the necessity of adjusting strategies to new situations (Leng, 1983). Successful experiences in the recent past are, for instance, more likely to lead to the repeated adoption of coercive actions. For the Bush administration, the quick collapse of the Taliban regime in Afghanistan was the source of considerable confidence in the invasion of Saddam Hussein's Iraq.

Group decision making

While motivational and cognitive processes hamper optimized decision outcomes, the quality of policy making is also compromised by the vested interests of various internal group forces. When a group makes decisions, the process is assumed to take longer, under normal circumstances, compared with individuals reaching a conclusion, due to the necessity of discussing a variety of options and reaching a consensus. An opposite phenomenon has, however, been observed in the decision-making process of highly cohesive groups, whose members are oriented toward conformity of values and strong moral convictions. This generates the complacency of group members about the perceived official position. Members are likely to refrain from raising questions about a group consensus favoured, in particular, by directive leaders.

Group processes may spawn destructive effects, especially when little internal diversity commits a collective decision more easily to escalating conflicts. An insulated group of decision makers tends to fail to seriously appraise the relative merits of various alternatives. The perception of invulnerability and strong belief in chosen actions prohibit group members from seeking external information and looking into other alternatives, underestimating the risks of the selected option. The absence of critical judgement encourages the preference for risky actions that can turn out to be disastrous. This type of decision making style, labelled 'groupthink' by Irving Janis (1982), characterizes the highly unsuccessful policy making that resulted in the escalation of wars in both Vietnam and Iraq.

'Groupthink' is known for concurrence-seeking, displaying decision-making behaviour ascribed to a pressure toward uniformity, along with self-censorship of deviations from the apparent consensus (Turner, 1982). Because group members tend to seek personal acceptance by, and approval of, others, the proper mix of consensus and dissent does not exist to moderate over optimistic views about the group's choice. The tendency to seek unanimity over realistic appraisal of diverse courses of action is likely to be strengthened by the stress of reaching an urgent decision (Brockner and Rubin, 1985). Policy-making deliberations become a kind of ritualized group approval of a predetermined course of action. The ostracization of critical members is accompanied by an intolerance of dissent in this type of decision-making process.

Group members look to high-status figures as a source of norms and rules for making judgements. Hence the opinions of other members reflect the prevalent views of a charismatic or authoritative leader, paying 'decreased attention to dissonant information and interpretations' (Vertzberger, 1990: 236). In the Cuban Missile Crisis, the Executive Committee of National Security Counsel provided rationale and details for President John F. Kennedy's decision heavily influenced by domestic political concerns (Robinson, 1996). Subordinates are encouraged to report information in support of the expectations and preferences of senior policy makers. In reality, self-censorship prevents adverse information from filtering into decision making.

Homogeneity of ideology or social background can lead groups to ignore information that threatens their belief systems. A strong sense of loyalty to the group reinforces shared complacency about the effectiveness and morality of its decisions. One's own inherent morality and negative stereotypes of out-groups desensitize self-doubt. Social pressures to adopt similar views about adversaries contribute to evil descriptions of opponents.

The defective decision making of 'groupthink' comes from a poor information search, a selective bias, a lack of objective appraisal of alternatives, and failure to work out contingency plans. Collective rationalization and closed minds discount risks of a preferred choice, underestimating warning signals and overestimating the group's risk management capabilities. Prior to its decision on the invasion of Iraq, the National Security Council of the Bush administration completely buried, or neglected, CIA analysis of the worst scenarios—such as anarchy and territorial break-up, the deepening of Islamic antipathy toward the United States, and a surge of global terrorism—in the aftermath of occupation. In order to justify its decision on invasion, meanwhile, high-ranking Bush administration officials put a spotlight on false or inaccurate intelligence on the Iraqi weapons of mass destruction despite prevalent scepticism.

Groupthink leads to the overestimation of one's own power and an illusion of invulnerability. In a small group setting, excessive optimism, reinforced by a lack of outside input, strengthens a willingness to push an unwarranted course of escalatory crises. Thus 'small groups are sometimes inclined to take more risks than individuals under the same circumstances' with risk-shift phenomena from individual responsibility to collectivity (Vertzberger, 1990: 236).

In a nutshell, the pathology of 'groupthink' stems from the desire for group cohesion at the sacrifice of a rational decision. An inclination to minimize each other's doubts and avoid counter-arguments brings about a shared illusion of unanimity. Conformity seeking is inevitable in groupthink with over-commitment to a cause. One way in which to overcome collective misjudgements, however, is to hear the opinion of outsiders as well as toleration of those within the group who disagree with the leadership and other members.

Factional and bureaucratic politics

Beyond the small inner circle of the elite, we need to pay attention to the interplay of powerful bureaucratic organizations that have competing interests in the wider political context of policy making. The interpretation of information about conflict situations by top government officials is often tinged with bureaucratic and political struggles. The choice is not an accurate representation of the deliberate and purposive action of leaders based on the 'rational' consideration of all the options. In the larger political context of government decision making, 'roles and interest are important determinants of preferred strategies of conflict management' (Holsti, 1984: 88).

A bureaucratic politics model strongly attributes the attitudes of decision makers to their institutional roles and functions (Allison, 1971). The escalation of a conflict has been ascribed to the prevalence of military, organizational routines. Decisions about strategies and tactics in international bargaining are derived from configurations of various interests and influence within a state. In their nuclear negotiations with American diplomats, North Korean foreign ministry officials frequently hinted to their American counterparts that the military are an obstacle to making concessions. In the negotiations with Britain, France, and Germany, the leaders of Iran's elite military unit, the Revolutionary Guard, have supported a hard-line position to reject threats of sanctions in support of continuing their uranium-enrichment programmes.

Political executives at the apex of a state power structure depend on information and advice provided by competing agencies. The Bush administration has been internally divided over how trustworthy Pakistani President Musharraf will turn out to be in the US war against al-Qaeda and how much pressure to apply. American diplomats and foreign policy makers believe in President Musharraf's credentials for being a committed US ally and are worried about the collapse of the US–Pakistan partnership in his absence. On the other hand, intelligence and military officials consider Pakistan's fight against terrorism to be half-hearted and advocate a 'hammer' approach to push the Pakistani leader to take a more aggressive stance.

A state policy making unit is not a unitary actor, given the diverse interests and perspectives held by bureaucratic factions. Even in a hierarchical political system, bureaucratic institutions play a critical role in a policy output. In spite of concentration of power at the top, therefore, decision outcomes reflect struggles among semi-feudal organizations whose leaders project their own organizational visions and interests. What they see is formulated by their organizational procedures and sensors that support a natural inertia embedded in a bureaucratic environment.

In the bureaucratic politics paradigm, therefore, competition within the government does not reflect the presence of a monolithic entity with a single, rational and identifiable interest. Policy preferences are advocated in the name of national or other collective interests often containing highly contentious ideological debate (Nossal, 1984). Internal bargaining is produced by 'pulling and hauling' between individuals and agencies, which are more concerned about administrative and managerial roles than substantive issues. In policy making, each group attempts to maximize its own interests and develop competing visions of collective goals.

Bureaucratic competition can explain incoherence and inflexibility in developing strategies of conflict management. Final decisions are made by a complex set of informal negotiations between the positions favoured by powerful factional interests. Even though some civilian cabinet members may not have been overly enthusiastic about direct incursion into the northern part of Iraq, the powerful Turkish military has successfully kept up pressure for attacks on Kurdish guerrillas across the border. In contentious conflict settings, a bureaucratic constituent pressure can limit the decision makers' ability to make concessions.

Notes

1 Stereotypes can be 'considered as a natural outgrowth of the categorization process, a consequence of the individual's need to simplify and order the world' (Brown, 1988: 235).
2 In coping with a conflict situation, tunnel vision is supported by selective perception.
3 Subconsciously motivated exclusion (derived from selective inattention) tends to manipulate our thought processes.

Part III
Process and Structure

Process of Conflict

5

As analogous to a natural life cycle, conflict originates from a particular situation, leads to escalation, and eventually must cease in one way or another after de-escalation. While almost every conflict is likely to go through the emergence of intense struggles, the transformation of conflict is not uniform, especially with its unpredictable outcomes. Internal party situations, inter-party dynamics, and contextual variables all affect the course of escalation and de-escalation in terms of their longevity and intensity.

The distinctive characteristics of each stage can be illustrated in terms of the transformation of relations between and within parties, along with changes in the salience of the goals, types of issue, and strategies. In addition, the dynamics of processes can be explained by modes of behaviour and types of strategies associated with coercion and conciliation. Many conflicts, as characterized by intense friction between Arabs and Israelis, rivalry between Catholics and Protestants in Northern Ireland, and civil wars in Sudan and Sri Lanka, have experienced more than a single cycle of conflict with histories of hostilities stretched over several decades. This chapter provides an overall picture of the manner in which conflict is initiated, pursued, and eventually terminated.

The transformation of latent to manifest conflict

Every serious conflict proceeds from the articulation of manifest interests, values, or needs by a social unit that is dissatisfied with the existing system or relationship. The expression of grievances and a demand for change can be made easier by the existence of certain technical, political, social, and psychological conditions. Prior to their manifestations, the latent conditions for conflict can be built in a structure that engenders a sense of injustice and resentment. If the antagonistic relationships arise from misunderstanding and misperception, the sources of conflict can be easily handled by promoting dialogue, or other facilitative methods of clearing disagreement or misinterpretations. This type of process would be successful, however, only in a social or organizational environment that does not suppress an expression of diverse views.

In every conflict, a certain event triggers the initiation of a manifest struggle, but behind the catalysing situations, there are structural conditions and socio-psychological factors that explain the nature and causes of conflict. The genesis of social conflict may include the rapid dissolution of initial cohesion among diverse categories of people which constitute a larger entity. Inequalities might have been justified on the basis of exclusive group status and identities. The sense of solidarity with and loyalty toward members of the same social category would be pivotal to setting off group mobilization and organized violence.

It has been commonly pointed out that frustration in deep-rooted conflicts often results from the failure of social systems to respond to the satisfaction of security, self-esteem, and other basic human needs. For instance, severe oppression of national minorities increases the chance of armed resistance (van Evera, 2001). In particular, a lack of adequate institutions or procedures to represent conflicting interests invites further potential for mass discontent or challenges of disenchanted groups. Killing and other atrocities against civilians by the military, as well as the denial of institutional change by non-violent means in Guatemala, Nicaragua, and El Salvador, were the main bedrock of civil wars in Central America in the 1970s and 1980s.

Structural and behavioural factors

The intermediate conditions for radical change consist of loss of authority and power deflation, related to dependence on mere coercive force for the maintenance of order. Whereas a catalysing situation triggers the manifest expression of conflict, organizational factors are essential to generating a prolonged struggle. Even though people may have been motivated by grievance or greed, they need to be mobilized along the lines of division on a sustained basis; otherwise initiatives for conflict would be likely to remain local or dormant.

The 'windows of vulnerability' exist at moments when particular stimuli provide exposure of the existing order to full-scale violence. The weakness of the overloaded system is revealed, especially during an economic collapse, civil unrest, political crisis or war. Any overt attack is facilitated by waning political support for the regime, in tandem with divisions within the ruling elite in support of, or opposed to, a status quo. Social violence is often indicative of hostile relationships following an emotional response to a triggering event (Horowitz, 2001). The disruption or breakdown of the system occurs much like any kind of spark that prompts an explosion when sufficient explosive gas has been accumulated.

Thus a fracture in a polarized society may erupt into violence, catalysed by certain events. Types of triggering event, which can bring latent conflict into public awareness through uncontrolled violence, include irregular elections, arrest and assassination of a key leader or political figure, a military coup, the sudden collapse of local currency, high unemployment rates, and increased prices or scarcity of basic commodities. Some of the well-known recent triggers range from the assassination of the president of Rwanda in the spring of 1994, which provoked ethnic genocide, to the fraudulent presidential election in Serbia, which led to ousting President Slobodan Milošević in October 2000.

While the trigger may be called 'random', or a 'chance happening', there are other specific behavioural manifestations that provoke an unpredicted chain of events. In the 1917 Russian revolution, mutiny by a military division and street demonstrations started off the monarchic system's collapse through the revelation of a weak elite's inability to control rebellion or to stop a demonstration. As illustrated by civil wars, for instance, in Sierra Leone and the Ivory Coast, various forms of ethnic protest as well as military revolts can ignite armed struggles between a government and rebellious forces. Disillusioned people can be stimulated to act upon the display of the regime's vulnerability, being encouraged by a belief in success. In general, internal disturbances, civil unrest, or war expose the system's inability to manage the crisis. When institutional capacities are inadequate to respond to increased protests, the elite are deprived of force for controlling violence.

In revealing the nature and causes of social conflict, the potential for cleavage, either economic or ethnic, among the members of a social system, often bestows the structural preconditions of struggle. Equally importantly, weaker state capability to accommodate ethnic and other sectoral interests with limited resources serves as a fertile ground for rebellion. The categories of the structural causes for social conflict range from unregulated group competition to an exploitative and corrupt system in support of the ruling elite. Social divisions may be underscored by the existence of an inherited or fixed status derived from differences in class, caste, religion, or geographic location.

Strong feelings of injustice are likely to be shared among disadvantaged group members if the costs of economic collapse or unequal distribution are borne along ethnic and religious divisions. In Sudan, the central government, controlled by a small group of military junta, imposed Islamic laws on the south and took oil revenues away from the region's development. This provoked one of the longest civil wars, prior to a peace agreement in 2005. In spite of the end of war in Southern Sudan, the crisis in Darfur was intensified to the level of internationally recognized genocide since February 2003. These atrocities are the outcome of government campaigns to quell discontent among residents which originates from the continued patterns of economic inequity and political marginalization.

A macro socio-political environment presents long-term structural features of the relationships within which the adversaries contend. In fact, uncertainties in transition (following modernization) bring out tension between various social groups whose welfare has been differently affected. The structural roots of conflict can also be ascribed to the pressure of population migration and urbanization.

In addition, transition toward democracy especially in the aftermath of the collapse of authoritarian regimes has exhibited great ambiguity. When an incongruent structure of expectations is clearly manifested, it serves as a ripe situation for random events to effectively set off a chain of actions leading to the demise of the old system. Revolts are likely to occur in many divided societies whenever repressive government policies begin to vacillate, or become more moderate toward reform, suddenly permitting the expression of diverse interests.

Highly repressive policies can hold off the initiation of challenges to the system, at least for a while, especially when the subversive groups notice the substantial costs of opposition and little likelihood of achieving their objectives. But a commitment to bringing about change, even with violent means, gains strength under conditions of continuing marginality and oppression. Even though repressive tactics may help to sustain the system of injustice, it will eventually face a crisis, either minor or major, that requires fundamental reform. Each society has a widely different capacity to cope with complex challenges and opportunities; constructive management of political, economic, and cultural dimensions of inter-group relations is essential to restraining the translation of grievances into acute violence (Clemens, 2002).

In an ethnic conflict, such external factors as material, military, and diplomatic assistance from kindred groups, sympathetic states or international organizations may shape the direction of contention. The United Nations accepted ethnic claims to independence made by East Timor at the end of the 1990s. In gaining independence from Pakistan, ethnic rebellion in Bangladesh would not have been successful without India's military intervention in 1971. Armed conflicts being fought in adjoining countries often create instability, through spill-over effects, especially in ethnically mixed regions. The flow of arms, refugees, and militants looking for safe havens has produced a general climate of insecurity in such countries as the Democratic Republic of Congo, Central African Republic and Chad.

Inhibiting factors

Some conditions retard, rather than advance, the organization of violence in a way that is analogous to wet wood resisting fire (Rummel, 1975). The inhibiting factors involve tight control of the populace, supported by the military and police, along with a lack of effective opposition leadership. In the absence of any restraining factors such as the tight imposition of surveillance over the masses, widespread violence can be more easily instigated by political campaigns of the counter-elite. While a mass revolt in Kyrgyzstan forced autocratic President Akayev to flee after the successful 'Tulip Revolution' in 2005, a mass protest in Uzbekistan at a similar time led to further oppression of dissenters. A protest in Uzbekistan following the 2006 fraudulent presidential election brought about short-term success, but was soon trodden on by state security forces. In the case of Burma, the iron rule of the military junta sealed non-violent political transformation despite the politically well-organized struggle by internationally recognized leader Aung San Suu Kyi.

The brutal crackdown on demonstrations organized by Buddhist monks in September 2007 has further sustained the longevity of the almost 30 year old military dictatorship in Burma. The survival of the military oligarchy is attributed to both the internal cohesion among top generals and their firm control over army units and government institutions. In this situation, external pressure is essential in supporting civic groups and ending the illegitimate grab for power by a small number of military officers. But Western efforts to bring sanctions have not been successful due to a lack of cooperation from China and other neighbouring countries which have vested economic interests in timber and mineral exploration.

The failure of the 1989 student and labour unrest in Beijing is contrasted with the collapse of the Eastern European Communist regimes. Chinese students protesting the autocratic nature of the one-party rule erected a model of the Statue of Liberty in Tiananmen Square of Beijing, calling for political freedom and rights to a free press and the organization of civic associations. After their initial reluctance, the Chinese leadership brought in military forces to shoot students and other protest groups as well as the execution of labour strike leaders in Shanghai and other places. The generation of fear, along with the severe restrictions of protest movements by state institutions, quelled the popular demand for change. In this incident, the control of police and military instruments within the leadership remained key in blocking the demands by disenchanted intellectuals and urban supporters.

The sudden collapse of the one-party socialist system in Eastern Europe at the end of the 1980s is ascribed to a lack of effective resistance of state institutions to unprecedented waves of popular street protests. The Eastern European leaders were intimidated by the show of public dissatisfaction and felt inhibited from the use of force. The establishment of normative political values, which prohibits shooting unarmed civilian protesters, following the spread of Gorbachev's political reform, also served as an obstacle for the Eastern European leaders to use brutal coercive forces against the masses. In addition, there was a strong Western enthusiasm with the mass revolts, contrary to more cautious, relatively lukewarm support toward China's popular protest, being limited to political rhetoric, without any attempt at diplomatic or economic sanctions that could have normally been applied to other situations.

The role of groups in social mobilization

Psychological causes, such as relative deprivation and collective grievances, facilitate group action, especially in combination with the emergence of organizational leadership, communication networks, and freedom of association. In particular, political and social organizations are essential to a collective movement with the support of material and human resources. In addition to strong inducements, ethno-political and other types of protests are bolstered by the territorial concentration of a disenchanted population. Pre-existing organizations may be ready to take on an opportunity forged by social instability. A group's capacity for sustained activities benefits from the intensity of shared identity and successful coalition building.

The articulation of manifest interests is, to a large extent, related to technical, political, social, and psychological conditions. The latent interests of base groups can be translated into organizational goals by the formulation of new agendas. Lost autonomy, government repression and increased political restrictions generate resentment which unites dispersed group members for rebellion and other types of collective action. The recruiting ground for conflict groups is typically comprised of social categories which suffer from power disparity in a polarized society. Unmobilized and unfocused interests need to be articulated by core groups for political representation. Degrees of central control and coordination among members have an impact on the efficiency of internal mobilization efforts.

Not all human and material resources can be converted into social power, some being lost in the organization of specific actions. Diverse group interests are not equally expressed or represented because of disparities in the structure of resource mobilization capabilities. Every group member may not have the same psychological state or disposition, but sharing a common objective would encourage each to act in concert with the others.

The effectiveness in the pursuit of organizational goals depends on a variety of factors: the level of consensus on core values within an opposition group, intra-group communication patterns, relationships between the leadership and members, and abilities to adjust to unpredictable demands. The successful formation of conflict groups is supported not only by improved communication but also by increased solidarity among group members. The presence of such legitimizing values as the rights of self-determination on one's own side strengthens protest movements.

The masses need to be mobilized by the counter-elite along with an emotional arousal before anger with an unfair situation turns into sustained struggle. Above all, the sense of injustice and threat is central to identity activation for group action. The interdependence of fate strengthens group bond and solidarity; violent social movements are indications of the breakdown of social control following discontent and grievances. In the group psychology of mobilization, a crowd can perform a deed that used to be unthinkable by individuals on their own (Brown, 1988).

The types of collective action, whether violent or non-violent, depend on the nature of manifest interests, belief systems, levels of discontent, and the scope of goals. Violence would be more readily employed at the initial stage of a conflict if the opposition campaign were aimed at the destruction of the existing order, rather than at a gradual reform, in a highly contested struggle. The adoption or rejection of violence as a strategy can also indicate which types of opposition, such as militia groups versus civil protest organizations, might be mobilized in what kind of process, being illustrated by intense ethnic hostilities turning into civil wars.

Overall conflict stages

In spite of their variations, conflict stages have, for analytical purposes, been portrayed in terms of an orderly evolution from initiation of struggles, escalation, entrapment, de-escalation and termination (as is illustrated by Figure 5.1). Thus, several phases progress from an incipient event, the manifestation of hostilities, through spiral dynamics, to a stalemate state, and eventual changes in the adversarial relationships (Cupach and Canary, 1997; Rummel, 1975). An outcome of one episode can become the starting point for another circle of renewed conflict if sufficient changes are not introduced to allay structural inequality.

The early stage of a conflict process includes precipitating events, public awareness, and consciousness of incompatible goals. In the manifestation of a conflict, one or both parties perceive or anticipate resistance from others when they make attempts to improve their situations. In general, conflict is more likely to be intense, especially when actual value and interest differences put partisans in a zero-sum contest. Opposing positions are recognized along with the emergence of concrete issues. More specifically, antagonistic expressions are manifested when one party makes demands for change in its

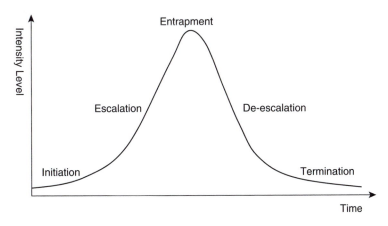

Figure 5.1   A conflict progression model

favour to an existing situation, but faces resistance by another group.[1] The emergence of overt conflict signals is characterized by moving from a latent stage to the pursuit of a unilateral solution.

A high priority assigned to specific issues vis-à-vis others may reflect the incentives behind full engagement in the conflict. Assertiveness in the demands of minority ethnic and racial groups for a new status brings tensions to the forefront of national politics. The pursuit of different priorities in a new, political atmosphere often raises issues that have not been significant in the past. The electoral victories of pro-Western presidential candidates in Georgia (2003) and the Ukraine (2004) have raised tensions with Russia, ending military and economic partnerships. Therefore, the salience of goals can be modified due to changes within the parties. The maintenance of good relations may not be considered any more important than pursuing unilateral interests.

Levels of unpredictability and uncertainty rise with emotional upheaval during the final shift from specific disagreement to general antagonism. As conflict emerges and escalates, it produces considerable confusion. Interactions between the conflicting parties change, at times radically and abruptly, as seen in the ethnic killings in Bosnia-Herzegovina. Enemy perceptions shape, in one way or another, boundaries of permissible acts. The circumstances of a conflict such as political chaos and competition among nationalist groups largely determine psychological perceptions of how costly a conflict will subsequently become. The alternation of behaviour is associated with changes in attitudes oriented toward increasing suspicion and mistrust.

Escalation is often drawn out by the eruption of new conflict spirals in which opposing sides search for every possible advantage in their battles and rally support for their cause. The use of relatively mild kinds of coercion or verbal threats is replaced with more forceful tactics of contention in win–lose settings. In the absence of trust, parties attempt to inflict one-sided solutions via coercion. Desires to induce capitulation substitute the initial promise of reward for yielding and the efforts of persuasion.

As the pace quickens, the issues become personal, leading to the use of insulting rhetoric such as George Bush's use of the word 'tyrant' in referring to the North Korean leader at the height of the nuclear stand-off. More adversarial communication patterns supplant formal contact, and at the later stages of escalation, parties become trapped in an action–reaction cycle that intensifies struggle. Entrapment in a cycle of coercion and counter-coercion is most likely to persist in the absence of an alternative to violent means of competition. The perpetuation of antagonism is even deeply ingrained in an ongoing violent discourse and its justification through the distorted construction of history.

Mutual escalation is likely to be carried on for a period of time after the point of actual use of, or commitment to, violence by one side and a coercive response by the other. A stalemate is understood in terms of a deadlocked struggle in the absence of a clear-cut victory, along with the inability of each party to curtail significantly the other's resistance. Inertia towards the continued course of escalation arrives with a total commitment to sacrifice for victory, commensurate to the psychological and political rationalization of heavy investments and swelling costs. Even after the emotional and material exhaustion, the parties may be less willing to accept some 'worthless' or 'unworthy' compromise. In fact, conflicting parties are often hesitant to cut their losses and quit, even when their goals seem more inaccessible.

As a consequence of the negative psychological orientations, adversaries may not be able easily to explore a genuine alternative. Escalation and stalemate endure so long as each party retains any little glimpse or hope of victory. Entrapment means a flat, unpleasant terrain stretching into the future with a damaging and potentially drawn-out impasse. A hurting stalemate, associated with the prolonged, high intensity of struggles, eventually results in pessimistic prospects for the outcome with dwindling will and capacity. The unbearable pain of loss, fruitless expenditures, and overwhelming damage are some of the main factors that drive the modification of behaviour.

Towards ending conflict

De-escalation may not come immediately after a decision on the cessation of escalation. Intensity in hostile behaviour can be diminished for strategic reasons without changes in intentions, namely, being designed towards a more economic and effective conduct of conflict. A genuine transition from a stalemate to de-escalation is more likely when the stalemate situation is mutually felt to be disadvantageous. This change depends on adjustment in subjective states of mind. Negotiation can follow the failure of further efforts to overwhelm the other side at the futile expense of resources. Contentious behaviour decreases with the transformation of a conflict environment, opening the way for tactical bargaining.

Successfully negotiating an agreement on termination may follow many failed attempts at searching for mutually acceptable solutions. Negotiated settlement may not be easy, in part, due to the difficulty of reducing enemy images and related misperceptions (Mitchell, 2000). The structure of the conflict, such as incompatibility in the objectives of the parties and the relative balance of forces, has a big impact on the outcome of the bargaining process. When violence creates an inhospitable environment for negotiation, victimization of each party by the other is a major obstacle toward de-escalation and reconciliation.

Thus conflict resolution is a reflexive process of overcoming negative, mutual emotions and psychology. If no agreement is reached, the conflict may escalate again into a test of strength and resolve, or it may remain frozen at the status quo. The renewed violence may end up with bringing the imposition of one party's will on the other. However, defeated groups or populations 'are typically soon ready to fight again so that [enemy] victories are symbolic and short-term' (Tainter, 2007: 77).

It is very difficult to transform conflict once it has become apparently intractable. The best that can be hoped for in the aftermath of a failed settlement is to guard against a further escalation of the conflict. A search for resolution can be complicated by the involvement of multiple parties with diverse behavioural patterns, combined with issues often embedded within each other. A dim prospect for conflict management or settlement may require the involvement of an intermediary who supports communication for lessening the differences between positions.

In resolving conflict, a different sense of identity may need to be created for one or both parties, as demonstrated by the development of a new national identity, embracing all races, in post-apartheid South Africa. Positive results of a conflict are generally achieved through the establishment of harmonious relationships. The fear of oppression and domination can be overcome by such means as power sharing and the reform of security and police forces for the guarantee of individual civil and group rights. New electoral processes were introduced to transition in Mozambique, Angola, El Salvador and most other post-conflict societies where opposition forces are given political voice through their representation in a cabinet or parliament.

Even when the end of the conflict leads to the previous status quo without meeting the original objectives of any of the partisans, it does not necessarily mean the return to an identical situation prior to the struggle. Active engagement in a conflict, itself, has a substantial effect upon participants and their relationships, even though the matter in contention may remain unchanged. The entity of a conflict goes through changes in leadership and collective identity. The outcome may generate new ways of redressing the grievances arising from the conduct of struggles, altering the initial conditions.

Variation patterns of conflict phases

In a linear progression model, intensity of conflict is described by a peaked curve on which the emergence of hostilities builds into violent interaction prior to any de-escalation attempts. While it is conceptually helpful to imagine a series of proceeding stages, protracted conflicts, in particular, do not progress in a uniform fashion. A rigidly bounded sequence is not easily applied to a long history of conflict, such as Arab–Israeli animosities, which have had many reversals with various events affecting each other.

Thus the path of conflict is full of discontinuous, transformative events in a non-linear, self-sustaining system. Due to volatility in human interaction, the transition from one phase to the next is not always subject to predictable models that suggest a specific duration for each stage. Representing different degrees of complexity, each episode also diverges significantly in terms of the nature of transition, being often acknowledged retrospectively rather than prospectively planned.

Diverse passages of a conflict are illustrated by the fact that most events do not go through a prescribed trajectory. The messiness does not fit into a simple stage-by-stage model that is within any particular actor's control. It is difficult to identify when the conflict advances from one phase to the next, given that the identification of markers signalling a movement can be, at best, ambiguous. Because one stage is not strictly differentiated from the other, a sequential order is not necessarily bounded in a rigid manner (Kriesberg, 1998).

These complexities engender numerous variations from a straight progression model. Instead of heading into intensive struggles, the emergence of violent incidents representing popular discontent can subside, through rapid control, especially in the absence of well-organized, opposing forces, as is illustrated by the Tiananmen Square protests of 1989. Following the strong show of initial resistance against the oppressive regime, military forces, loyal to the autocratic president, crushed protests in Uzbekistan, leaving the conflict dormant for a future occurrence. The translation of latent conflict into another opportunity for manifest struggle may have to wait longer following its initiation.

If one party suddenly loses its organizational ability to sustain the struggle, conflicts can be rather promptly terminated, following the intense, initial period of confrontation. Immediately after escalation, a struggle may lead to a sudden ending if one party capitulates, is subdued, overwhelmed, or otherwise intimidated with the minimum use of force. Such a situation as the collapse of the Iraqi army facing the US invasion provides a poignant example of this. Urban protests after the fraudulent elections in Georgia (2003) and the Ukraine (2004) led to a shift in power after the governments' failed attempts to control the opposition crowds.

The changes in conflict dynamics, such as an abrupt eruption of armed insurgency, can be set by an accumulated period of agonizing interaction between existing forces. The introduction of new policies, such as the deprivation of an ethnic language's official status, may pave a way for a new level of fighting. A more organized insurgent movement in Macedonia, manifested by attacks against the police in January 2001, proceeded from sporadic protests and other clashes between the Albanian minority population and the government.

While Macedonia obtained independence from Yugoslavia in 1991, it put curbs on the Albanian language university in 1996 and prohibited the use of Albanian flags in 1997, antagonizing approximately 25% of the minority population in the territory. The armed conflict ended with the Ohrid Agreement of 2002, which accepted a new model of decentralization. While the Albanian minority agreed to give up any separatist demands, the government pledged greater cultural and educational rights, adopting Albanian as an official language, as well as increased representation of the ethnic group in the government, armed forces, and police.

Lasting entrapment

In many civil war situations, violent phases of escalation are often prolonged with heavy civilian sacrifices. In fact, '[s]talemated military conflicts are among the most damaging of human circumstances' (Tainter, 2007: 77). The failure of a revolt by a group of junior military officers in 1960 lent itself to the organization of an armed insurrection against the Guatemalan government. This event became the origin of Guatemala's 36-year civil war. Major counterinsurgency campaigns launched by the government in 1966 and 1982 led to recapturing many portions of territories held by the insurgent movement, but the guerrillas showed military resilience by concentrating their attacks in Guatemala City in conjunction with the employment of hit-and-run operations.

The partial victories won by a series of military, or military-dominated, governments were based on an enormous cost in civilian deaths. Right-wing death squads, as well as government military units, were engaged in torturing and murdering students, professionals, and peasants who were suspected of sympathizing with leftist activists. In particular, the brief presidency of Ríos Montt in 1982 was the most violent period, involving the deaths of thousands of unarmed indigenous people. Despite condemnation of government conduct by the Conference of Catholic Bishops and other moral voices, summary executions, forced disappearances, and torture of non-combatants did not cease, further polarizing Guatemalan society. Most of the civil war period was marked by massacres and political assassinations, undertaken by security forces and affiliated paramilitary groups, leaving only a very few bystanders unharmed. The violence finally ended with the 1996 Peace Accord. Even though the duration of the Salvadoran civil war was relatively short, the leftist coalition was also locked in a similar struggle with the government between 1980 and 1992.

The entrapment period of internal conflicts in Sudan, Angola, and Mozambique is characterized by more than two decades of brutal warfare. In these civil wars, a periodic intensification of armed fighting alternated with a relative subsiding of military encounters. The fight of the non-Arab populations in southern Sudan against the Arab-dominated government lasted from 1955 to 2005 with the exception of an 11-year cease-fire. The process of independence from Portugal set off decades-long civil wars in Mozambique (1977–92) and Angola (1975–2002) after opposing factions made exclusive claims to control government institutions. Even though civil wars in Sierra Leone (1991–2002) and Liberia (1989–96 and 1999–2003) were comparatively shorter, the long entrapment period caused tens of thousands of civilian deaths and millions of displaced people (well over one third of the population in the case of Sierra Leone). Although many civil wars finally go through cease-fires and negotiated settlements, the extended period of violence represents difficulties in establishing de-escalation once various parties are entrenched in testing each other's resilience and ability to absorb heavy costs.

Enduring status quo after escalation

In contrast with the above, the escalation stage can be stabilized through a frozen stalemate over a long period of time by accepting, even tentatively, the outcome of violent clashes (as demonstrated by the history of Israeli–Syrian relations since the 1967 Six-Day War).[2] In this kind of situation, hostilities tend to subside prior to the emergence of a new desire to change the uncomfortable status quo. Even though an urgent need to regulate any uncontrollable violence may have been met, neither international nor domestic contexts may provide a propitious time for settlement. As seen in the examples of the Cyprus conflict, a long-standing, low level of antagonism may not be worsened, but neither may it develop any urgency in settlement.

The outcome of war, reflected in the occupation of territory and the division of land, often seals a new status quo that may need to be transformed, either through negotiation or renewed fighting. Neither side has the capacity to sustain the fighting or alter the status quo permanently due to either external or internal circumstances. The conflict may stay inactive or frozen without real efforts for resolution; the eventual emergence of a new balance of power between the antagonists might generate another fight unless the discontent can be redressed through negotiation.

The current status of the drawn out conflict between Armenia and Azerbaijan is represented by a situation of no-war-no-peace. At the end of the Karabakh war that erupted in the late winter of 1992, Armenians managed to gain full control over not only their small enclave Nagorno-Karabakh, but also approximately 10% of other Azerbaijani territory. Since a Russian-brokered cease-fire in 1994, the two former Soviet republics have held peace talks, but negotiation over the enclave's status stalled. While active fighting stopped for more than a decade, both countries have become enveloped in a protracted status quo; Azerbaijan has, meanwhile, been attempting to curb a secessionist movement in Nagorno-Karabakh via diplomatic efforts.

Rupture in enduring hostilities

Ending a conflict after a long struggle may sometimes follow dramatic changes in the balance of forces. The independence of East Timor was granted in the aftermath of the sudden collapse of the Suharto government in Indonesia, caused by the Asian financial crisis of 1997–1998. Such changes as a collapse of currency, inability to pay back foreign debt, or diminishing assistance or diplomatic support for continued armed insurgencies often considerably weaken the will of primary antagonists to fight by removing significant sources of financial and military strength. In fact, unforeseen changes in a conflict environment may contribute to dramatic, discontinuous leaps into a new stage rather than a slow change at a constant rate.

A relatively abrupt, unanticipated de-escalation may be accompanied by a long-term escalated conflict condition (as exemplified in the release of

Nelson Mandela after 27 years of imprisonment; the sudden end of the 27 year-old civil war in Angola). Particular events might provide sharp turns toward winding down hostilities, as is illustrated by a secret meeting between the white minority government's leadership and Nelson Mandela prior to his release or by the battle death of rebel force leader Jonas Savimbi in the case of Angola. In sharp reversals, psychological and behavioural adjustments are needed for sudden ruptures. In particular, it may take time to soothe simmering antagonism derived from intense hostilities of the past. Even if adversarial actions might immediately cease, long-term reconciliation would be required to support the endurance of settlement.

The nexus of escalation, de-escalation, and re-escalation

Intractable conflicts tend to go through a complex cycle that comprises perturbations in escalation, continuing stalemate, de-escalation, and re-escalation. Thus a core set of interrelated dimensions of activities is better explained by a dynamics model that has more than one peak with valleys between them. Following a quick initiation, a conflict can be sustained, though without major armed clashes and heavy casualties, for a longer time-span in a state of stalemate that is full of many small and brief episodes. Once a struggle is further escalated, however, a protracted phase may go through intense entrapment prior to the eventual erosion of each other's capabilities and will (as seen in the civil wars in Bosnia-Herzegovina).

In the Democratic Republic of Congo, Burundi, and Somalia, many attempts to control violence faced setbacks due to the difficulties of coordinating and harmonizing diverse factional interests. The Northern Ireland peace process is a typical example of discontinuity and leaps in progress prior to the devolution of most central government power to a Northern Ireland Assembly, as envisioned in the Good Friday Agreement of April 1998. Negotiations on the future of the Northern Ireland government were conducted over a period of nine years, against the background of the reversal of a ceasefire by the IRA and bombings of London's Canary Wharf in February 1996, and other violent events. The tumultuous process was eventually overcome by the creation of a coalition government after direct talks between Democratic Unionist Party leader Ian Paisley and Sinn Fein's Gerry Adams in early 2007.

The reversals of a conflict sequence, prior to its ending, are not uncommon, because the progression of many conflict situations does not move in a linear fashion. Following some sorts of de-escalation, a larger cycle of conflict may move back to a new mode of escalation. The stumbling Israeli–Palestinian negotiations to implement the Oslo Peace Accord, best illustrated by the collapse of the Camp David summit in July 2000, served as a backdrop for a more entrenched struggle with the introduction of suicide bombers by radical Palestinian factions. Such provocative actions as right-wing Israeli politician Ariel Sharon's visit to the Haram al-Sharif/Temple Mount (regarded as a sacred symbol by both Jews and Arabs) in September 2000 ignited this new cycle of violence, known as the second intifada. The Angolan civil war also experienced several reversals of a peace process, with the repetition of cease-fires, elections, and a renewed warfare, prior to the 2002 agreement on permanent demobilization of rebel forces and their integration in a new political framework.

This back-and-forth, non-linear character often defies a temporal logic and developmental inevitability of conflict phases. A complex system of conflict processes can be characterized by a set of interlocking sub-processes of various events that are mutually influencing. In conflicts persisting over a long period of time, lower level tension prevails with sporadic eruptions of more intense confrontations. Whereas brief cycles of hostile incidents modify the fluidity of struggles, the parameters of the conflict are often entrenched in larger and more enduring psychological relationships.

The course of a conflict can be branched and rebranched to extra issues, creating an expanded movement (d'Estrée, 2003). The efforts to bring about the denuclearization of North Korea have been derailed after the American government froze North Korea's foreign bank accounts with charges of Pyongyang's involvement in the counterfeiting of US dollar bills. The emergence of this new issue prevented progress in further talks based on a preliminary agreement in September 2005, since North Korea refused to return to continued discussion about its nuclear programmes without removal of the unilaterally imposed sanctions. Thus the main concern was hijacked by other developments, adding another complex dimension to the negotiations. The prospects for negotiated settlement were further complicated by North Korea's missile tests in 2006, which provoked US and Japanese condemnations. Since the inception of renewed confrontations over the US charges of North Korean nuclear programmes in 2003, the above and other subsidiary issues such as human rights have been layered on top of the core contentious issues.

Re-escalation may be accompanied by failed negotiations and the revival of mutual coercion with periodic intervals of dormancy. The nature of struggle may evolve in a response to several rounds of escalation that have changed the character of both internal and external dynamics of a conflict. If one side begins to feel that it increasingly overwhelms the other, it may want to adopt a war of attrition strategy to impose its preferred settlement.

In the absence of a shift in the balance of forces, however, a cycle may continue between lower level endemic fights and crises. The intensification of struggles can be avoided only after attempts to overwhelm the adversary become too costly or comprise unacceptable risks. In situations of power symmetry, neither side can have any successful end in sight, owing to difficulties in destroying or neutralizing the other. Negotiated settlements are not easy if irreconcilable differences arise from various characteristics of antagonistic values and systems.

In many ethnic conflicts, illustrated by the Tamil guerrilla warfare in Sri Lanka, peacemaking may draw to a close, only tumbling back into violence in the absence of the cooperative potential which is essential to tolerant relations. The destruction of faith and trust tends to persist over time, damaging future prospects for peacemaking. The images of negative encounters overshadow any positive aspects of experience, since friendly gestures are now misconstrued, with suspicion, as aberrations, if not as attempts at deception.

A movement toward de-escalation involves each party's ability to defuse a crisis and entails successful withdrawal from an episode of coercive tactics (Pammer and Killian, 2003). Negotiation is not likely to be productive in the perpetuation of repetitive patterns of threats, provocation, blame, and retaliation. In transforming destructive exchanges embedded in a high-stake game, escalation, crisis, and coercive bargaining are some of the dynamics to be managed.

In some situations, conflict dynamics run their due course until a more powerful party perceives that coercive means are ineffective in breaking the will of a weaker party in a costly contest. If strong, negative synergy within a conflict system continues to drive an unending struggle, it needs to be compensated by more assertive de-escalation efforts to control a rapid escalation or re-escalation leading to violence. In the absence of synergy or counterbalance to control destructive, escalatory dynamics within a system, a de-escalatory initiative may come from an outside intervention such as peace enforcement functions designed to contain ethnic killing or genocide.

A curvilinear path of a large conflict system

The life cycle of a conflict is more likely to follow a curvilinear path, with protuberances, rather than a straight line. This is well illustrated by the three major wars between India and Pakistan (1947, 1965, and 1971); the Middle Eastern conflict (after the creation of Israeli state in 1948); and the Bush administration's abandonment of the 1994 Agreed Framework on North Korea's nuclear weapons programmes accompanied by efforts for a re-negotiated settlement since 2003. A conflict path comprised of blips and bulges illuminates changes in a diverse context of evolving events. Moreover, structures of conflict relationships are shaped and re-shaped by the replacement of political leadership and re-alignment in external ally relationships.

A conflict history can be divided by watershed events that feature attempts to change the status quo, reflecting the balance of antagonistic forces within the system. In its 35-year history, a large conflict system, representing US–Soviet relations, went through the Cold War, détente, renewed hostilities, conciliation, and the eventual demise of the socialist system (as demonstrated by Figure 5.2). Many of these key events can be described in the context of escalation and de-escalation. Each of the major struggles—the Berlin blockade of 1948, the Korean War of 1950–53, the Cuban Missile Crisis of 1962, the Vietnam War of 1964–75, the Arab–Israeli wars of 1967 and 1973, and the Soviet war in Afghanistan of 1979–89—entails its own internal dynamics, swayed by evolving international relations. The Cuban Missile crisis brought the two superpowers close to the brink of a catastrophic war, whereas the Berlin blockade and the Soviet threat of intervention in the 1973 Middle East War went through controlled escalation

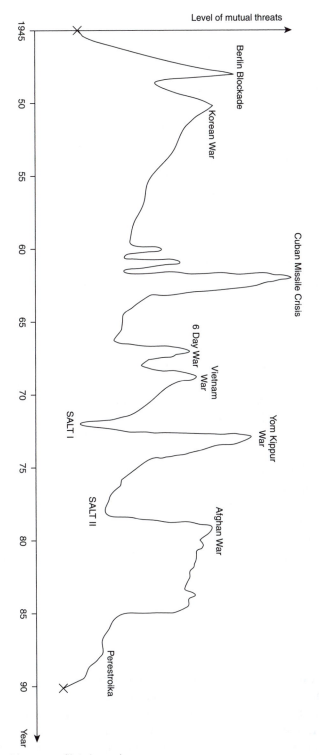

Figure 5.2   Macro conflict dynamics

prior to the final subsiding of confrontation accompanied by Soviet yielding. In between these major events were such mini-crises as the U-2 incident of 1960 (the shooting down of an American spy plane over the Soviet Union) and the construction of the Berlin Wall in 1961.

The US containment policies of the late 1940s and early 1950s led to the direct American military intervention in Korea as well as the creation of NATO. The Berlin Blockade became the first major US–Soviet confrontation with a big stake. In his efforts to ease enmity, Soviet Premier Nikita Khrushchev promoted the doctrine of 'Peaceful Co-existence' beginning in 1953, and was actively engaged in meetings with American presidents. In spite of these new initiatives, a quest for one's own military security, along with lingering deep mistrust, generated intense struggles between the American and Soviet leaderships, most dramatically presented by the Cuban Missile Crisis of 1962. In the aftermath of this near catastrophic incident, tension gradually declined to reach détente, culminating in the conclusion of the Strategic Arms Limitation Talks I and II (of 1973 and 1979 respectively), aimed at limiting the development of costly anti-ballistic missile systems and offensive nuclear arsenals.

The harsh US response to the Soviet invasion of Afghanistan of 1979 and astronomical military spending by the Reagan administration, totalling US$ 2.2 trillion over eight years, brought the height of new tensions in the early 1980s. Direct military attacks were deterred by the potential for mutually assured destruction using deliverable nuclear weapons. With the democratic reform programmes called 'Perestroika' and 'Glasnost' of Mikhail Gorbachev in 1987, however, the Soviet Union permitted the transformation of Eastern Europe and its own dissolution by 1991 (Leatherman, 2003; Odom, 2004).

The directions of various conflict events have been shaped by the emergence of new leaders, including Nikita Khrushchev and Mikhail Gorbachev, and their decision-making choices. The behaviour of each protagonist was constrained not only by intra-party demands such as public protest against war but also by external, sub-system-level pressure, for instance, derived from divisions within an alliance as well as system-level dynamics of arms race between the two opposing blocs. Fortunately, one side, or both sides, were able to decide to pull back from the brink of a crisis to prevent a runaway spiral, as exemplified by the Berlin Blockade and the Cuban Missile Crisis.

Meanwhile, intermittent decreases in conflict intensity coexisted with occasional outbreaks of new animosities, often encouraged by external circumstances (for instance, regional wars) beyond each protagonist's control. Even through the détente, indirect conflict between the superpowers continued in the developing world, particularly during the political crises in the 1973 Arab–Israeli war and the Angolan civil war. Each power served as a patron of local antagonists by supplying military hardware and economic assistance. In spite of coercive activities to undermine each other's influence on the global arena, the superpower rivalry was managed, without provoking World War III, prior to the collapse of the Soviet system.

The nature of conflict movements

Various characteristics of conflict dynamics can be distinguished by an increased or decreased level of hostilities, their continuity or reversal as well as duration. The direction of a conflict can be identified in terms of the overall, combined balance between pulling toward and pushing away from intense struggle. Wars and other violent acts expand hostile dimensions of interaction and have a long lasting impact on conflict participants. The effects of certain modes of action such as the declaration of war can be characterized by their irreversibility.

Intensity

A conflict can be intensified with a series of increasing pressures from initial verbal threats, economic sanctions, displays of force and the limited use of force, to all-out war. In a crisis situation, on the other hand, a sudden burst of animosities generates an unpredictable course of interaction. An attempt can be made to subdue the risk of violent struggles, but new forms of confrontation might surge with unexpected events such as accidental firing of missiles or uncontrolled collision of forces.

The intensification of a conflict is observed when formerly non-violent acts are accelerated to a violent level. Escalation is almost certain in a switch from limited armed struggles with medium intensity to a high-stake struggle, often comprising severe crises or wars with a large number of casualties. Intensity scales can be observed in terms of an increasing level of psychological pressure and mass destruction with heavy casualties.

Rates of change: general patterns

Different types of conflict have a diverse time span, according to the fluidity of a conflict cycle. In crisis situations, both escalation and de-escalation processes are likely to be of short duration in almost a symmetrical manner. This is best represented by the Cuban Missile Crisis and the Yom Kippur War. On the contrary, many protracted civil wars are full of tumultuous histories which have different impacts on escalation and de-escalation dynamics.

Whereas it may not be exactly symmetrical, both escalation and de-escalation dynamics can evolve for a long time span. In the case of Northern Ireland, it has taken almost two decades for de-escalation initiatives to produce a more tangible outcome of power sharing and effective cessation of hostilities. At the same time, the most intense period of escalation comprised of bombing campaigns by the IRA was also sustained for at least two decades beginning with the establishment of the terrorist organization in 1969.

In many incidences, the rates of change are asymmetric, reflecting diverse characteristics of actor relationships. Steep escalation (of short duration) can be followed by slow de-escalation dynamics, comprising long-term efforts to bring an end to the fight. While it took only a few days for the Soviet Union to invade Afghanistan in 1979, three to four years of exit strategy were needed to withdraw from fighting with Islamic guerrilla forces in 1989.

In internal wars initiated by the suppression of popular discontent (for example, El Salvador and Guatemala), subsequent military violence against ordinary citizens and violations of civic rights gradually slipped into decades-long, armed resistance by organized anti-government forces, with fluctuations in intensity levels. Once protagonists decide to de-escalate their fighting and are seriously devoted to settlement, a negotiation process can be wrapped up in one or two years. Thus, compared with long histories of struggles, it tends to be relatively short to wind down the fighting prior to concluding a peace treaty in the majority of successful negotiated settlements.

Modes of escalation

After discontent is expressed, some conflicts may burst rather quickly into flames, while others would go through a slow slope curve of escalation (as presented in Figure 5.3). Steep escalation of adversarial behaviour and protracted stalemate can normally be observed in a long-term rivalry. In contentious relationships, various types of provocations may unexpectedly release an intense escalation movement owing to deep emotional enmities rooted in past grievances (for instance, the 1965 India–Pakistan War).

On the other hand, the nuclear stand-off between Western allies and Iran has been slowly escalating with cautious moves to test each other's resolve. Even though threats and warnings have been issued, bullying tactics did not translate into direct military action which can ignite an all-out war. In some situations (exemplified by Sri Lanka), a long period of animosities (mostly manifested in unarmed protests) can be passed on to a totally new stage of

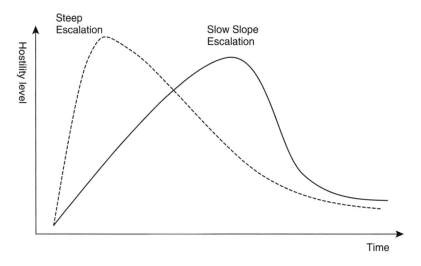

Figure 5.3   Modes of escalatory change

conflict characterized by guerrilla warfare with the organization of armed groups. Then the stalemated escalation stage produces many military gains and setbacks for both parties.

Modes of de-escalation

In a similar manner as escalation, de-escalation dynamics are also subject to diverse movements of changes, tumultuous or cumbersome (as illustrated in Figure 5.4). It is not difficult to find examples of a tenuous transformation of long-term adversarial relationships. In a dead-locked struggle, with other conditions being equal, the longevity of de-escalation tends to be an inevitable part of a pro-tracted history. Despite minor setbacks, a steady transition toward de-escalation may take root in a consistent movement through the accumulation of many con-ciliatory moves prior to a more visible and distinctive departure from old policies. It took at least a decade for the governments in both South and North Korea to develop the momentum toward conciliation that eventually culminated in the visit of President Kim Dae-Jung in 2000 to the North Korean capital Pyongyang.

In contrast with the above example, de-escalation dynamics may be intro-duced in a relatively short time frame. In such instances as the Oslo peace process between the Israelis and Palestinians in the early 1990s, and the American–China rapprochement in 1972, the initial point of a de-escalation movement represents a sudden rupture from the previous patterns of antago-nistic interaction. As is best demonstrated by the end of the Cold War, unin-tended internal and external changes may permit one or both parties to pull out of a long-running conflict completely (Singer, 1999).

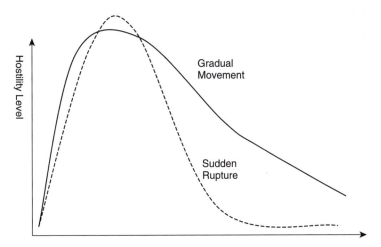

Figure 5.4   Modes of de-escalation

Irreversibility

New balances are constantly re-established, as a conflict evolves. Each stage has its own processes, which are different from those that preceded it or those that will follow. Remarkable changes in the seemingly short term may represent the effects of the previous occurrence. Even in a relatively short-lived, intense conflict, we are most likely to observe structural and other changes engendered by the initial escalation. Actions during the intense phases of the struggle cannot simply be nullified, retracted, or revoked (Mitchell, 1999).

For example, in a civil war, the insurgent groups may have dispelled regular armed forces and may begin to control a new territory to weaken support for the government (Kriesberg, 1998). This was the case in the internal wars of Mozambique and El Salvador, within which anti-government forces established their own administrative functions in the 1980s. Resentment and grievances resulting from the conflict casualties and destruction of infrastructure are not quickly abandoned, because of the reduction or even complete cessation of military and other types of coercive action. Even though active warfare ceased in Bosnia-Herzegovina, civilian deaths caused by Serb and Croatian militia forces have made it difficult for Muslims to reconcile with their loss.

Regulating potential

Different conflict cycles generate distinct dynamics of change. The protraction of a conflict is ascribed to insufficient resistance against development of antagonistic interactions as well as abundant elements pushing for competition. The relative balance of forces drives the course of conflict, defining the role of each action at any given moment. Motivational and systemic characteristics involved in limiting conflict formation and progression include the fear of destructive effects coming from escalation, the benefit gained from an interdependent relationship, weak support of major allies, conflict-control institutions, internal divisions, and negative public opinion against belligerent actions.

Every conflict context contains a different combination of regulating potentials. In controlling conflict, a stronger party may rely on cooptation or neutralization strategies to discourage resistance. Internal divisions may be manipulated to restrain an adversary's effective engagement in conflict. Propaganda is likely to be used to discredit the leaders, goals, and tactics of an adversary. These methods may be combined with threats, harassment and other forms of coercive interference, being followed by a show of overwhelming strength.

Instead of repressive measures, concessions can be utilized to help to diffuse tension. Major concessions, timely made, may reduce the potential for catastrophic collision or violence. When the leaders want to cut their losses in domestic conflict, they may permit social or institutional changes. In Nepal, for instance, the king gave up his omnipresent power, capitulating to public protests in the spring of 2006. The ineffective military campaign against the Maoist guerrillas significantly weakened the king's position against civilian opposition parties that were demanding the transfer of power from the monarchy to parliamentary rule. Government control over the opposition in divided societies clearly becomes weaker during a civil war.

Various types of intervention are important in regulating international confrontation or the initiation of a full-scale civil war. When there was a mass demonstration in protest against Japanese Prime Minister Koizumi's visit to the World War II criminals' shrine in April 2005, the Chinese government initially encouraged public protests as a means of putting pressure on the Japanese government. However, the Chinese leadership soon stepped in to crack down on mass rallies, being concerned about losing beneficial Japanese investment. The dispatch of NATO forces to Macedonia, in response to the insurgence of Albanian minority guerrilla movements in the early 2000s, cooled down the hostilities between the government and the ethnic minority group.

The mechanisms of conflict regulation are utilized to hold unrestrained negative changes in check. The existence of shared interests and belief systems within the EU enhances the appreciation of the intrinsic value of a mutually beneficial relationship. The recognition of each other's legitimacy brings with it a sense of permissible and non-permissible boundaries of behaviour. The cross-pressure of multiple commitments of parties to other simultaneous conflicts also serves as an obstacle to the further intensification of fights.

A tipping point

Reflecting on the inner logic of conflict movements, each step in the chain of events creates conditions that stimulate the next. In the progression of a conflict from one state to another, some junctures are more noteworthy than others. In tracing how to link one moment to the next, points of change are represented by 'tipping points', or thresholds, between which semi-permeable boundaries exist. In essence, certain salient moments serve as a threshold marker that, once passed, is denoted as a point of 'no return'. Tipping points may be considered to be events that catalyse a break between past and future trends. Indeed, a sharp change in a function or relationship often heralds a watershed which translates into an entirely different state.

In considering that thresholds are departures from routines, they may possibly be irrevocable, radically changing the context of events. For instance, the London terrorist bombings may reflect disenchantment with British policies and feelings of isolation among the Muslim youth. While the meaning of the incidents can be found in the transformation of attitudes and emotions, the acts have created a new relationship between the minority population and the larger society. The precipitants can be generated in a diverse context to challenge or preserve the existing equilibrium. As relational moments, tipping points are marked by significant shapers of subsequent events that induce strategic 'turns'.

A tipping point brings about the loss of equilibrium with constant instability and chaos. Psychologically or socially collective thresholds may entail the final recognition of a change in the status quo. The sum total of all of the small events, including the 'final straw', can be heaped upon each other before the collapse of the existing structure (Gladwell, 2000). However, the maximum limit, necessitated for a crucial change, may never be known until it is exceeded.

It can be contagious when one party adopts the other's behaviour, either constructive or destructive. Individuals tend to be immediately mobilized via a primitive, contagious process with the emergence of a collective mindset that creates homogeneity in people's feelings and actions (Reicher, 2001; Kruse, 1986). Thus a new, more conflict-intensified state might be built by the emergence of attitudinal consensus and group solidarity derived from a sudden external pressure or crisis. Contagious behaviour may initially subsist on seemingly small incidents among participants, but it can instantly be sensationalized in a large public domain.

Behaviour originally involving a few individuals in the larger collective can spread in a way that is analogous to the transmission of germs (Goldstein, 2002). The 2005 youth riots in Paris mushroomed very rapidly to Lyon, Berlin, and other European cities, providing an opportunity for the expression of anger and frustration ascribed to social discrimination. The 2005 'Muhammad' cartoon controversy originated from Denmark, but implicated most of Europe in its cultural war with the entire Islamic world, inviting violent protests from the Middle East to Indonesia. The initial publication of the cartoons in a small local Danish newspaper *Jyllands-Posten* in late September 2005 drew nearly 3,500 peaceful demonstrators in Copenhagen, but the re-publication of the images in several European papers in November set the course of widening protests, economic boycotts, and even burning of Danish diplomatic facilities in Damascus and Beirut by early March 2006.

A tipping point may arrive from a major re-evaluation of policy by a series of tragic events or an impending disaster. Threats, made with limited military action, can easily be misinterpreted, changing the characteristics of a struggle. Large changes in the status quo can sometimes happen at a single dramatic moment as a result of the manifestation of violent events. For example, the '9/11' terrorist attacks have developed clear demarcation lines in US relations with other parts of the world. The perceptual gaps between the Western and Islamic worlds have further deepened after the US invasion of Iraq.

The contradiction between what is espoused and what is actually happening may itself constitute a critical moment of initiating challenges to the status quo. An unexpected verbal or physical attack can manufacture uncertainty by facilitating events that knock the relationships off balance (Putnam, 2004). These occasions of interactive engagement or intense emotional experience, involving surprise and anxiety, may serve as critical moments. Having reached such a 'crossroad', the salience of those moments is often spotted only in hindsight.

Timing becomes an important factor for understanding a critical moment and threshold (Druckman, 1986). 'Ripeness', interpreted as appropriate conditions for de-escalation, requires the arrival of certain emotional and physical states that are reached only at a critical moment. Such events as concessions, offers, or reduced threats are considered markers to be reciprocated at critical moments toward de-escalation. Thus the effects of each action in the midstream of a conflict are contextually bound. On the other hand, a new momentum for escalation can be created by a shift in strategies, for example, a switch from non-violent to violent actions.

Forces of change: agency versus structure

The forces of conflict dynamics can be investigated as to motivations associated with aggression and political alliance as well as the nature of a movement toward a different stage of struggle. These questions have often been asked in discussion about the initiation of World Wars I and II, and the rise and fall of rivalry between major powers. We can further develop two broad perspectives in answering questions about the forces driving conflict behaviour. Does each interaction have its own unique character, only being shaped by actors, or does it merely reflect the effects of uncontrolled mechanisms? To what extent can uncontrolled forces or individual actors determine a conflict outcome?

If we take a voluntaristic perspective, the process of conflict is geared toward an outcome sought intentionally by a particular agent. Thus a conflict relationship is driven by conscious actors who know how to control various tides of dynamic movements implicated in their interaction with adversaries. In systems perspectives, however, the consequences of any action are regulated by a series of events in the social environment. This process is expected to produce a particular outcome under given structural circumstances.

The focus on different characteristics of actors helps to identify behavioural styles of the adversaries and motivations behind decision making and various institutional characteristics (Filson and Werner, 2002). Parties themselves have an ability to influence, albeit to varying degrees, how conflicts begin and terminate. If the intervention of external forces is minimal, the capacities and will of an individual agency are likely to have more impact on conflict dynamics.

The main limitations of an agency model are that actors are not likely to have all the knowledge and information which is necessary to make the most suitable decisions to control conflict dynamics in their favour. In addition, misinterpretations of external events, as well as misunderstandings of other actors' intentions and misperceptions of their behaviour, skew their judgements. Even though deliberate strategies are considered to be an initiating force for change, it is often the case that the unintended consequences of particular actions are almost inevitable.

Individual actors can make choices in determining the outcome of certain events, but the level of their effects differs according to how others react. The number of alternatives available for reacting to an external stimulus affects each party's decision making abilities. Indeed, a stronger party has more options simply because it has extra means available to negate the effects of an adversary's action or external environment.

In a more mechanical perspective, transition from one stage of group dynamics to the next is attributed to the process itself in analogies to the passage of one season to another, driven by the orientation of the earth to the sun. The behaviour of groups surely evolves, but it is only reactive to inevitable changes stimulated by dynamics embedded in the mutual effects of multiple individual actions. If individual actors are assumed to have a very limited impact on the intensity, duration, scope, and other qualities of events, the movement of a conflict has its own internal logic and patterns of resurgence and subsiding. Individual actors may be swept away by overwhelming social and political forces inherent to a conflict cycle.

On balance, the will and capacity of actors need to be present to generate major historical events, but they are not the sole determining factors in any serious change. If we emphasize voluntaristic—more specifically, psychological, motivational—aspects of action, then the alteration in dynamics stems from each agency's increased or decreased ability of destruction, for instance, in inter-state conflict. Nonetheless, hostile intentions serve as one of the major factors behind major wars, only combined with underlying forces driving escalatory dynamics. In fact, '[m]acro social structures constrain individual motivations and interaction patterns' (Ellis, 2006: 160). Overall, we may safely conclude that a conflict situation is created by the interaction between actors in a given structure.

The sequence of events can be more meaningfully explained in terms of a dynamic system that stimulates interaction. Each interaction is not merely a reflection of actors' individual strategies, cognitive frames, or decision-making styles in isolation from one another. Nor can each dynamic be viewed as a mere aggregate sum of individual strategies. Major changes are, instead, imperative within the structure of a conflict system that is constantly reshaped by actors' intentions and desires.

The trajectory of change is derived from twists and turns in the strategies, orientations, and goals of various actors. At the same time, many structural and situational circumstances also deflect the intended effects of any action. Personal perceptions, relationships, social processes, and political institutions are touched upon by those changes. Indeed, critical transformations such as ripeness for de-escalation can be sought in terms of the internal decision-making of each party and the structure of the overall conflict system. Propitious timing for conflict transformation is, then, the convergence of interests among two or more major adversaries created by a new institutional environment and psychological situation.

Notes

1 The existence of two clearly identifiable opposing categories generates the stimulus for initial actions. In a social comparison, other groups 'serve as vital reference point for the evaluation of our abilities and validation of our opinions' (Brown, 1988: xi).

2 In this war, Syria lost the Golan Heights to Israel and has not accepted that outcome; Israel, meanwhile, vowed not to return the land to Syria without the full Israeli demands being met. These conditions include Syrian cooperation to control anti-Israeli militant groups in Lebanon. The post-war status quo has been maintained by the fact that Israel has not initiated full residential, commercial development, but neither domestic nor international conditions have yet materialized to alter the entrapment.

Interlinkage and Context

6

As conflicts do not often have clear temporal and spatial boundaries, they are interlocked in terms of their impact on each other's dynamics. When conflicts are not completely resolved, they are downgraded or contained, with the reconstitution of the divisions among conflicting parties or a reorientation of issues and grievances. Even if one conflict loses its salience and simply fades away, others may become more intense, perhaps embracing violent escalation. It is not unusual that new struggles supplant previously settled conflicts. An old conflict draws less attention as participants engage in new issues or pursue new relationships.

In a long series of struggles, actors, issues, and temporal contexts are intricately linked to each other. The course of a particular conflict is affected by an unpredictable series of circumstances connected to other conflicts. Due to complexities arising from different sets of issues and relationships, some conflicts become more intractable than others, with poignant examples being the current wars in Afghanistan and Iraq. After the invasions of these countries, the US government has not yet proved capable of achieving its goal of providing stability even despite its mighty military strength. No one can fully control the course of conflict under fundamentally changing internal dynamics. In Iraq, constant realignments among multiple types of insurgents with varied agendas have created not only great uncertainties but also difficulties for transformation. Parties to conflict are bound by their own actions as well as the policies pursued by adversaries.

Unless the interpretation of rules and norms is easily handled within the system, serious discontent in the relationships would spill over to more serious demands for structural change and justice. Every conflict tends to be magnified, albeit at different degrees of complexity, by the formation of a new local, regional, and international alliance among parties that might have different ideologies, values, political systems, and military capabilities. These complexities evolve over the course of a conflict, along with changes in the behaviours and attitudes of the protagonists. This chapter investigates the manner in which a series of conflicts are interconnected in terms of actors, issues, and temporal order.

The intricate web of conflict dynamics

Every struggle with a long duration inevitably entails multilayered structures of relationships among parties, both internal and external. One layer of the relationship consists of rivalry and allegiance among primary contestants, whose interests diverge and coalesce according to changes in the dynamics of a conflict. The second layer entails the overarching relationships between external parties that have their own dynamics of struggle, but which nonetheless influence the processes and outcomes of local conflicts.

These layers are then interwoven with various forms of connections among primary contestants and external actors. The horizontal relationships are complemented by the vertical relationship between primary contestants and their supporters, who are external to the conflict. While events in the higher levels of the system are likely to impinge on lower levels of relationship, sub-conflicts may furnish an impetus for larger events beyond self-containment. For instance, tension between the Austrian–Hungarian empire and Serbia in 1914 eventually evolved into the participation of even non-European countries in the first major world war. Most intractable conflicts are subject to dialectical interactions among all of the multifarious forces of larger structures.

Different motivations and power dynamics get involved in the formation of layers of conflict relationships. Whereas the USA is not directly engaged in disputes involving gas prices between Russia and Georgia, Russia's decision to increase previously subsidized prices in early 2007 was seen as Russian retaliation for Georgia's pro-Western stance and an expression of Moscow's fear of expanded American influence in former Soviet republics. In this case, Russia's conflicts with its former republics over seemingly economic transactions have been characterized by triangular relationships that also involve an external power.

As is portrayed by the conflict in Lebanon, multiple actors—composed of two opposing blocs of local adversaries interlocked with their external environment—produce a complex web of interactions. At a national level, the resolution of the conflict in Lebanon must overcome deep divisions along lines of class, religion, and regional interests that transcend the simple notion of 'Christianity versus Islam'. For example, Hezbollah, the Shiite Muslim movement, draws its main support from a low-income population, in contrast with a more moderate Sunni faction. Hezbollah is allied in a struggle against the Sunni Prime Minister with one of the Christian parties, which is in a rival relationship with a right-wing Christian movement. At the external level, the American and French governments are wary of the interference of Iran and Syria in Lebanese politics and their support for Hezbollah. The US allies have been supporting the Lebanese government, based on the coalition of Sunni and conservative Christian political parties, as a means of reducing the influence of anti-Western regional forces.

Transboundary penetration and foreign meddling tend to both fuel and stretch out ethno-political rivalry in Africa's many regional conflicts. Tutsis in Rwanda, Burundi and the Democratic Republic of Congo (DRC) in the Great Lakes region of Africa have often been drawn into the internal conflict of neighbouring states in support of their ethnic kin group. After their defeat in 1994, Rwandan Hutu extremists escaped to DRC and began to attack Tutsi residents in Eastern Congo. This invited counter-attacks by the Tutsi dominated Rwandan military. Fights among ethnic groups may focus on political, economic and ideological dimensions of relationships that cut across external and internal boundaries.

The external dimensions of civil wars often represent intrusion by neighbouring states claiming security threats. Militias and insurgency groups, allied with foreign sponsors, have competing agendas and motives, ranging from political grievances to financial greed (for example, the diamond and timber trade in Sierra Leone, Liberia and Angola). Internal warfare, predicated on criminal activities in such violent regions of the world as the DRC, Somalia, Sudan, Ivory Coast, Chad, and Colombia, is driven by money and power rather than a cause. Realignments among numerous state and non-state actors in these wars are often unpredictable, given the tentative alliance of astounding bedfellows.

Multilayered structures of relationships: the case of Iraq

External players can contribute to the mitigation or intensification of local struggles by providing different types of support. The complexity of conflict in Iraq is derived from internal divisions as well as the relationships between external actors. While external allies add intricate dimensions to the internal conflict, religious sects, economic interests, and competition for power divide many Iraqi factions. In their intense engagement with Iraqi politics in 2006–7, the US government was allied with Prime Minister Nouri al-Maliki's Dawa Party and the Supreme Islamic Iraqi Counsel (SIIC), headed by cleric Abdul Aziz al-Hakim. At the same time, US soldiers were battling with anti-American cleric Moqtada al-Sadr's military group. Given that these Iraqi groups stand for Shi'ite Islamic sects in Iraq, Iran has maintained close relationships with not only the anti-American al-Sadr group but also the SIIC and the Dawa Party. As opposed to Iran's alliance with Shiite factions across the political spectrum, Saudi Arabia and other moderate Arab states provide funding and political support for Sunnis, who have been alienated from national political institutions.

At the national political level, Sunnis bitterly object to Shi'ites, allied with the Kurds who were suppressed during Saddam Hussein's era. In spite of this overall structure of a national political struggle, al-Sadr and his Shi'ite allies were opposing constitutional changes and political divisions, pursued by the Dawa Party and the SIIC, sharing their concerns with the majority of Sunnis. The al-Sadr Shi'ite position embodies the fear of any arrangements which would leave oil-rich regions in their rivals' hands. At a regional level, in particular, in Basra, their rivalry in Baghdad did not hinder al-Sadr's Mehdi Army from being allied with SIIC's armed wing, the Badr Corps, in violent clashes against militias of Fadhila, which broke away from al-Sadr. The opposing alliances in Basra have been fighting over the oil industry and fort facilities, the control of which is critical to financing political and military operations.

Even though their alliance in Basra was built for tactical reasons, the rivalry between al-Hakim and al-Sadr at a national level has been reflecting political and economic divisions in Iraq. While al-Hakim draws support from established, property-owning Shi'ites, al-Sadr commands strong popularity among the poor, especially in the Sadr City ghetto of Baghdad. By calling on his followers not to attack Sunnis, al-Sadr has been attempting to emerge as a voice of Iraqi national unity. He has repeatedly condemned the US presence in Iraq and has demanded an immediate withdrawal of all foreign coalition forces in an effort to stand as a symbol of anti-American resistance. In the meantime, US army commanders have been accusing Iran of aiding Mehdi militias with the supply of explosives and arms.

The connections of external parties to primary parties are manifested in many different ways. Along with ever changing lines of allegiance, an adversary's enemy automatically becomes one's own ally. The presence of an external party may further extend complexities by inviting the participation of their adversary into the local conflict (Lobell and Mauceri, 2004). Iraq is an example where divided societies often become a battleground for outside rivalry.

Interlocking of actors: patterns of vertical alliance

A powerful external party may instigate a local conflict with its political and material support. At the same time, local parties might drag external allies into their struggle with opponents who are also allied with outside forces. The extent to which external parties can mould the actions of local parties varies due to different types of dependency relationships (Taras and Ganguly, 2005). External parties would not be able to control local parties if the latter were to have their own autonomous support bases for self-sustenance. Given their illusive representation, it is difficult to bring responsibility to self-organized groups such as insurgents and militias that are seeking narrow, exclusive interests with genocide and other extreme forms of violence.

Local parties' interests and fates can diverge and converge alongside those of their external supporters. Moscow, for example, refused to provide advanced offensive arms for Egypt, in the early 1970s, as part of efforts to sustain détente with the United States. While local parties may not want to compromise their own interests and agendas, external allies may see less significance in the value of a continued conflict that is initiated by a junior partner. Local agents may act independently, creating difficulties for their supporters. The strategies of each internal faction have shaped various forms of subdivision and allegiance in the turbulent history of Kashmir. The local groups demanding independence are not easily controlled by their external allies such as the Pakistani military, but any provocative actions taken by extremist groups (for example, terrorist bombings in India) have become a liability for Pakistan in managing its relations with New Delhi.

On the contrary, allies can be surrogates of their patrons, the interests and resources of which cannot be overstretched. Cuban involvement in Angola on behalf of the Soviet Union during the Cold War is an example. Local parties such as Hezbollah have been created in support of external actors, before beginning to develop their own internal structures, leadership, and interests that coincide with external supporters.

In the wars in Korea and Vietnam, the Soviet Union did not engage in direct combat operations with the United States, being restricted to the supply of arms and logistical support for their local allies. Both Washington and Moscow precluded a direct war by means of restricting their engagement in regional wars that were initiated by the other superpower or its allies. Local conflict can be expanded into a larger crisis involving the direct clash between patrons in the absence of mutual restraints. The war in the Middle East of 1973 might have brought about a direct military confrontation between the United States and the Soviet Union, following the latter's threat to intervene, on behalf of Egypt, in response to the Israeli violation of a ceasefire, had it not been for the Kremlin's decision not to act on its warning. The main patrons of local participants have to cooperate even implicitly to circumvent the uncontrolled escalation.

External and internal relational contexts

The level of flexibility in the formation of external and internal alliance has an impact on the manoeuvrability of multiple actors to control conflict dynamics at different layers. The images of Muslims in European societies have been re-defined by the terrorist attacks of 11 September 2001 in New York and the 7 July 2005 London underground bombings. In turn, the prejudices, as well as social marginalization, have brought about further disenchantment of the Muslim population in the Western world. The unsuccessful bombing plots in London and Glasgow undertaken by medical doctors from Iraq and India in July 2007 have further strained relations between European societies and the Islamic world, creating heightened fear and new stereotypes.

External conflicts may provide opportunities for marginalized groups to demand a new status within a system. The end of World War I resulted in the collapse of European empires and the promotion of national aspirations that contributed to the formation of newly independent states and the promotion of the principles of self-determination. The territories under the Austro-Hungarian and Ottoman empires were split, giving birth to independent Poland and Czechoslovakia. Recently, the participation of female soldiers in the civil wars of African countries brought them a sense of their own rights and a desire for an improved status following the end of war.

Interlocking issues: convergence and divergence

Each issue may have different stakes for diverse participants, along with multiple implications for conflict strategies and the formulation of goals. Diverse issues can be connected through the convergence of complex conflict dynamics. The interests of various actors may diverge over new issues in a different conflict.

There is a variety of patterns of issue convergence in conflict relationships. Issue convergence and divergence have different implications for settlement. Israel, for example, refused to accept solutions through multi-party negotiations on comprehensive agendas, in considering that it is more advantageous for them to respond to one particular issue (as it did in concluding a peace treaty with Egypt) than getting involved in simultaneous negotiations with multiple Arab states over diverse issues.

Multiple issues, comprised of security, human rights and trade, may underline a broad conflict relationship between two countries, as seen in the current US–China relations. In contrast with the involvement of multiple issues in bilateral relations, one party can get involved in a dispute with several different parties over single or similar issues. For example, China has been facing complaints from the European Union administration and American government about its violation of copyrights, counterfeiting of Western brands, and undervalued currency, which facilitate a huge trade imbalance.

The settlement on the same issue with one country can have implications for resolving differences with another country. The Bush administration has opposed the development of nuclear reactor and uranium programmes in Iran and North Korea. The US policy toward Iran has often been compared with its policy toward North Korea. The agreement on the North Korean nuclear programme is likely to put pressure on Teheran. American opposition to North Korean and Iranian nuclear programmes is further contrasted with the US willingness to supply nuclear technology to India that could then be equipped with the production of several hundreds of nuclear bombs each year. In handling the nuclear proliferation issues, the American double standard has undermined its persuasive power to dismantle the North Korean and Iranian programmes.

Issue convergence can generate synergetic effects of settlement in one area for other arenas either positively or negatively. The improvement in one issue area (for example, arms control) can spill over to economic cooperation or other areas. For instance, an agreement to demolish North Korean nuclear facilities would lead to Washington's lifting trade sanctions. In the 1970s, the US export of agricultural grain to the Soviet Union was often tied to such conditions as the improvement in human rights conditions or freedom of migration for Jews to the West or Israel. As negative linkages of issue arenas, the Soviet invasion of Afghanistan provoked the boycott of the 1980 Moscow Olympic games by the Carter administration and its allies. The Soviet Union retaliated by boycotting the 1984 Olympic games held in the American city of Atlanta.

Temporal links

Many conflicts are characterized by a struggle in interlocking and asymmetrical power relations of multiple actors over an extended period of time. Through mutual interlinkages, existing relationships produce a new context for recurrent or concurrent conflicts. Particular characteristics of system dynamics (such as the denial of minority rights) may resonate through recurrent conflicts. The resurfacing of the same issues regarding the guarantee of self-determination has been frequently observed in a protracted conflict across multi-ethnic societies. A conflict that has been suppressed, or merely put on hold, can be reignited by outside manipulation or by the spillover effects from other conflicts running simultaneously.

Temporal links can also be made in terms of opportunity costs derived from a simultaneous engagement in multiple struggles. A concurrent conflict is characterized in terms of the indirect or direct links that are created by participation in various types of struggle at the same time. Engagements with one conflict reduce the ability to make synchronized efforts to respond to every other important event occurring concurrently. Although every conflict might be equally important, simultaneous engagement in several conflicts cuts down the available time, efforts, and resources to be devoted to each of them. To focus on a new one, some other conflicts can be disregarded, discounted or toned down. The American war in Iraq has, for example, severely restricted US options in dealing with other crises, making it more dependent on ally support, such as the leading role of its European allies in negotiation with Iranians.

Recurrent conflict

A protracted conflict may flare up for a while, be intensified by destructive elements, become less visible, and then simply fade away without even resolution. In a recurrent conflict, the existing relationships are likely to be transformed within a period of time through changes in, or reinforcement of, past dynamics. Even though recurrent conflicts may involve new issues and parties, they are part of developments in a long-running series of similar situations. Regardless of leadership changes within each party, a new balance in the relationship can, at least, in part, be derived from the experience of previous conflicts.

A higher level of intensity may result from an unforeseen event that ignites the old animosities without any reconciliation efforts (Olzak, 2006). Whereas a unique situation could emerge that is not connected to any preceding events, the historical context of many conflicts, for instance, in Rwanda and Cyprus, often defines the new circumstances. The legacies of past events involving one party or both revive old experiences in the current conflict. Each episode of a recurrent conflict tends to facilitate progressively more harmful behaviour and negative attitudes, without any internal or external restraining mechanisms, through a conflict-reproducing structure—for instance, the vehement fighting put up by the second Palestinian intifada (uprising) in the early 2000s. In the case of fighting in former Yugoslavia during the mid-1990s, the ethnic killings were reminiscent of the World War II atrocities that saw Serbs victimized by Croats who collaborated with Nazi troops in the Balkans.

Antagonistic behaviour associated with previous events reinvigorates a distrust of the opponents; the new conflict is also reinforced by strong emotions that are carried over from the past and by a desire to retaliate for a prior loss. The stereotypes of the opponent, even if new participants enter the conflict scene, will continue to manipulate the images of the other side. The Israeli–Palestinian conflict has, for example, been made even more intractable due to the stereotypical images passed over from one generation to another.

The continued participation of the same leadership produces an expectation of similar types of behaviour from adversaries, even in a totally different, new situation. If one party feels that it was successful in past negotiations, it is likely to expect the same result from the newly emerging leadership. This leads to resistance in making concessions that are perceived to be unjust, compared with deals made in past settlements. In the negotiation with the Bush administration over the nuclear weapons issue, North Korea has held the same or similar expectations, as it had of its negotiation with the previous Clinton administration a decade ago, despite the two administrations' dramatic political differences. The election of former general Ariel Sharon (accused of responsibility for the atrocities against the Palestinians in the Israeli invasion of Lebanon in 1982) to Prime Minister in the early 2000s sent the Palestinian authority a pessimistic signal for any tangible negotiated settlement in the near future.

A previous struggle leaves vivid memories for the participants of a future conflict. As violence, displayed by the 2005 French civil unrest with the participation of minority youth, lies dormant, the same patterns of struggle become latent, awaiting the next triggering event. The attitudes and perceptions of the participants such as minority ethnic groups will, in the next episode, be embedded in the residual memories of the previous events. The legacies of hostility and mistrust left over in the earlier struggle over particular issues are likely to subscribe to the exacerbation of relations between the parties in a new conflict. The persistent recurrence of escalation tends to leave lasting damage to any efforts for reconciliation.

Recurrent civil wars in Africa

Sudan and the Democratic Republic of Congo (DRC) have experienced the deadliest civil wars in the modern history. The recurrent civil wars in Sudan represent repeated patterns of economic exploitation and interference by the Arab-dominated government in socio-cultural life. In the case of the DRC, ethnic rivalry was exploited by neighbouring states, which reignited internal conflicts for the expansion of regional influence and economic interests. The recurrent civil wars, ascribed to multifaceted causes, have been redefined by changes in the realignment of forces as well as the legacies of the previous conflicts.

The First Congo War of 1996–97 set a foundation for the beginning of the Second Congo War in August 1998, with the heavy involvement of Rwanda and Uganda in the rebel force's military operations to end the thirty years' reign of President Mobutu Sésé Seko. New President Laurent-Désiré Kabila soon parted with his former backers after dismissing all ethnic Tutsis from the government, and ordered Rwandan and Ugandan army officials to leave the country. By taking advantage of the outbreak of renewed conflict with minority groups in the eastern Congo, Rwanda and Uganda sent troops to aid rebels attempting to overthrow Kabila, triggering the Second Congo War.

The war was soon expanded, following the arrival of troops from Angola, Sudan, Zimbabwe, Namibia, Chad, and other African countries in support of the new regime in Kinshasa. The Second Congo War has thus been characterized as the widest interstate armed conflict in modern Africa, involving not only eight countries, but also around 25 armed groups (Carayannis, 2005). The fighting had taken roughly 3.8 million lives, prior to its end in 2003 and the establishment of a transitional government. The casualties were mostly as a result of the starvation and disease brought about by one of the bloodiest wars since World War II.

The southern, non-Arab populations in Sudan have long resented the northern, Arab-dominated government's exploitation of oil fields and other significant economic assets as well as the imposition of Islamic rule (Idris, 2005). Even though southern Sudan was granted wide regional autonomy on internal matters at the end of the first civil war in 1972, President Nimeiry decided to institute Shariah law as part of a drive for Islamicization, touching off the second Sudanese war after 11 years' ceasefire. Mainly non-Arabic rebel groups fought against the central government in an attempt to establish an independent Southern Sudan.

The second Sudanese war is marked by a fight between the primarily Muslim north, and the Christian and Animist south, as were the 17 years of the first civil war that raged between 1955 and 1972, and which left half a million dead. More distinctively, the second war, waged for 22 years, has been recorded as one of the longest lasting and deadliest wars of the twentieth century. The Second Sudanese Civil War of 1983–2005 killed almost two million civilians and left more than four million refugees. Ending the conflict became protracted, due to several significant changes in the central government, military coups, splits and realignments among the armed resistance groups.

Spillover effects of concurrent conflict

The simultaneous occurrence of multiple conflicts can generate unexpected effects in the course of each. As the Sudanese war in the south was wound up, the crisis in Darfur led to over 400,000 civilian deaths and as many as 2.5 million displaced persons toward the end of 2006. A series of major assaults on non-Arabic land-tilling farming communities were organized by the Sudanese military and the Janjaweed, a militia group recruited mostly from the Arab Baggara, camel-herding nomad tribes of the northern Rizeigat. The massacres in western Sudan have been destabilizing the neighbouring Central African Republic and Chad, creating lawless conditions through the infiltration of armed criminal groups as well as refugee flows.

The majority of civil wars in Africa have been ignited, intensified, or reignited by troubles in neighbouring countries. Any new development in existing conflict dynamics is often initiated by changes in the external context. The onset of hostilities can spill over to an external domain of other conflicts through issue or actor linkages. The severity and scope of the Congolese wars are, to a great extent, attributed to the Great Lakes refugee crisis that originated in the influx of the two million Hutus from Rwanda to Eastern Congo after the Tutsi military victory in July 1994 (Khadiagala, 2006). The militia groups linked to political parties, accountable for the Rwandan genocide, soon dominated refugee camps set up in eastern Congo, and clashed with Zairian Tutsis and Rwandan troops. Much of eastern DRC remains insecure, primarily owing to the infiltration of illegitimate, privately armed gangs.

Embedded conflict

Many issues beneath structural tensions in the twentieth century signify antagonistic relationships between rival political and economic systems. Conflicts embedded in the Cold War corresponded to fundamental frictions between adversaries that resided in opposing system characteristics. A multifaceted struggle to defeat the other side can be seen as part of a large system conflict. In considering that the catastrophic outcome of a direct military confrontation was obvious, an endeavour to undermine the other's strength was extended to economic warfare such as trade restrictions and economic blockades. In addition, psychological warfare employed propaganda and sabotage to subvert the enemy as well as rallying supporters. The interlocking patterns reformulate the meanings so that the significance of a fight is largely circumscribed by overall system features.

Multiple events are embedded in a larger conflict system either spatially or temporally. A series of armed confrontations, for example, arising from Arab–Israeli relations since the foundation of Israel in 1948, have exposed various overall system characteristics that delineate the issues and behaviours of adversaries. In a larger history of adversarial relations, each conflict is interlocked with those that preceded it. The Israeli victory in the first Arab–Israeli war in 1948 led to many Palestinian refugees and a loss of territory, with simmering Arab emotions. The Six Day War of 1967 grew out of increasing tension in the aftermath of the 1956 Suez Crisis, which culminated in a temporary occupation of part of the Egyptian territory. The 1973 Yom Kippur War was initiated by Egypt, Syria, and Jordan to recover territories and reputation lost in the Six Day War.

Each conflict adds new dimensions to the larger Arab–Israeli conflict. Arab humiliation and defeat in 1967 meant deep wounds to the myth of secular Arabic nationalism. The newly gained territory, including Jerusalem, Hebron, and Jericho, was suffused with religious symbolism and transformed the secular modern Jewish state identity, adding a new dimension to the regional conflict. The pursuit of unilateral peace by Egypt after the Yom Kippur War, meanwhile, divided the Arab world, virtually eliminating the future possibility of a major war against Israel. The defeat of the Arab standing armies has yielded more prominent roles to armed insurgent movements in such instances as resistance against the 1982 Israeli invasion of southern Lebanon and its occupation until 2000. The Israeli control of Palestinians in the West Bank and Gaza Strip (newly acquired in the 1967 war) provoked the first and second intifada (respectively 1987–91, 2000–05), along with the creation of Hamas and other more radical Islamic resistance groups.

Whoever championed the Arabic side, political tensions and open hostilities have been filled with shame, pride, and other deep emotions that re-characterize present and future conflicts. In an embedded conflict, any intense level of struggle, aimed at changing power relations, can be considered to be part of continuing conflict dynamics. Worldwide attention has been drawn to Arab–Israeli conflicts, in spite of their involvement in a comparatively small area of land and a fewer number of casualties, as a consequence of religious and cultural bonds with Christianity, Islam, and Judaism, on top of political-strategic, economic and human rights reasons (Fawcett. 2005).

A base structure of multitudes of fights can easily provoke destructive spirals through expanding negative mutual interactions. The intensification of one conflict may strengthen negative dynamics of other conflicts in the overall structure of adversarial relationships. The rise of new contentious issues can highlight the magnitude of the existing tensions emitting from antagonistic system characteristics. Even though each struggle may not play a decisive role in the outcome of the overall conflict, the combined trends of various types of competition influence a larger, longer conflict, like battles occurring within the broader context of a war.

A series of conflicts can be set off by the same structural conditions, for instance, arising from the collapse of a federalist system with competing relationships among many ethnic regions. The down fall of the former Yugoslavia served as the bedrock for a series of ethnic wars: the 1991 Slovenian War; the Croatian War of 1991–95; the Bosnian War of 1992–95; the 1999 Kosovo War; the 2001 Macedonian conflict. These conflicts in the Balkans since 1991 have been attributed to underlying ethnic, religious, economic, and political tensions after the 1980 death of Yugoslav president Josip Broz Tito. Slovenian independence in 1991 after the Ten Day War left a decisive mark in signalling a series of upcoming ethnic conflicts by forcing the Federal Republic of Yugoslavia (later Serbia and Montenegro) to make a series of major shifts. The idea of preserving a unitary Yugoslavia was substituted by Serbian President Slobodan Milošević's conception of 'all Serbs in one state', widely known as 'Greater Serbia'.

Superimposed conflict

The meaning of local conflicts can be imposed or altered by other events at an external system level. When a superimposed conflict transforms the nature and surrounding environment for many struggles, relations within a system at a macro level reproduce dynamics at a lower level. As distinguished in the era of the global war on terrorism led by the American government and its Western allies, everything is related to a superordinate goal of wiping out fundamental Muslim networks. This has dramatically changed the dynamics of many local conflicts around the world, in the same way that US–Soviet rivalry did in the second half of the twentieth century. In particular, the global war on terrorism has been manipulated to delegitimize parties to any local conflicts that rely on methods of struggle that can be easily branded 'terrorist tactics'.

Even in many ethnic conflicts around the world, one faction is favoured over the other by the US government simply because of being suspected of terrorist connections. To garner American support and expand political ambitions, local and regional groups often portray their opponents as having connections to al Qaeda or other terrorist groups. Every suspicious local faction has been drawing direct US military strikes, whether they are in Somalia, Pakistan, or Afghanistan.

The rise of new, contentious events at a large system level easily magnifies the role of previously insignificant conflicts in re-characterizing the existing tensions. By seizing post-September 2001 reactions, oppressive governments have escalated their efforts to suppress groups that they claim to be terrorists and thus illegitimate. Many Islamic ethnic groups fighting for self-determination in Kashmir and Uyghur, for example, were depicted as terrorists by the Indian and Chinese governments, respectively. While reframing an internal conflict as being perpetuated by terrorists, India, China, and Russia have even stepped up police arrests and detention along with further abuse against suspected rebels and anti-government activists. Pakistan and India have undermined human rights protection by activating emergency and extraordinary military power. At the same time, the Indian government has been exploiting the context of the war on terrorism to criticize the Pakistani government's links to militant Islamic groups in Kashmir. On the whole, a superordinate conflict has served as a negative environment for the protection of rights for many ethnic, political groups engaged in local struggles.

The superimposition of one conflict on another presents a potential for amplifying even seemingly trivial strategic concerns and issues. The ups and downs in the relationships between the two superpowers during the Cold War period had an immense effect on many regional struggles, often exacerbating their intractability (Brune, 2006). Each superpower lent support to its clients, thereby adding more fuel to local conflict.

Past civil wars waged largely in Africa and Central America thrived with military and other kinds of assistance granted by external sponsors. Most significantly, the 'superpower rivalry' imposed a context that largely accounted for a 'proxy war' in such places as Angola. The Arab–Israeli, Korean, Vietnamese, and Afghan wars all began as internal or regional wars that soon attracted foreign intervention, owing to their implications for US–Soviet competition in the global arena.

The trajectory of each conflict is impacted, to a varying degree, by a multitude of external conditions that echo various traits of superordinate social systems, mirroring a historical context. The flow of a local conflict replicates, by and large, the ups and downs of a superordinate ideological and political struggle. Indeed, armed conflicts in Mozambique, El Salvador, Guatemala, and Nicaragua subsided and settled, within a neo-liberal political, economic order, after the superpower competition was over.

The superimposition of regional rivalry in post-Cold War Africa can also explain the sustained internal warfare in Liberia, Sierra Leone, Somalia, Burundi, the Democratic Republic of Congo, etc. Neighbouring countries may become directly engaged or may simply supply weapons or extra funds with an offer of safe havens for militia groups preparing to launch new attacks. Such aid often enables combatants to escalate fighting. Internal strife has been seized as an opportunity to weaken a rival state's capacity along with expanding control over the region.

Focal conflict

Some conflicts rally those who advocate particular values and ideals symbolized by the struggles. They regenerate intense emotions attached to the existential values. A focal conflict sharply divides not only partisans but also both external opponents and supporters on a particular issue with a sustained struggle. It tends to persist until the issues are resolved or terminated by one-sided victory. It has been difficult to end long-term hostile relations between Pakistan and India without bringing resolution in the Kashmiri conflict (Paul, 2005). In three interstate wars between India and Pakistan, especially in 1948 and 1965, each adversary closely linked their struggles to the unresolved conflicts inside Indian-controlled Kashmir.

One of the best-known contemporary focal conflicts is the decade-long international campaign against the white South African government before the establishment of the majority black government following constitutional changes in 1995. A global anti-apartheid campaign in the 1980s was spurred by the strong symbolism entailed in the white South African government's discriminatory policies against the indigenous black population. Not only blacks but also many educated whites in the West joined divestment initiatives and supported other economic sanctions, as well as the exclusion of South African white minorities from many world cultural and social events. The symbolic meaning attached to 'anti-racist' struggles helped to sustain the movements, drawing many supporters who otherwise may not have been interested in the issue.

Another example includes the Israeli–Palestinian conflict. Many Arabic leaders have referred to this conflict as an underlying issue that is embedded in the overall diplomatic relationships in the Middle East (Fawcett, 2005). It has, to a great extent, symbolized the American government's role in the Middle East and injustice for the Arabs. Middle Eastern countries have emphasized that, without a proper settlement over the status of the Palestinians, normal relations between the state of Israel and the entire Arabic world will not be established. In addition, every war between Israel and its opponents in the Middle East has played a unifying role among the Arabic populations, regardless of differences in their religious sects and political affiliations

Diffuse conflict

In a diffuse conflict, different patterns of struggles are organized at geographically separate sites. Each episode of struggle is treated as part of a much wider, single whole of a campaign that is focused on key values through the convergent participation of people who have compatible motivations, desires, and needs. The contagious spread of emotion, grievances, or religious zeal, either conscious or unconscious, triggers a spontaneous release of previously controlled behaviour. In spite of differences in outcomes and tactics, the principle may remain the same, and parties in widely dispersed organizational and geographical arenas can carry out a struggle. A diffuse conflict can be transformed into a single, complex (national or international) one as a result of a coalition to achieve specific goals or bring about changes. In a diffuse conflict, party boundaries shift with the growth and decline in the number of organizers of the movements and their sympathizers.

The events mobilized by various types of people on the same or similar issues can converge or diverge, as seen in the historic US civil rights movement. The December 1955 incident of the denial of a bus seat for African American activist Rosa Parkes in Alabama spawned many other types of racial protest and civil disobedience within a larger struggle for equal treatment of black and other minorities. New energy was infused with 'sit-ins' at the lunch counters of several local stores in Greensboro, North Carolina and Nashville, Tennessee, that spread throughout the South, by the end of 1960, with a rash of student campaigns in protest of segregation. In a similar, dramatic manner, the Greenham Common anti-nuclear women's movement of the early 1980s served as a symbol of nuclear disarmament until the Reagan administration decided to withdraw the plan to install intermediate range missiles in the UK and elsewhere in Europe.

A wider struggle increases the pertinence of the cause by challenging conventional notions of existing system values (Opp, 2001). A struggle at one place may inspire other campaigns that embody a larger goal. Some diffuse movements may be spontaneous and die down naturally until the next round. The October–November 2005 ethnic youth riots in the Paris suburbs spread to other cities not only in France but also in Germany and other parts of Europe. Without any particular organization committed to sustain them, the violent protests by Muslims in Europe did not persist.

Social and political issues such as the war in Iraq have instigated new diffuse struggles. The multiplication of new groups and attacks in Spain and Britain, following their governments' support of the war in Iraq, suggests that the war on terrorism would not end by simply wiping out al Qaeda. The war in Iraq has deepened the pool of terrorist groups globally and has produced new sympathizers for Jihad movements, even among European Muslims beyond the traditional Islamic countries (such as Pakistan and Indonesia). At the same time, the aggressive tactics of the war on terrorism, even including the endorsement of torture advocated by the Bush administration, are likely to intensify and prolong more resentment in the Islamic world.

With the growth of movements, the boundaries of their activities are likely to be poorly defined, owing to a broad mobilizational base drawn from a variety of sectors of the society (Lobell and Mauceri, 2004). As in the peace and environmental movements of the 1960s and 1970s, when the initiatives begin to expand, rival factions may vie for control over the agendas in the overall direction of the struggle. Tightly organized core groups may be able to maintain their participants' discipline better than a diffuse set of actors that are loosely aligned under an umbrella coalition. However, it is very difficult, in a diffuse conflict, for one group to dictate the overall direction of a struggle.

In a large coalition, various lines of previously insignificant cleavage may emerge in a disagreement on eventual goals and strategies. Not only internal cleavages but also a lack of consistency in actions become major factors in the break-up of broadly organized movements. The networks of movements will eventually die down or fade slowly, as fatigue begins to predominate, leaving a core organizational infrastructure behind for the future conflict.

The projection of values engendered by larger campaigns may induce or proliferate local conflicts. Home grown drives, for example, in US anti-abortion crusades, may have been cajoled and coaxed by national initiatives rather than stemming from an endogenous origin. In this case, local mobilization is mainly reactive, involving significant non-residential staffing, in that it has been developed for a strategic opportunity. On the contrary, conflict events can also be initiated and staffed by resident members or adherents of local branches, as though they can eventually be supported either technically or financially at the central headquarters. In spite of overarching issues, shared values and social networks, local and national actors may have divergent views about immediate objectives with subsequent organizational friction.

Part IV
Dynamics and Escalation

Part IV
Dynamics and Perception

A System of Conflict Dynamics

7

The dynamics behind conflict progression, comprising emergence, persistence, and transformation, can be revealed by a general systems theory that illuminates elements geared toward either sustaining or disrupting a status quo, and their relationship to the internal and external environment. In complex systems theory, a conflict path is viewed as more than a simple, static, and dyadic process. While some might depend on a linear system to explain changes, cyclical patterns may better illustrate how seemingly unrelated events and processes conspire to shape outcomes (Gleick, 1987). Each conflict is considered contextually unique, but its main features can be explained by shared common foundations (Golden, 2007).

Society is interlaced by orders created at various levels, but segmented in diverse ways. In considering that conflict systems are not necessarily linear, the course of any event does not always produce controllable and predictable outcomes. In contrast with a fixed structure, adaptive response systems can generate novel and creative outcomes in a complex environment (Jones and Hughes, 2003). This chapter sheds light on action–reaction modes of conflict dynamics, diverse types of behaviour, and contextual variables involved in influencing the patterns of interaction between actors.

System perspectives

Relationships between conflict components can be explained in terms of system processes and their outcomes. Persisting trends in mutual interaction and consistent patterns of behaviour characterize each stage of conflict. The changes in a conflict system move through a cycle of grievance expression–escalation–suppression. An action–reaction process is considered cyclical with a punctuated equilibrium. With the manifestation of escalation, a latent conflict turns into a crisis. Then the crisis eventually has to be turned back to a latent condition of conflict, for heightened tension is not the normal state of relationships.

A system is imagined as a complex set of interaction patterns, constituting forces beyond the features of individual components. By nature, a system is continuously shifting from one stage to another in the process of adapting to a new situation. Although a dynamic interaction within a given structure changes from moment to moment, it is not chaotic, representing instead 'a set of self-organizing forces that keep the system on track' (Littlejohn and Domenici, 2001: 218). Thus system dynamics are best captured in terms of an equilibrium embodying a succession of identical or similar states.

In general, events activated at an earlier point can come back to affect the original event with a tendency toward greater intensity. For example, additional pressure from a supervisor results in more resistance from employees, eliciting greater directive responses from the boss. On the other hand, the interaction can be 'self-correcting, and perpetuate a steady state' if the relationships between the boss and employees are self-regulated without involving patterns of abusive orders and withdrawal (Littlejohn and Domenici, 2001: 219). A complex set of interactional patterns is, of course, modified as a result of a deviation of the system, subsequently restructuring rules that govern relationships.

Changes can, therefore, be elaborated in terms of any action that causes system disturbance. Equilibrium is a normal state of many dynamic interaction patterns. Some systems are characterized by cyclical repetition of an indefinite sequence of states. Thus conflict may be seen as a movement away from an orderly normal state of relationships regulated by existing norms. The main question that remains, however, is how groups move from harmony and equilibrium to a manifested conflict, and vice versa.

In a system's model, the dynamic paths may all converge into, or diverge away, from the equilibrium point. The loss of equilibrium sparks off movement toward the previous balancing point. When system components lose the ability to interact in equilibrium, parties experience a breakdown in regular interaction patterns. Once a new system emerges, the laws of the old system are not valid any more.

The larger picture of US–Soviet history between 1945 and 1979 epitomizes the repetition of a particular sequence of events, moving to and from a certain equilibrium point. The Cold War pendulum vacillated between the opposing poles of containment and détente before the collapse of the Soviet bloc socialist systems. Détente in the early 1970s was followed by an unstable equilibrium, ascribed to unilateral arms build-up, the pursuit of military superiority by President Ronald Reagan and his ideological rhetoric in the early 1980s (rivalling that of the worst days of the Cold War in the late 1940s). The US plan to install intermediate-range missiles in Western Europe and the renewed nuclear arms race created anxiety and pressure to recover a stable equilibrium.[1] This pressure eventually brought about renewed arms talks and a superpower summit. With the demise of the Soviet system, the old patterns of rivalry were replaced by new rules that govern different dynamics in the relationship between post-Soviet Russia and the United States.

Being accompanied by more than 40 years of antagonistic relations, the US–North Korea nuclear weapons agreement in 1994 created a stable equilibrium point at which to open up the possibility of diplomatic normalization. The pendulum swung in the opposite direction in 2000, however, with the election of President Bush and his administration's abandonment of the agreement. A tit-for-tat escalation of conflict between the American and North Korean leadership led to the latter's testing of nuclear weapons in 2006. Since then, the conflict has been moderated only by the renewal of bilateral talks and the withdrawal of US financial sanctions, as an effort to explore a new equilibrium point that restores normalized channels of communication.

These events are denoted by divergence from, and return to, behavioural and normative expectations found in stable relationships. Incompatible, unregulated patterns of interaction are the hallmark of negative relationships represented by disequilibrium. Whereas intractable conflicts escalate towards a more destructive end, many normal adversarial relationships can be managed through a relatively stable system, oscillating between periods of tension and equilibrium. An action–reaction model suggests not only conditions that facilitate escalation, but also conditions that encourage stability.

Action–reaction functions

A system's perspective reflects action–reaction functions that have been applied to the analysis of arms races, which create the vulnerability of each side to destruction by the other. The joint functions of two or more interacting countries can be said to form a system with an equilibrium point at which each side feels that its security interests, protected by military, technological, and economic strengths, are balanced against the other's threats. This equilibrium impinges upon the structure of expectations that are derived from the combined effects of interests, capabilities, and wills.

In understanding changes which affect the maintenance of the equilibrium, we can focus on a self-reinforcing spiral of actions and reactions that might either instigate the initiation of war or spur conciliation. The exchange of the moves and countermoves drives conflict either downwards or upwards. By moving away from mainly adversarial relationships, associated with an overall increase in a range of hostile behaviour, accommodation can be reached at the balancing point.

In an action–reaction process, the behaviour of one party is, in large part, a function of the other's move. The concept of interaction functions was originally formulated from an arms race perspective (Richardson, 1967). This research originates in the classic work by Quincy Wright (1942), which correlates national interests and respective levels of armaments to the increased likelihood of hostilities.

In the processes of the arms race envisaged by Richardson (1967), one country reacts to increases in an adversary's armament levels by strengthening its own arms expenditures, pushing, in turn, growth in the initiator's military spending levels. The threat of the other party, denoted by even higher levels of arms, will cause one party to boost its military strength again. The perceived threats coming from the rapid arms build-up of the opponent are a main factor leading to an upsurge in armaments; the level of responsiveness in military build-up reflects the intensity of the impact of an adversary's armament on one's own perceptions of threats, fears, and grievances.

In the mutually aggravating process of an arms race, therefore, the rate of change in each party's military build-up is a direct result of the combined effect of a rival country's military strength and an accumulation of grievances that sharpens a sense of threat. The level of arms production is checked only by the cost of procuring arms systems, and such internal constraints as limited economic strength, budgetary restrictions, and other indicators of fatigue.

A desire for balance in the dynamics of arms competition is driven by fear of the other's superiority in arms levels. While the perceptions of threat (resulting from feelings of insecurity) are magnified by increasing grievances toward the other party, motivating further arms build-up, each party must be able to afford continuing armaments. The capability to keep up with the other's expenditures is bound to preserve a threat-arms accumulation reaction system. Thus mutual parity in arms procurement is an essential condition for safeguarding equilibrium and deterring all-out war.

The system is regarded as stable if forces tending to recover the equilibrium point effectively counter a disturbance. When the differences in arms procurements are relatively small, disturbances move within a certain range from an equilibrium point. Noticeably, a small deviation does not result in a general war. Gradual and continuous adjustments to arms levels reproduce stable interactions between perceived threats and costs. In contrast, equilibrium in the existing interaction would not be sustained if an arms race were to end in either total disarmament or war.

The failure to attain equal arms development with disparities in economic capabilities produces conditions for disequilibrium. An unstable equilibrium is created by large disturbances from the system's present state. The rising level of threats, following an uncontrolled exchange of hostilities, in tandem with a clear manifestation of opposing interests, is expected to unleash catastrophic events that are beyond defensive reactions. In this situation, predomination of the arms build-up is likely to precipitate overt armed conflict.

The accumulated mutual grievances from each other's threats generate runaway conflict spirals. The ability of parties to intensify a conflict can be constrained by emotional and physical costs. The strength of disequilibrium factors needs to be overshadowed by braking factors, such as a fear of a possible war, along with the accumulation of goodwill.

If equilibrium in the arms race is not stable, instances of hostilities can have a chain effect, leading to a specific outcome of war. The retention of high levels of arms outweighs goodwill by generating the need to keep pace with the increasing arms competition and heightened threat levels (Richardson, 1967). Large disturbances in the system's state result in a failure to return to the equilibrium point.

Intense overt conflict is irrevocably tied to the destructive capabilities of parties as well as perceptions of threat and grievances derived from unequal relationships. In order to uphold stable action–reaction dynamics, the conflict system has to balance threats and arms control. In the end, system transformation is essential to de-escalation and conflict resolution.

In parallel to an arms race between rival states, ethnic mobilization, accompanied by the collapse of the central authority in Bosnia-Herzegovina (1992 to 1995) or militia armaments in Somalia (since 1988) and Liberia (1989 to 1996), demonstrates competition among antagonistic groups for control of the state. Each group may want to take advantage of a window of opportunity to expand its power and exploit the vulnerability of others in an all out competition to capture state legitimacy and material assets (for example, timber and minerals) or infrastructure such as ports. In enduring ethnic rivalries, one group's increased strength creates a sense of insecurity for others, whereas neighbouring groups practice self-help to ensure their own security.

Competitive, especially armed, mobilizations generate 'a hostility spiral of action and reaction' (Lobell and Mauceri, 2004: 4). Even a seemingly defensive move is seen as an offensive posture by rival groups. Each hostile action is likely to be reciprocated by an adversary's counter-offensive operations. In total anarchy, ethnic groups seek counterbalance with their opponents' fighting capabilities, believing that offensive strategies are the most effective in pursuing their survival. While each group either implicitly or explicitly takes measures to protect themselves by balancing the rival's strength, the mobilization dynamics result in further escalation of hostile actions without increasing one's own group's security. This process ultimately ends either with the emergence of one dominant group or external intervention to bring stability through new institution building.

The modes of interaction

Sanctions are often regarded as legitimate and acceptable methods of coercion in the international political system. The transmission of threats specifies the negative consequences faced by parties who defy the demands of a coercive opponent. Hostilities, war, or other negative forms of social influence are contrasted with persuasion and incentives (Franck, 2006). While a negative mode of action involves economic or diplomatic sanctions that are intended to increase costs or to take away benefit, positive measures focus on rewards or recognition.

The attributes of interaction may consist not only of a mode of behaviour, but also different levels of intensity in movements (incremental versus sudden) and directions of a particular measure (an increase or decrease in punitive action). The degree of severity and consistency of sanctions produce diverse interpretation and reciprocal action over time. The consistently increasing harshness of sanctions is likely to signal the demand for capitulation rather than a move toward conciliation. The increasing or decreasing pressure is inclined to be adopted in a manner that bears a direct relationship to the other party's compliant or defiant acts.

Different degrees of positive inducements, ranging from diplomatic recognition, humanitarian relief and economic assistance to military aid, can be employed as an appeasing influence strategy. Economic incentives such as lower import tariffs and free loans have often been aimed at inducing a favourable response and fortifying ally relationships. In its pursuit of the war on terrorism, US economic assistance has, for example, been granted to Pakistan and strategically important Central Asian countries.

The initiation of a negative mode of behaviour (such as violent acts as well as hostile statements) tends to be easily reciprocated through retaliatory measures. The transmission of coercive messages may have undesirable repercussions with uncontrolled consequences via escalation. To prevent a run-away acceleration of violence, coercive action needs to be applied gradually, with a greater magnitude, in specific areas. The effects of threats and punishment as a mode of influence generally focus on the costs originating from non-compliance. This strategy is contrasted with a promise made to engender trustworthy perceptions and deliver good intentions.

In most conflict interactions, the imposition of pain is combined with the remuneration of benefits (Mitchell, 1999). Whereas coercion is likely to constitute a dominant form of escalatory action, the mixture of both collaborative and coercive strategies is typically associated with conflict diminution. Even with the introduction of de-escalatory measures, bullying and intimidation tactics may not completely disappear if pressure needs to be put on adversaries to act. When a conflict is controlled to bring about settlement, the ratio and frequency of conciliatory behaviour increase vis-à-vis those that are coercive.

Threats and coercion may be accompanied by persuasive efforts made through the promise of rewards. For example, the USA and its European allies promised limited types of nuclear technology to Iran in return for Teheran's freeze on uranium programmes. When Iran declined the proposal, Western powers threatened to initiate UN-sponsored sanctions. In the post-conflict settings of Mozambique and El Salvador between 1992 and 1994, guerrilla forces temporarily ceased a continuing demobilization process when the governments were slow to take promised measures such as changes in election rules and land reform, respectively.

In antagonistic relationships, sanctions may serve as a means of communication to constrain an adversary's behaviour. On the other hand, the unmanaged expression of hostile intentions inadvertently instigates the rival party's misperceptions. The prevalence of an aggressive mood in one country is likely to invite similar reactions from the other. Prior to the Six Day War of 1967, both Arabs and Israelis were reacting to each other's intense emotional fever for war.

The same action causes different consequences, depending on the opponents' perceptions. Provocative behaviour by one side generally brings about the other's harsh response intended to deter continuing provocation. Even if stronger reactions entail a risk of inciting further escalation through a negative spiral, it might be feared that modest reactions are seen as a lack of will to challenge an aggressor. The breach of normal expectations, accompanied by extreme violence, sets off a malignant spiral of escalatory acts. Witnessing atrocities encourages vindictive behaviour against enemies.

High-stakes competition, especially in conjunction with an ability to inflict pain on adversaries, most likely rouses voices of complaint about excessive concessions. While conciliatory counter-proposals can be made to meet, at least partially, an adversarial demand, this might not soften the stiff position of the opponent who feels a sense of victory and seeks total capitulation. The concessions proffered unconditionally by one side may generate expectations of continued gains from the other, who may not want to believe in, or be convinced of, a limit on what can be achieved. If the adversary's goal is confined to low antagonistic interactions, they can be placated through friendly gestures and symbolic recognition of their claims.

Prior to the abandonment of antagonistic measures, competitive behaviour may increase temporarily in signalling the possibility of a return to a tough stance, commensurate with an adversary's future strategies. Aggressive moves for short-term gains can be misinterpreted, however, unintentionally producing retaliatory reactions. The hard question becomes how to avoid provoking the other side into an escalatory track while adopting contentious tactics in a measured manner to strengthen one's negotiating position.

The other's intention can be misconstrued due to the multiple functions of communication methods. Whereas specific actions may have been taken to shape the opponent's interpretations of the situation, these may also have to be considered in terms of the morale of one's own constituents. The efforts to send out both conciliatory and harsh messages to multiple types of audience often bring about misunderstandings and unintended reactions. Ambiguous meanings can be crafted to show intransigence to the domestic audience, while intimating an intention to lower hostilities toward adversaries. Even though the tough messages are constructed for public consumption and to allay domestic critics, they can proliferate ill feelings and enmity in the enemy camp.

Specific expectations and standards about acceptable and unacceptable contentious behaviour may differ among the parties. Words and acts ought to be interpreted in the specific context of past and present events. Every action does not have the same value. In fact, some can be intentionally ignored or dismissed. For instance, even after the North Koreans detonated nuclear weapons in the autumn of 2006, the USA and Japan declared, as part of efforts to reverse their adversary's claim to a nuclear power status, that they do not recognize the ownership of nuclear bombs by Pyongyang as a factual matter.

Even in escalation, implicit or explicit sets of rules may emerge to inhibit excessive conduct intended for total destruction. In the midst of a violent struggle, tacit communications can be devised to constrain each other's attempts at further escalation. Without official acknowledgement, the Israeli military refrained from bombing Beirut's main commercial centre, during the 2006 Lebanese war, in part, due to Hezbollah's threat of retaliatory rocket attacks on Tel Aviv.

A threat mode of action

Threats can be designed to force the other party to abstain from particular actions or to push them to pursue new policies that favour the threatening party. Compliance with another's threats and accompanying demands hinges, in part, on the likelihood of the actual implementation of the impending actions in the event of defiance. The threats are seen to be more credible if the imminent attack appears to be well prepared for causing real harm. Credibility also rests on the actor's reputation for adhering to their own words with a show of determination (Patchen, 1988).

The cost of acting on a threat has to incorporate vulnerability to counteraction by the target. Even though the United States has the military capability to strike Iranian nuclear facilities, the American government is less inclined to employ force because of their vulnerability to destructive counterattacks. The price of actually carrying out the threatened military strikes needs to be compared to the cost of not doing so.

In response to coercive steps, the target party has multiple choices, ranging from unconditional or partial compliance with the demand, ignorance by inaction to defiance with a counter-threat. The recipient of the threats may choose to placate an adversary with an alternative reward, opt for conditional compliance in return for the satisfaction of their own demand, or simply counter the other's threat with their own. When the threatening side is unlikely to accept any response short of unconditional and outright compliance, threats and counter-threats can be further escalated as far as to war. Serbian rejection of the Austro-Hungarian empire's key demands, in the aftermath of the June 1914 assassination of Archduke Franz Ferdinand in Sarajevo, set a chain effect into motion. The series of fast-moving events finally spiralled into World War I.

Compliance to demands under intimidation is more likely if the punishment is of high magnitude, if a low cost for concession making is worthwhile evading the reprisal, and if other means are available by which to achieve the goals to be abandoned. Power differentials make compliance inevitable in order to end the current pain and to avert an imminent, even larger one. The target may choose to respond to low-level coercion, instead of waiting for the infliction of much more severe retribution if the current loss is considered a less costly option in the long run.

Threats, especially carrying excessive demands, can be a gamble if they push an adversary into a corner. The target of deterrent threats is less likely to yield if it has to give up its vital needs without any alternative routes to satisfaction. In particular, the appeal of compliance would not be great without the availability and attractiveness of alternative options after the desertion of one's objectives.

Resistance is likely to come from concerns relating to the precedent-setting effect of yielding under coercive pressure. This anxiety increases if the issues at stake are repetitive in nature and so likely to be brought up again. In addition, compliance under coercion is likely to be discouraged if what has to be conceded carries value of a high magnitude.

The intrinsic costs originating from accepting the threat terms take account of a loss of reputation for being firm as well as damage to status, self-esteem, and pride. The price of complying with a public threat can be particularly difficult to absorb due to a loss of face. Such harm to one's standing can result in the encouragement of new demands and threats even from other adversaries fighting on different issues.

Giving in or making a concession might be taken to be evidence of general weakness for opponents who are inclined to issue further challenges. The outcome of the current conflict can then set expectations about future resolve. For instance, Germany adopted more assertive strategies and invaded Poland in September 1939, after the Munich crisis of 1938 that ended with Hitler's partial annexation of Czechoslovakia.

A target may defy the threat despite possible vengeance, or even send out a counter-threat as an attempt to discourage the adversary from carrying out the original plan. Furthermore, pre-emptive action can be taken against the warning party in order to neutralize their coercive capabilities. A high cost of compliance with the threats and also the perceived illegitimacy of the attached demand are likely to augment a prospect for such defiance. Since the counter-coercion needs to be backed up by necessary force, not every actor is capable of forceful resistance or counter-retaliation.

In general, threats are made under the assumption that the target will react rationally to make an objective calculation of costs and benefits. The opponent's response may, however, become unpredictable, with the involvement of miscalculations, especially under the stress arising from having few options but highly destructive outcomes except capitulation. In this situation, policy making is more likely to be dictated by emotion than rational considerations (Gordon and Arian, 2001). Even though a high level threat is successful in creating fear, it fails to engender an attitude change. The magnitude of threats should, therefore, be adaptable to the target of influence.

The nature of threats ought to differ according to the target's strength and the odds of resistance. For example, the US threats of trade sanctions against Iran would have a different leverage from those targeted toward China. The threat of a sanction (for instance, the imposition of high tariffs) would be effective if the positive incentives (the continuing benefit of trade relationships) exist for compliance with the demand (the protection of property rights).

Behavioural, psychological, and organizational dimensions

The situation of each conflict stage is configured by particular behavioural and psychological parameters. At the same time, the perception of structural conditions by parties is likely to mirror changes in the dynamics of conflict. The situational variables in antagonistic interactions elucidate the definitive effects of confrontational actions. The mitigation of a conflict is typified by a transition from violent to non-violent strategies.

The patterns of interaction, associated with a particular conflict phase, impinge on certain psychological and structural conditions. Behaviour is adjusted to various periods of perceptional change in relation to themselves and the opposition. Adversarial behaviour is unlikely to be moderated in a meaningful manner if each contestant desires to keep up coercive strategies with the goal of domination. Various types of action and strategies can be accounted for by the intensity of a fight.

The different degrees of coercive power have an impact on choices of actions, thus altering the dynamics of contest. Besides a value commitment to non-violence, the use of threat or the actual exercise of force becomes asymmetrical if there is imbalance in the capacity to reciprocate the other's aggressive behaviour. In asymmetrical situations, the stronger party is in a position to dictate its favoured settlement terms. While extreme power inequality is likely to motivate the superior party not to make concessions, the worst escalation is more likely to happen in the moderately unequal balance of power (Pruitt, 2005).

The imposition of a unilateral solution may be met with fierce resistance under normal circumstances, especially when the weaker party in possession of their own means of reprisal lacks alternatives for redress. The more important the issue is, the more difficult it is for the parties to give up their struggle, even in disadvantageous situations. Through persuasion, each party may attempt to convince the other to assent by arguing that its desired goals can serve the interests and values of the other party. The loss of capacity and will to continue to fight eventually leads to the contraction of goals.

The degree of power to impose one's own will differs according to the types of issue in contention. Protagonists have diverse levels of ability to control agendas in different issue areas. The extent of asymmetry in issue salience has an impact on each party's decision on whether to fight. The achievement of a particular goal is probably more critical to one side than the other. The other side's coercion is more likely to be endured with a greater will of resistance if vital interests are at stake, containing a high magnitude of grievance. The pertinence of the issues in contention, embedded in a historic struggle, inspires a highly committed fight in the longer time horizon.

The commitment to the exchange of coercive actions during escalation and stalemate is based on a balance between a party's ability to endure the costs and its perceived potential for victory. A weak party's strong will and capacity to resist raise the cost to a more powerful party with the consequence of drawing out a struggle. Dominant parties may refuse to change their positions unless they notice that the conflict cannot be won without unbearably heavy costs.

Mounting costs test social, psychological, and military resilience in intense conflict situations. Each party has a different degree of ability to absorb costs. The infliction of pain has a limited effect when the other side has already anticipated some cost and has been prepared for that. If an adversary perceives pain to be an investment, the higher price to be paid for the sacrifice only strengthens their resolve. In such situations, therefore, reversing the other's decision through heavier coercive tactics is likely to be counterproductive.

Gross asymmetry in psychological and organizational resilience is contrasted with asymmetry in military power. In the 2006 war in Lebanon, Israel had far superior military power, but, despite a high-tech Israeli military assault, Hezbollah demonstrated more resilience, in absorbing higher conflict costs than generally expected, forcing Israel to retreat after its re-entry in southern Lebanon. In the 1991 Slovenian War, local, irregular militia groups had far superior morale, in contrast with that of their counterparts in the Yugoslav army. Without a big stake in the fighting, many of the Yugoslav soldiers, composed of diverse ethnic groups, initially mistook the military operation as an exercise. As a consequence of the lack of a clear direction or goal for the war, the federal government easily gave up the war in ten days, granting independence to the breakaway republic.

The trajectory of a conflict's intractability is shaped by the effects of grievances in psychological commitment and mood as well as the level of incompatibility in the goals and methods adopted to dominate others. Psychological changes at each stage of conflict can be explained in terms of not only perceptual variables but also emotional intensity. A collective trauma results in the development of shared emotions such as fear and hate. Indeed, deep feelings of animosity and rage contribute to destructive behaviour. In conflict mitigation, a reduced level of enmity and hostility is necessary for the control of coercive action.

Not only social and psychological, but also organizational developments generate new conflict dynamics. New perceptions, thoughts, and feelings of solidarity can emerge along with the development of new organizational culture. Group activities are adapted to the acquirement of new members, technologies and tasks (McGrath and Argote, 2001). The strategies of conflict may count on the prevailing cultural and institutional patterns as well as the capabilities of the adversaries. Organizational ability for a continued struggle is limited by fatigue, derived from difficulties in the recruitment of new members and internal cleavages. The exhaustion of organizational will and capacity saps the desire to pursue even a once sacred goal.

Organizational behaviour

Parties with diverse sizes, membership structures, and goals have different organizational inclinations and skills in adopting particular methods of struggle (Hogg, 2001). Resistance groups in civil war situations may rely on economic sabotage, destruction of government installations and attacks on security forces. In contrast, many civic organizations are purely committed to strategies of non-violent mobilization with open, horizontal communication structures. Greenpeace and other environmental advocacy groups have rallied a great number of protesters in an effort to bring public attention to global warming and the loss of species. The Tibetan government in exile has remained committed to non-violence even though the Chinese government killed several thousand peaceful protesters in 1957 and has continued to use highly coercive and repressive tactics, including torture.

Broad-based non-violent movements can be contrasted with terrorist organizations, characterized by the tight, cell-like leadership structure which carries out relentless violence against any enemy targets. A relatively small group is more adapted to upholding violence as a strategy to challenge state authority, even though violent means do not enhance their cause. It is very difficult to negotiate with terrorist groups that refuse to give up mostly destructive tactics, especially because their goal is illusive and is not amenable to compromise.

Some organizations advocate violence as a means of taking a strategic advantage, or due to a lack of peaceful means by which to achieve their goals. Non-violence and violence strategies have even been used by the same organizations in diverse situations against different adversaries. While Hezbollah preferred guerrilla warfare tactics against the Israeli troops, they have been restrained from armed tactics against their domestic opponents. In March 2007, they set up tent towns in central Beirut as part of their sit-in protest to demand the resignation of a pro-Western government, even controlling the temptation to retaliate against killing of their members and other provocative actions by adversarial groups. This avoidance of violent tactics by Hezbollah can be, in part, attributed to efforts to conserve their capabilities to fight with a much more onerous foe.

In principle, non-violent resistance has been used to change a dominant party's behaviour by generating public sympathy and support for the cause of the oppressed. In applying moral pressure on the dominant power to recognize injustice, non-violent engagement counts on clear communication of intentions for persuasion (Sharp, 1973). Non-cooperation and civil resistance are juxtaposed against violent, malignant strategies of government oppression. Violence can be rejected on the grounds of a moral or religious principle.

Non-violence may also be a more practical means by which to overcome a physical power imbalance, in that it can lower the costs of a struggle for a weaker party that is not adapted to militant strategies. Unfortunately, however, non-violent struggle against the government's continuing coercive tactics did not ease the degree of suppression in Burma and China, though it has helped to inspire international support for the causes of human rights and self-determination (Kriesberg, 1998). The success of non-armed, persuasion strategies is contingent on the existence of a viable civil society as well as freedom of the press and reasonably well informed public opinion. Non-coercive strategies can be more easily embraced in societies with relatively little repression, and less government control over dissent and opposition groups.

Political and normative dimensions such as the quest for justice play an important role in conflict analysis to the extent that moral opinions provide constraints on a powerful party's ability for non-discriminatory destruction. A subordinate group yearning for justice may refuse to accept the status quo and continue to struggle for the recognition of their moral cause. Escalation via non-violent struggles may take account of a strategy of transforming asymmetric conflict for subordinate groups. The attitude of a dominant party may fluctuate under the weight of moral and political costs brought about by sufficient external pressure.

Internal, external, and contextual variables

Not only internal but also external dynamics shift with the evolution of adversarial interaction. The overall characteristics of conflict dynamics can be determined by any combination of 1) internal changes in the contending parties, 2) the predicament in the inter-party relationship, and 3) an overarching context. Various compositions in the modification of these three components may either strengthen or weaken negative conflict dynamics.

Intra-party changes such as the emergence of a new leadership may instigate an adjustment in inter-party dynamics. The effects of positive changes within a party can be constrained by a negative external environment. For instance, efforts to bring stability to the Central African Republic have been hampered by the spill-over of armed conflicts into neighbouring countries such as Sudan. Therefore, modifications in one component such as intra-party level decision-making structure (considered favourable to de-escalation) can be negated by an opposing movement toward escalatory directions made at an external level (Putnam, 1988).

Internal changes might take place in either one of the parties, or both. A negative attitude on one side may have contagious effects on the other. The hawkish positions of one party resonate in the other's switch toward hard-line views. This relationship dynamic would, in turn, make it more difficult for conciliatory positions to be formed within each party. Moreover, forces external to the party may lay more road blocks across the path toward settlement. The overall outcome of conflict dynamics hinges on how stabilizing and destabilizing forces balance each other out.

If one party is ready for change, while the other is not, positive initiatives may be cancelled out or undercut by adverse actions. If one party's action toward intensification of conflict is stronger, the other party's efforts toward de-escalation are likely to be outbalanced. Overall, the nature of interaction between parties is featured by communication patterns, content of messages, the level of incompatibilities in each other's activities, and the number of adversarial groups (Ellis, 2006).

External influence

Conflict transformation might arise from adaptations in external dimensions as well as internal dynamics. Internal support of escalatory moves can be mitigated by an opposite external effect towards the weakened military capabilities of adversaries. On the contrary, an external environment, related to military and economic support for war efforts, can further fuel the underlying force of self-perpetuating conflict spirals.

In a struggle with a dominant party, weaker parties may be empowered by both technical assistance and moral encouragement. If external intervention on behalf of a weaker party is designed to redress asymmetric power relations, it can compel a stronger party to cease escalatory tactics. External pressure on the parties who refuse to negotiate will, however, be more effective if there are organizational or psychological changes within each party such as a rising level of fatigue combined with deteriorating capabilities to fight.

The regional or international context has an impact on inter-group dynamics, for example, in civil wars. In the Cold War period, many internal conflicts started off because of, or were aggravated by, the US administration's political and military backing of corrupt authoritarian governments or right-wing military dictatorships worldwide from Chile and Guatemala to Zaire. In 1954, a CIA-organized covert operation toppled the democratically elected President of Guatemala, Jacobo Arbenz Guzmán, who was known for being socialist in leaning. The increasingly autocratic rule of the newly installed military government set off an armed insurrection that turned into 36 years of civil war. In September 1973, US Secretary of State Henry Kissinger masterminded the Chilean coup d'état that overthrew the democratically elected Marxist president of Chile, Salvador Allende, whom the Nixon Administration feared supported the Soviet Union. The subsequent military dictatorship by General Augusto Pinochet instituted a brutal campaign against the leftist political parties, which led to the execution of around 3,000 people, the incarceration of 27,000, and the torture of a great many others.

As is illustrated in the global war on terrorism, all factors (related to parties, goals, issues, scope, and domains of conflict) are interrelated. Ethnic conflicts, combined with competition between radical and moderate Islamic groups, began to draw US attention, because the extremist groups may become potential allies for al Qaeda or other terrorist networks. The conflict in Somalia, ignored for the last ten years by external powers, now has a new dimension as a result of US suspicions that the fall of Mogadishu to religiously oriented groups might provide a breeding ground for terrorists. The Bush administration even militarily supported the Ethiopian government's invasion of Somalia, in January 2007, to nullify the military victory of the radical Islamists in an effort to bring moderate groups back to the control of the country.

Many casualties in African civil wars were, in part, attributed to the availability of small arms flowing from neighbouring countries that experienced internal violence (Lobell and Mauceri, 2004). Funding for internal violence comes from the existence of international black markets that permit rebel forces to profit from the illegal sales of timber, diamonds, and other minerals. The system of antagonistic inter-group relations is often interlinked to external forces that have vested interests in prolonging the conflict rather than undercutting destructive dynamics.

Inter-group dynamics

The rivalry between opposing blocs of protagonists has driven decades of conflict in Somalia, Burundi, Sudan, and Nepal. In these and other divided countries, settlement has been hampered by the necessity to involve multiple actors who are not necessarily representing broad constituents. In Nepal, the dissolution of the government by King Gyanendra in February 2005 and the imposition of a state of emergency united all of the established opposition political parties and eventually contributed to his loss of traditional monarchical power in April 2006. This helped Maoist guerrilla groups reach agreements with the coalition of various political parties that began to run the government.

The fate of many ethnic and political conflicts rests on more than two parties which may form different alliances or complementary relationships on a united front against a common enemy. Opposing blocs may try to take superiority or keep up with a balance in the power struggle by recruiting diverse new allies. In opposing one dominant group, all others may build a natural alliance simply for the sake of their survival. Many opposition organizations may coalesce to develop joint forces in bringing down an authoritarian government. In a civil protest against an autocratic state, varied political parties often work together with the single aim of political change.

The rebel movements, composed of disparate, ethnic contingents, may build up a unitary force against the existing political establishment, dominated by a single elite faction or ethnic group. But once the shared enemy is gone, fresh conflicts flourish among former allies. The major ethnic groups joined the

Ethiopian People's Revolutionary Democratic Front (EPRDF) to topple the Mengistu regime. Since the government's fall in 1991, the movements representing the region of Eritrea successfully sought independence in 1993, but the 1999 border clashes between Ethiopia and Eritrea evolved into a year-long war. Meanwhile, the EPRDF was battling with two major opponent blocs, many members of which used to operate under a broad umbrella of the previous rebel movements. In particular, the opposition groups consisting of the Coalition for Unity and Democracy and the United Ethiopian Democratic Forces protested the denial of victory in the 2005 parliamentary elections ascribed to the ruling party's fraud.

Intra-party dynamics

External conflict either exacerbates or undermines internal dissension, depending on the existing level of group loyalty among members. The means chosen in pursuing goals are generally adaptable to a group's internal structure. In its struggle against the Serbian government, the Kosovo Liberation Army, for example, had vastly different political ideologies, tactics and relationships with its constituents compared with those political groups that advocated non-violence.

Internal party divisions often centre on who is genuinely representing the community. In-fighting creates an obstacle to the negotiated solution of a larger conflict, but at the same time, a protracted intra-group struggle erodes the will to fight external enemies, contributing to subsiding violence. There are always complicated relationships between those engaged in armed struggles and those who seek political solutions.

Tamil guerrilla forces removed voices for compromise with the violent eradication of a moderate political leadership (that shares the same ethnic constituent base), further aggravating the Sri Lankan conflict. In contrast, the Basque Homeland and Freedom (ETA), engaged in a bloody campaign against government institutions and personnel, has lost wide support among the constituent population due to the success of moderate nationalists in gaining concessions for regional autonomy from the Spanish government. In the Kosovo conflict, the Albanian community has been politically represented by those who advocated non-military solutions, undercutting the power of armed resistance groups heavily oriented toward intimidation tactics with an ethno-nationalist ideology.

The nature of a struggle has an impact on the group's identity, morale, and self-respect as well as a general level of material well-being. The degree of commitment to a conflict, and types of strategy and tactic selected for the struggle can have lasting implications for group cohesion and values. The use of violence by oppressed groups is often ascribed to self-affirmation of their identity and esteem especially in a situation within which non-violence is not feasible (Fanon, 2004).

The impact of a conflict on each contending party differs, depending on group structures such as the degree of membership unity and the extent of centralized control. Each party has unique decision-making procedures and rules related to power distributions and diverse methods of regulating internal divisions.[2] Morale may decrease, due to an unfavourable trend in the balance of power between parties, accompanied by a loss of battles or international isolation. Low morale, following economic sanctions or destruction in war, sways the mood of the rank and file, in tandem with the loss of confidence in the leadership, demanding an adjustment of goals.

A struggle with outside enemies has unforeseen consequences within each society or group. The need to engage in extreme struggles may effectively justify the expansion of hierarchical control. In addition, further centralization of decision-making power is frequently rationalized in such instances as a major socio-economic crisis that has dire implications for survival. A group involved in a political, military battle with a much stronger adversary calls for stronger membership commitment and blind loyalty. Militant or revolutionary forces engaged in unconventional strategies necessitate a hierarchical, command system based on absolute obedience (Coser, 1964).

The image of a demonized opponent helps to submerge internal differences, in that group members believe that internal divisions jeopardize the chances for their survival in the face of a vilified enemy. On the other hand, an internal discord over strategies, in the absence of a unifying leadership, can be exposed and aggravated in the midst of an uphill battle, eventually serving the demise of the group's campaign. During the Algerian civil war, for example, the split between the two main rival Islamist rebel groups, namely, the Islamic Salvation Army and the Armed Islamic Group, in 1994, undercut their capacity to arrange an efficient campaign against the military-run government, contributing to the struggle's cessation by 2002.

Contrary to this, however, well coordinated insurgent groups demonstrate an ability to share information, techniques, infrastructure sometimes with reorganization or more centralized management of their relationships. After experiencing internal divisions with the creation of new splinter groups, in the Second Sudanese War, 13 opposition groups set up the National Democratic Alliance (NDA) in June 1989. This was instigated by the necessity to work out collective agendas and strategies against the newly established regime of Omar Hassan al-Bashir who seized power in a military coup. In ending the civil war, the NDA successfully negotiated with the government and signed a peace agreement in June 2005. Similarly, after almost two decades of fighting, four principal left-wing guerrilla forces in the Guatemalan civil war were combined to establish the Guatemalan National Revolutionary Unity (URNG) in 1982. This group conducted effective negotiations with the government in 1995.

The ability to fend off the external pressures is reinforced by a strong sense of group loyalty. Identities play an important role in the translation of grievances into mass sentiment as well as the formulation of goals and methods. When the commitment to the cause is not strong, for instance, in the US wars in Vietnam and Iraq, mounting costs, especially accumulated by unlimited war spending and human suffering, are likely to be an important source of internal discord. In autocratic states, defeat or failure to fight effectively against external enemies emboldens opposition, raising questions as to the legitimacy of oligarchic control.

Internal discord can be put aside again by revitalizing popularly accepted beliefs or myths. Any overt expression of dissent is accused of interfering with the pursuit of collective goals, being condemned by group members. Pacifist opposition to a total war has been suppressed even in Western democratic societies. World-renowned philosopher Bertrand Russell, for instance, was imprisoned for his pacifist activities against World War I in 1916. If continuing struggles rely on the recruitment of new members and volunteers, tolerance and inclusiveness might be needed to expand a constituency base.

Besides members' total conviction of their shared future, unity, discipline and loyalty cannot be insisted upon or retained without a strong leadership capable of keeping the group together especially during the discouraging moments. The costs of maintaining coercive strategies, especially for a large population, are generally unpopular if the sacrifice is made without the promise of a tangible reward, either psychological or material, or if it exceeds what people originally estimated. Dissension is subdued by even such means as execution to artificially craft support under an authoritarian leadership, but universal values or nationalist ideologies are more emphasized in democratic relationships.

Internal decision-making structure

Decision-making can be protracted with a more diverse input in the development of options. The influence of individuals and groups in the course of a larger conflict can be undermined by decision-making procedures. In fact, weak group cohesiveness, internal rivalry, and differences in intra-party belief systems may complicate the development of official positions. In winding down the El Salvadoran civil war in the early 1990s, the UN and external mediation yielded a successful result, in part, owing to a united negotiating position of opposition guerrilla forces and their ability to impose internal discipline. On the other hand, ending a civil war was more challenging in the Democratic Republic of Congo and Burundi, because of a loose coordination of multiple rebel groups, their different interests, and a lack of self-control needed to abide by the agreements.

Intra-party decision-making structures become more complex in state bureaucratic institutions. State behaviour, in part, illustrates an outcome of a complex negotiation of policy-making organizations. The top leadership may also have to consider the levels of economic strength, resource base, and popular support as well as an appropriate type of fighting. The economic burden and rising casualties are borne disproportionately within a group. Internal bargaining entails difficult balances among disperse factions, subsequently nailing down common denominators in a variety of institutional interests. The existence of perceptive leadership helps overcome political and personal differences that drive internal factions apart (Gerzon, 2006).

Leaders have a diverse set of relationships within their collective entity during the course of a conflict. The types of relationship between the elite and constituencies, by and large, determine the extent of leadership power to formulate group strategies and goals. The capacity to keep up escalation comes from internal solidarity as well as a strong resource base. In addition, the leadership's flexibility to explore better relations with adversaries comes from success in the minimization of internal resistance and the preservation of trust among key constituencies.

The low degree of internal unity and the existence of extreme or militant factions present the leadership with a challenge to overcome factional divisions. Hawks are more likely to amplify internal divisions with their intimidating tactics against even other group members. The necessity for internal negotiations between the elite and its followers, as well as between different factions, can protract the final settlement. Such crucial decisions on ending or continuing a struggle may have to await not only the shifting balance between hawks and doves but also the political leadership's effectiveness in the persuasion of key constituents.

Notes

1 Reflecting on the public fear of nuclear war in November 1982, ten-year-old American Samantha Smith sent a letter to the Soviet leader, Yuri Andropov, pleading with him to work toward peace. Her visit to the Soviet Union, in 1983, upon the invitation of Mr Andropov, served as one of the prominent incidents which helped reverse a dangerously low point in US–Soviet relations.

2 The course of external conflict can be affected by the outcome of internal power struggles. External negotiation becomes more complicated if there is a challenge to the leadership with the ascending demand of radical factions. The US pursuit of al Qaeda has become more tricky, for example, as related to Pakistani President Musharraf's wishes to avoid clashes with tribal group leaders in the lawless region of western Pakistan, where terrorist suspects are believed to reside.

Escalation and Entrapment

Conflict escalation is noted for its rising levels of hostility, driven by the severity of the tactics. New patterns of interaction are accompanied not only by the involvement of extra parties in the struggle, but also by changes within each of the parties. An increase in the intensity of a conflict tends to bring about an expanded scope of participation that engages more people. At the same time, conflict groups are further divided with de-individualization, due to adversarial socio-psychological processes and organizational developments in preparation for an entrenched struggle. Enemy images, stereotypes, and lack of trust result in the destruction or loss of important links of communication, both formal and informal.

The escalation of a conflict is associated with proliferation and generalization of the initial specific issue, the polarization of relationships among parties, deep feelings and the personalization of the situation. The continued escalation reflects efforts to rally allies and the dehumanization of an enemy with hardening attitudes. The value placed on winning substitutes a more pragmatic goal, along with the rise of hard-line leaders, curbing the possibility of seeking alternatives. In a nutshell, the self-fulfilling expectations of contentious behaviour are further fuelled by the development of enemy perceptions and decreased contact between the parties as well as strained communication. This chapter examines the various characteristics and processes that are related to conflict intensification and entrapment.

Dynamics of escalation

The emergence of a number of contentious issues pushes the parties to move further apart, accentuating differences and submerging similarities between them in order to justify a desire to inflict harm on one another. The increased mistrust of enemy motives hinders an ability to sympathize with the other party and strengthens a tendency toward zero-sum calculations. Fixed assumptions about the conflict result in the distortion of each party's positions, even generating a strong sense of threat to a group's central values. A disputed territory may have been perfectly divisible, but the fighting and its consequences attach symbolic meaning to the contested land; denying it to the enemy becomes, in itself, a gratifying goal.

In a highly contentious struggle, issue proliferation produces new flashpoints along with the emergence of obdurate positions. Narrow, specific complaints become universalized, with the development of antagonism predicated on the denial of the other's legitimate rights. The shift from a specific disagreement to general group hostilities may shed light on hidden agendas that were previously considered taboo. The prohibition on wearing a headscarf in French schools, for example, provoked a protest against the suppression of Islamic culture; forced assimilation and intolerance of non-French ethnic traditions has resulted in the resurfacing of discussion about French government policies, and mainstream society's attitude toward African and Middle Eastern minorities.

The enlargement of contentious issues is likely to highlight the competitive positions of opposing groups. A widening conflict is inexorable in a clash involving multiple types of contestant over a broad set of issues arising from deep divisions of basic values or interests. When one adversary extends their list of demands, the other may be willing to enlarge an opposing list of contentious issues. Even technical, mundane matters may evolve into attacks on personal or group attributes, being framed as integral to collective identities and even to the party's own existence. Great symbolic significance can be attached to seemingly separate, minor incidents of collision once there is a rising sense of grievance. Any harm caused by the imposition of sanctions is attributed to the other's strong desire for vengeance by the use of any means, even if the sanctions may have been carefully introduced, with limited objectives, so as not to alienate the entire population of an adversarial state.

The expansion of a conflict demands heightened personal commitment in conjunction with the devotion of more resources to the fight with optimism. Conviction in the feasibility of total victory generates increased confidence about the achievement of desired objectives (Kriesberg, 1998). This is well illustrated by the euphoria and surge of Arab nationalism, prior to the 1967 Six Day War, along with a call for sacrifice, exhibited in the capitals of Egypt, Syria, Jordan, and other Middle Eastern states.

Parties are unwilling to make concessions and take positions of non-compromise with high aspirations for a victory across a wide range of issues. Embracing more assertive patterns of behaviour complicates the original conflict that became expanded with the growth of issue complexity. Once the solidification of enemy perceptions is tied to one's own survival needs, ideologically or morally characterized struggles defy compromise. The war on terrorism was monolithically defined by the US government in terms of a fight against 'evil', leaving very little room for the analysis of the political and social causes that might be related to the US role in the Middle East. Such positional rigidity is further strengthened if there are no efforts to properly interpret an adversary's motives.

A fight over an extended list of issues is more likely to solicit support from a wide spectrum of sympathizers with the expansion of recruitment bases. Splinter groups might be formed to push their own agendas to the fore. As people react to calls for outside support, a conflict gains new complexity through an increased number of partisans, each of whom is likely to have their own understandings of the original issues entrenched in primary antagonism.

The creation of opposing camps in support of different protagonists enlarges the conflict with the addition of new ally or patron–client relationships (Maoz, 2006). The tendency toward enlargement exerts pressure on non-aligned parties in the periphery of the conflict to take sides, pulling more groups farther away from moderate positions. Formerly neutral observers are increasingly more attuned to the polarized centres in a widening conflict in which vying for external support becomes the latest game of competition.

There are diverse motives for the participation, ranging from shared interests with one of the protagonists and a search for allies in their own conflicts (through links to other conflicts) to the evasion of future costs incurred from non-involvement. The Pakistani government revealed that the US threat through informal channels of 'bombing [its] country back to the Stone Age' forced its participation in the US fight against the Taliban and al Qaeda in Afghanistan despite domestic opposition.

A high level of polarization accompanies inadvertent escalation associated with very little trust or miscommunication (Anderson, 2004). The bifurcation of groups between 'us' and 'them' puts up psychological and physical barriers that reduce interaction with the formation of negative images. Severe forms of violence wipe out cross-cutting ties that used to link multiple sectors of society and sub-groupings across political, cultural boundaries. In the aftermath of various terrorist attacks by al Qaeda and its proxies or sympathizers, the number of Arab professional visits, other travels and students studying in the United States has dramatically declined, deepening social distance. Most significantly, inter-group polarization produces a synergy for in-group solidarity with less tolerance of favourable or sympathetic views about a common enemy.

Thus polarized attitudes emerge, in part, from conformity to extreme in-group normative positions along with the derogation of other groups (Cooper et al., 2001). A lack of interest in accommodation is reinforced by such motives as seeking a sense of 'justice' and yearning for revenge as well as the expression of anger. These sentiments are supported by the adoption of a militant ideology that rationalizes the high cost of fighting adversaries as psychologically redeeming. In the patriotic post-9/11 era, any opposition to US military campaigns in Afghanistan was ridiculed or was subject to ideological criticism, raising very little doubt about extravagant government spending on 'the war against terrorism' despite the sacrifice of essential domestic, social and economic necessities.

The projection of fear onto the opponent plays a critical role in rationalizing highly destructive, retaliatory tactics in lieu of persuasive argument. Tenacious enemy images, rooted in the predominant public sentiment, are exploited in the justification of a win–lose orientation. The contentious strategies prevail in anger and hatred, seeking costly, undesirable consequences for opponents and shutting the door for the promise of reasonable discussion. A stronger party is inclined to bully antagonists into submission when their substantial power superiority would easily subdue the aspirations of the other.

The magnitude of value incompatibility is misapprehended in a switch from pursuing narrowly defined objectives to an attempt to annihilate adversaries. The original aspirations are reinterpreted in the overall preferences of goal hierarchies, supporting agendas seen as integral to the protection of the group's essential core identities. The intense pursuit of uncompromising goals, combined with the use of threats and force, is primarily responsible for destructive conflicts.

Psychological and behavioural aspects

Escalation is characterized by an increase in quantity, intensity and scope of coercive exchanges among protagonists. The perpetuation of a violent struggle invokes a 'upward spiral', comprising a cycle of attacks and counter-attacks. The intensification of violence may proceed from a series of actions, ranging from the denial of rewards to economic threats and boycotts prior to military moves. An increasing employment of deception and pressure tactics becomes the main means of influencing an adversary in seeking an advantage. Even greater coercion is advocated as the only way to curtail resistance from the other side.

A high level of escalation is advanced by a variety of socio-psychological processes such as misperception which stimulates the distortion of the other side's traits and motives. Fear anchored in the distrust of the other's intent might encourage provocative actions that prompt escalatory moves. In general, any conciliatory conduct by an adversary is inclined to be overlooked or, even if it is acknowledged, regarded as deceptive. The amplification of negative stereotypes assists in depicting the opposition as menacing, invigorating the belief that the enemy would completely violate one's own rights (Abrams, 2005). These rising tensions cause deformed patterns of communication with every message viewed through an antagonistic lens. Non-existence of communication at the height of escalation begets dangerous conditions for misjudging the other's intentions and taking risky behaviour.

Negative emotions attached to a locked-in struggle encompass a subjective, ethical legitimization of violent acts. An outlet for the mounting hostility depreciates the ability to empathize with the other's needs. De-individualization of enemy group members, based on ethnocentric values and attitudes, spawns demeaning behaviour, along with a display of superiority to outsiders. In particular, a moral disengagement rationalizes harm to, or exploitation of, certain 'kinds' of people deemed to be an obstacle to one's own prosperity. Harsh measures are more easily taken with a feeling of contempt for opponents seen as inferior or evil.

In a long-term rivalry, the motivation to inflict physical and psychological injuries is ascribed to a profound desire to seek revenge for one's losses. The parties' ability to envision alternatives is further constricted by a breakdown of open and direct communication. This interruption of communication, in conjunction with a high level of distrust, engenders the misrepresentation of factual matters. Damaging propaganda adds yet further difficulties for blocking fruitful discussion about substantive issues. Most importantly, vicious escalation spirals are stoked by malicious intentions, castigation and revenge.

Once a total commitment is made on the basis of the justification of previous investments, complete withdrawal from even a failing course of action is not considered to be an option despite continuously rising costs. With very little prospect for reaching settlement, an escalatory path of ever increasing commitments is built over a longer time horizon, perpetuating a tendency to persist in the existing course of action. Independent of its originating sources, each action represents a momentum of its own, while the original causes become less relevant. Increasingly hateful confrontations are geared to hurt opponents rather than boosting one's own interests.

A malignant interaction

A threat by one group spurs the other side's counter-threat in a spiral of new coercion and defence. Every escalation step taken by one party provokes the other's defensive hostilities in the absence of any willingness to compromise. Tensions exacerbated by unregulated responses push the upward-spiralling dynamics of a more damaging conflict. In a malignant social process, retreat becomes more difficult, owing to vulnerability to an unacceptable loss of pride and self-esteem. Self-amplifying action–reaction dynamics are founded on the intentional or unintentional instigation of violent acts which become normalized patterns. Brutalized relations, revealed in terrorism or total warfare, are based on the excessive means and extent of destruction without any regard for an adversary's welfare (Eckert and Willems, 2005).

At the initial stage of the second intifada, Palestinians were angered by the killings of a growing number of children following gun battles between Israeli troops and Palestinians in September 2000. After Ariel Sharon's election as Prime Minister, Israelis launched F-16 warplanes against Palestinian targets for the first time in May 2001. In the ensuing months of June and August, Islamic Jihad began its campaign, with the recruitment of Palestinian suicide bombers.

They blew up a disco in Tel Aviv, leaving more than twenty people dead and more than sixty others injured. This was followed by another suicide attack on a crowded restaurant in the heart of Jerusalem, claiming the lives of 15 people and injuries to about ninety others.

In the subsequent years, approximately ten more Palestinian suicide bomb attacks detonated buses in Haifa, Jerusalem and Beersheba, a hotel event in Netanya, a social club in Rishon Letzion, a Haifa restaurant, and a popular nightspot in Tel Aviv. The levels of casualties reached their highest between 2002 and 2004. The Israelis reacted with an incursion into the Rafah refugee camp (causing at least forty Palestinian deaths), a massive military assault on Jenin and other West Bank towns (even reaching Yasser Arafat's Ramallah headquarters) as well as the assassination of Hamas leaders with missile strikes and aircraft bombs. In spite of a seven-week truce in the summer of 2003, these attacks had lasted until a ceasefire between Israel and Palestinian militants in February 2005.

Progressively destructive interactions, represented by strident rhetoric and assertive strategies, push each side to expect a higher degree of coercive action by their opponents (McAdam et al., 2001). A rise in hostilities might even be derived from the anticipation of an enemy's fresh attacks. Higher levels and new types of offence, exemplified by suicide bombs, missile strikes and assaults by F-15 fighters on residential areas, can be introduced to alter expectations about future actions and outcomes. The permissible amount of force may go beyond previous boundaries with direct attacks on an enemy's top leadership (for instance, the Israeli missile strike against Hamas leader Abdel Aziz al-Rantissi in May 2004 and air strikes on the spiritual leader Sheikh Ahmed Yassin in March 2004). The indication of an expanded boundary for one party's attacks signals a heightened level of pressure on the other side to concede.

The retaliatory spirals driven by blame, anger, and vengeance intensify the desire of one party to hurt the other in response to actions that it finds offensive. The growth in negative stereotypes relaxes inhibitions against the employment of harsh measures. The experiences of each party are justified by hostility originating from past grievances or feelings of injustice in relation to the other's atrocious acts. As perceived injustice exacerbates rage, the harm suffered becomes a lasting source to seek revenge.

The belligerent actions are reproduced with each round of exchanges in an upward spiralling driven by action–reaction processes. In a mutually damaging interaction, a growing list of grievances is further expanded, while each retaliation action stirs a new provocative action. In malign, escalatory spirals, therefore, every exchange of contentious behaviour aggravates protagonists to step up their pressure. The retaliatory actions of one are countered by the other's coercive responses at even a higher level in a 'tit-for-tat' logic. The lower end of the intensity scale, meanwhile, is elevated to an intolerable level with the replication of an enemy's escalatory moves.

This higher pressure, along with a growing perception of threat, arouses self-fulfilling expectations in which one's worst suspicion is confirmed by the other's behaviour via one's own false beliefs (Bordens and Horowitz, 2002). False expectations and negative perceptions elicit the feared response to become reality as a consequence of inflamed emotions. Once one's initiatives are based on the anticipation of an antagonistic action, this, in turn, evokes its actual realization. Thus self-fulfilling prophecies are materialized by the parties' irrational images of, and behaviour toward, each other, in the context of deadly confrontations.

Even if the intention of the initiator is proactive (for example, the construction of a 640-kilometre West Bank barrier by the Israelis in 2002), actions may be seen as menacing by the opponent. The attribution of adversarial behaviour to harmful intentions provokes further engagement in a hostile reaction. An excessive reaction to a perceived threat is attributed to growing suspicion and mistrust in conjunction with the miscalculation of an adversary's likely move. A mutually destructive spiral is predestined for a highly competitive process felt simultaneously by adversaries. In the mutually assured destruction (MAD) of competition for nuclear armament during the Cold War period, an adversary's move was often regarded as an unacceptable peril with concerns about humiliating defeat. Stereotyped enemy images and historical analogies further tighten a commitment to absolute victory.

A mode of escalatory spiral

In a linear arrangement, qualitative and quantitative changes occur in each repetitive pattern of interaction. In an incremental escalation model, a spiral whirls upward in a step-by-step process, with roughly the same, or similar rates, in each antagonistic response. Tension may rise over time through a chain of incidents, each provoking a new level of hostility, eventually reaching a point of crisis. The endpoint of mutual escalation is likely to be an exercise of physical force; a series of events can prompt one or both parties to determine the outcome of contest by attack.

Research on foreign policy-making behaviour suggests that conflict is more likely to escalate into an intense crisis level if it entails a threat to basic values, finite time to react, and a high likelihood of military hostilities (Brecher and Wilkenfeld, 2000). After the establishment of the Reagan administration in the early 1980s, the exchange of hostile rhetoric between the leaders of the United States and the Soviet Union (exhibited by the 'evil empire' and 'a mad man' respectively) drastically grew into a dangerous psychological warfare and a renewed arms race, despite mutual avoidance of military provocations. Fortunately, the psycho-political aspect of the confrontation was not further escalated beyond the competitive military build-up and antagonistic emotional responses.

The course of challenging and protecting the status quo can be featured by gradual escalation when each party attempts to test the other's strength and resolve with a series of increasing provocations. The unstable competition for advantage, in general, ends up with uncontrollable violence without any steps taken to reverse it. Turkey invaded Cyprus in 1974 and occupied a significant portion of land inhabited by the Greeks as a final step to break through the continual standoff with which neither side to the conflict felt comfortable. The invasion was set in the context of Turkish threats of military intervention in the mid-1960s to alter the political landscape in favour of minority Turks on the island vis-à-vis the original Greek inhabitants.

Prior to the invasion, each clash further escalated the conflict, producing a higher level of political tension. This coincided with a Turkish weapons shipment and aerial bombing as well as Athens' support for hard line Greek nationalists. The Turkish government used a coup orchestrated by Greek militants to depose Cyprus President Makarios as a pretext to dramatically tip the territorial balance. The Turkish action created about 160,000–200,000 Greek Cypriot refugees who comprised 82% of the population in the north.

By taking advantage of Greek inaction to the military provocation, the Turkish government was able to further escalate the tension and imposed a new status quo desired by them. In the above case, '[t]ensions and vulnerability build up slowly, until they reach a critical point at which something snaps or some parties decide to force a break-through'. In this situation, a long and gradual onset contributes to the unfolding of a pattern of critical incidents with a relatively abrupt termination after 'the stage was set psychologically and politically for a showdown' ('tHart and Boin, 2001: 32).

Escalation behaviour is not necessarily restricted to military actions or direct threats of their use (Hewitt, 2003). In the majority of international conflicts, severe political acts encompass antagonistic alliance formation, severance of communication, violation or abandonment of treaties, territorial claims, denial of political legitimacy and diplomatic sanctions. One-sided escalation, imposed on an adversary, can be taken more seriously by virtue of either stronger verbal or physical acts even if the adversary might not have initially taken the threat seriously.

A status quo is ultimately disrupted by the escalation of a non-violent, diplomatic mode of exchange to military action. Even an escalatory ladder of war entails various types of threshold, ranging from demonstration attacks on the interior zone and limited bombing against the infrastructure to increasing assault on the military. Thus a constrained disarming attack and some other forms of controlled warfare may precede full military attacks. A series of thresholds may be pushed further up the escalation curve, while each party is eager to display its own capabilities for and commitment to entrenched battles.

In cautious bullying, adverse statements may escalate to shows of strength, military preparedness, and manoeuvres before an ultimatum being accompanied by the employment of force. Intimidation tactics may not necessarily be intended to move farther up escalatory steps and might have been prepared as part of a 'carrot-and-stick' strategy. Pre-threat is devised for probing to get a sense of the other's strategy prior to the first signal of threat along with initial steps toward escalation. Escalating threats culminate in the actual application of destructive force at the end of assertive bullying.

The initial exchange of threats and low-level coercive actions can continue to grow in magnitude and pass one or more salient points, finally crossing the border line of an all-out war. In fact, adversarial actions implicated in a war might denote the failure of manipulating enemy psychology with a gradual escalation strategy built initially into diplomatic pressure and warnings as well as a demonstration of strength. In the two US invasions of Iraq in 1991 and 2003, the advance of military actions proceeded from diplomatic efforts to form a coalition in support of American policy along with the psychological manoeuvres to scare Saddam Hussein.

As opposed to a progressive escalation of hostile exchanges, a spiral for the eruption of sudden hostilities is embedded in a long-term rivalry. This is well demonstrated by the massive Israeli retaliatory air strikes in Lebanon following Hezbollah's abduction of three Israeli soldiers in summer 2006 as well as swift Israeli bombings on Syrian targets of suspected nuclear laboratory sites in fall 2007. Unrestrained, emotional reactions to any provocations may slip into open warfare quickly without a regulation mechanism. In surprise attacks, intentions of aggressive moves, exemplified by the Argentinian invasion of the Falklands, may not be so clearly expressed. The Korean War of 1950–53 was also initiated without much of a warning signal. Even though there were a series of antagonistic political and diplomatic moves, no one predicted the North's major military offence in a short time span.

Tensions are easily exacerbated by unregulated responses to surprise attacks. In many crisis situations, quick military strikes are taken to catch enemies off guard. In a show of dramatic offensive moves, the higher end of the intensity scale might be reached without much of a spiral process; adversaries may promptly mobilize the highest destructive forces with great intensity.

A crisis mode of escalation

An engagement in intense hostile behaviour is often reinforced by a sense of crisis which stems from warnings of acute danger requiring immediate reaction. In many escalation cases, the stakes unintentionally rise to crisis levels, especially when each party does not fully assess the broader consequences of individual actions. In the lead-up to World War I, a series of events, escalated by antagonistic diplomatic manoeuvres and the mobilization of coalition armies within a short time frame, rapidly got out of control.

The Indo–Pakistani War of 1965 originated from the Pakistani troops' attempt to infiltrate Indian Kashmir and instigate local armed resistance. Initially it was planned as a quick military campaign to tilt the balance in the disputed territory of Kashmir. After several skirmishes, India attacked Pakistan on multiple western fronts in retaliation. This war started with the miscalculation of Pakistan's leader General Ayub Khan to easily stir a rebellion in a region controlled by India. The Pakistani leadership underestimated the Indian military's strength after the latter's loss in the 1962 war with China, and misconceived India's will to fight.

The exacerbation of a high-stakes struggle into a crisis evolves from negative reactions to each other's threats. In a vicious spiral of escalation, each party justifies its action as defensive, while perceiving the other's action as offensive. Behaviour involved in such escalation situations as the Cuban Missile Crisis illuminates the fact that the posturing of one side elicits similar behaviour from the opponent who is reluctant to show weakness. Neither party is willing to make concessions, given that the mutual reinforcement of hostile expectations involves higher stakes in the outcome of the struggle.

In the absence of caution, competitive risk taking, as part of manoeuvres for advantage, may evolve into a spin-off escalation. Inflicted pain may have been designed to change the behaviour of the adversaries, but its effects would be the reverse if the other side were to overreact out of fear. It is also ineffective if an adversary has anticipated some cost and has been prepared to provide counter-threats.

In a crisis situation, an interaction pattern of contentious behaviour impels high emotional arousal with feelings of anxiety and surprise (Brecher, 1998; Rosenthal et al., 2001). Intense stress and negative emotions stir a chaotic interaction process. Quick escalation leaves limited time to act, developing a sense of urgency with fewer creative, moderate options. In this situation, particular stages are dictated by the leader's emotional resilience and bureaucratic decision-making styles. Urgency is often generated by public announcements of a deadline or ultimatum. The short time span of conflict alters the quality of decisions by demanding swift action with dire consequences.

Decision makers are usually uncertain as to the effects of particular actions within the crisis context marked by a high level of instability. In general, great uncertainty is unavoidable in the absence of information about the other actors' intentions. An intense level of stress is produced by the elements of surprise, characteristic of an unexpected event, in tandem with time constraints which prohibit full investigation of decision-making choices (Robinson, 1996). Conflict behaviour in crisis conditions is consequently handicapped by fear, panic, rage and other intense emotions. Being overwhelmed by extreme anxiety, decision makers are subject to reacting more erratically and dysfunctionally, being less concerned about the effects of reckless choices.

Irrevocable commitments tend to be made by narrowing options to force the other side to back down. When one party has an ability to cause damage, aggressive policies serve as a means to subjugate an adversary to put down resistance. A dangerous situation can be pushed to the verge of disaster after opponents depend on brinkmanship for obtaining the most advantageous outcome. As a manoeuvre to press the opposing camp into making concessions, each adversary attempts to fabricate an impression that they are not hesitant to employ extreme methods. In some escalatory processes, thus, a willingness to risk precipitating a dead-end battle by means of such acts as the issuance of ultimatum may be intentionally designed for false impression of invincibility while putting unbearable pressure on an opponent.

Eagerness to back up threats is often displayed by a high level of provocative action. However, such intentional shows of commitment further exacerbate volatile situations with an adversary's inclination to adopt a similar strategy. Thus escalation may be an outcome of inadvertent steps that follow each party's miscalculated moves (Lebow and Stein, 1994). Escalation to war is more likely to happen in instances of power parity combined with mutually exclusive confidence in success. In a coercive interaction, the majority of communications is presumed to be threatening. As long as an adversary's intent is not to go to an all-out war, each party can reduce the potential for escalation by cooling down the other's provocative actions with a restrained response.

Escalation and deterrence

In general, manipulation via threat tends to be a primitive method of controlling contentious social relationships. As a matter of fact, adversarial interaction, especially in an international conflict, is more likely to be managed by deterrence based on punishment capability and hostile intent. Threats and intimidation have long comprised a major strategy for deterring others from taking antagonistic actions. The administration of threats entails committing certain acts construed as detrimental to the adversaries.

In a stable deterrence system of checks and balances, the opponents may be discouraged from resorting to violence, assuming the availability of information about each other's objectives and intentions. A recognizable risk of war can be deliberately created by displays of the will to deploy destructive forces. Being concerned that an opponent would exploit any sign of weakness, however, protagonists are more earnest to exhibit toughness to mobilize military force even to the point of risking mutually devastating destruction. A party may even believe that inflexible, stringent positions are necessary to prohibit another's aggression.

Escalation is an inescapable outcome of dysfunctional deterrence systems that favour the threat of equal or superior force as a main tool of controlling the chances for potential aggression. The failure of deterrence stimulates spiral dynamics, as exemplified by a war resulting from an arms race. A historical collapse in international deterrence is evident in the Japanese invasion of Manchuria and German aggression against Poland prior to World War II (Choucri, et al., 1992).

So long as the capability to ensure severe damage to the other is a basic premise of deterrence, mutual threats are actually intensified once each side engages in certain prohibited actions beyond a permissible boundary. In spite of serious warnings, Hitler believed and hoped that Britain and France would not organize a military campaign to save Poland (van Evera, 1999). On the other hand, the allies felt that there would be no limit on Hitler's demand for endless concessions unless they stood up against Nazi Germany's military occupation of Poland in 1939. The disastrous outcome is inexorable, as a mutual deterrence system unleashes, instead of controlling, a high magnitude of destructive capability.

In a realpolitik approach, a threat to escalation continues to be part and parcel of deterrence mechanisms, with a belief that the demonstration of a resolve to retaliate would successfully check an aggressor's behaviour. Escalatory exchanges of sanctions are commonly associated with engagement in punitive actions. Negative intentions and attempts to inject fear in the other's calculation bring threats and counter-threats to the forefront of an adversarial relationship. Escalation may even have been designed as a move in strategic bargaining that combines threats with offers to be made later (Schelling, 1960).

Threats intentionally made in crisis situations are, however, likely to produce more antagonistic reactions with each round of hostile exchanges. Even the verbal expression of extreme acts may ultimately backfire, inviting preemptive strikes when ostensibly well-calculated increases in threats end up provoking unintended destabilizing incidents. In an intense conflict situation, limited escalatory activities are not likely to be interpreted as a probe designed to seek local advantage. The actual exchange of punishments means the breakdown of a deterrence system supposed to prevent destructive consequences through the fear of violence. If the opponent is not discouraged from resorting to violence, deterrence systems are a sure avenue to conflict escalation (Morgan, 2005; Reiter, 2003).

The danger of escalation strategies to deter the other's action is attributed to psychological decision-making characteristics. There is a tendency that threat or coercive acts harden the attitudes of an adversary instead of yielding submission (Gordon and Arian, 2001). Regulating the adversaries' behaviour through military strength is not successful in inducing changes in the positions of determined adversaries for whom sacrifice equals investment. The containment of antagonistic behaviour cannot be solely dependent upon creating the fear of devastating fighting. The attempt to reverse the adversaries' decision through inflicting pain may even reinforce the enemy's resolve. The resentment of an enemy who causes the suffering in the first place further strengthens the positions of a hawkish leadership.

In more cautious actors' calculations, escalated commitments must cease to thwart ever more costly outcomes. It would be preferable to react rather cautiously to an adversary's provocations (especially limited to little damage) by avoiding the option of retaliation. In general, past setbacks in the same or similar clashes are likely to be attributed to the development of a more guarded approach to subsequent escalation decisions. But a high level of simmering grievances ascribed to earlier loss can lessen the fear of continuing loss.

In 1973, the Egyptians and Syrians decided to begin another war with Israel, despite their military inferiority, in order to regain self-respect and vindicate pride lost in the 1967 War.

Owing to its high price tag, a commitment to escalation as a means for achieving goals is not always based on a rational calculation of obtaining a desired endpoint with minimal costs. If the other party is willing to display destructive capabilities without any apprehension, tensions over minor issues may easily erupt into costly, protracted battles.

Strategies for controlled escalation

In international politics, the exhibition of firmness has been advocated as a main strategy to confront a competitive adversary seeking unilateral advantages. However, a clear demonstration of resistance against domination can be combined with efforts not to invite unintended risks by signalling one's non-aggressive aims. Threatening messages could be applied, with diverse degrees of intensity, in an attempt to change the behaviour of opponents. A high or low scale of severity in the prospective outcome has a dissimilar psychological impact on the parties.

A sudden administration of sanctions is contrasted with small increments over an extended time period. Unexpected escalatory moves leave less control over the development of events in the hands of the initiator as well as the target, especially when the spiral dynamics are more difficult to manage. Independent of its initiating rationale, each action may produce unpredicted consequences along with misjudgement of the target's intentions and probable responses. In the pre-World War I crisis, Austria wanted to punish Serbia without inviting Russia to a brawl, but its move brought about a chain effect of escalation that led to the catastrophic war, eventually involving Germany and France as well as Russia.

An escalatory mode of strategies can be adapted either to the higher or lower ends of the intensity scale, depending on changes in each actor's calculations and behaviour. One way in which to avoid uncontrolled escalation is to take gradually punitive steps instead of introducing sudden provocative actions that catch the other side off guard, making them react in panic with disproportionate means. Temporary tactical escalation with restricted punitive measures might be waged to elicit the other's concession without provoking a retaliatory spiral despite an element of pressure (Brzoska and Pearson, 1994).

In some instances, a warning shot could be undertaken to deter the other's shift to aggressive strategies, while leaving future options open. A lower level threat of punishment at the initial stage of escalation provides more flexibility, given that it can be used merely to send a signal of further action. The intentions of the messages ought to be clearly declared, given the possibility that the adversaries may initiate new levels of hostile moves in a reaction even to cautiously taken measures. The frequency and magnitude of coercive actions and counteractions might grow, but the process can be halted, and even be reversed, prior to explosion into all-out conflict (Patchen, 1988).

The gradual escalation may be stabilized by hostile, yet predictable, patterns of interaction that are governed by the implicit or explicit rules of the game. A controlled mode of escalation is more easily managed to avert reaching a threshold for initiating a catastrophic spiral. In US–Cuba relations after the 1962 Missile Crisis, the American government did not resort to military action, being content with the four decades' old economic embargo. Despite its rhetoric and occasional emergence of contentious issues, the Castro government in Havana largely held back provocative action that might raise any security concerns in Washington.

There are various types of condition that inhibit the increasing level of escalation. In general, stability is likely to be fostered by the necessity to maintain strong social bonds as well as the fear of a dangerous escalation. The need for contentious tactics is minimized by the existence of conflict management institutions and forums that cultivate conciliatory norms. Broadly based interdependent relationships serve to buttress stability instead of uncontrolled enmity. A short-term intensification of conflict is, however, more likely to happen in the event of a power imbalance that generates perceptions of a quick victory. In addition, a lack of options, combined with high expectations about a successful fight, encourages the parties to go for a more contentious approach.

While adversaries have different choices about escalating their commitment, non-violent tactics are preferred as a more viable means of confrontation in more stable relationships. The rules of a struggle can be transformed by accepting institutionalized channels for protest. For tactical reasons, some struggles may transition from violent fighting to non-violent confrontation and vice versa. During its four decades old campaign for independence, the Basque separatist movement ETA in Spain has occasionally switched its tactics to declare the abandonment of terrorist attacks, with the emergence of a more liberal government, only to resume the armed struggle later.

Entrapment

After a sustained period of escalation, a conflict may end up being trapped in a longer course of action that is justified by an increased commitment to the pursuit of goals. A malign conflict spiral maintains high cost struggles with no chance of either party backing away. Once the thresholds have been crossed for the intensification of overt coercion and outright violence, a conflict is more likely to be entrenched. In a stalemate, perpetually polarized and malignant processes are accepted as a normal and natural reality.

The Sri Lankan government has been locked in armed battles, over the last two decades, with Tamil guerrilla forces, characterized by repeated territorial gains and losses. The conflict originally started with a protest against the government's exclusion of the minority language from an official status, leading to communal uprisings by the Hindu Tamil minority in the late 1950s. Once the conflict turned into deadly military insurgencies with the establishment of well-financed Tamil Tiger rebel forces and attacks on government troops in 1983, the armed struggle has defied any logic of sensible compromise despite various attempts for external mediation.

The government is not willing to give into the rebels' demand for an independent Tamil homeland in the north and east, being undeterred by the death of more than 60,000 people and damage to the economy in one of South Asia's potentially prosperous societies. The exhaustive nature of internal warfare is well characterized by the government campaign 'war for peace', being matched by guerrilla forces' counter-offensive with the atrocious killings of civilians and assassination of political and military elites. Even cease-fires and tentative political agreements reached between the government and rebels in late 2002 easily faded away in an atmosphere of deep mistrust, only serving as an interval to re-charge armed strength. The entrapment has been marked by a periodic switch between low intensity fighting and all-out war.

Reflecting various characteristics of a war of attrition, a stalemate and impasse are typical conditions of entrapment. When increased demand levels by adversaries reach the limit of concessions, heightened resistance to further compromise brings a deadlock (Faure, 2005). Neither side has been neutralized or destroyed without losing the capability to fight completely. Bailing out of a costly war on baseless commitments is difficult due to too much investment. However, the main goals may not be obtainable despite all the dedicated efforts. Frustration is attributed to the recognition of little prospect for a clear-cut victory, following the initial underestimation of the other party's capacity and determination to get involved in an entrenched struggle as well as the inflated estimates of one's own commitments.

Although it may belong to the end stage of escalation, entrapment is not necessarily part of an escalatory spiral (Brockner and Rubin, 1985). Whereas each partisan may not be psychologically ready to escalate a degree of commitment to fight further, adversaries may feel that their past struggle has been in vain if they do not continue to devote themselves to a chosen course of action. If someone is absorbed in a certain cause, then they are less likely to be concerned that their decision would increase the duration of being embroiled in the impasse.

Being stuck in a particular type of hostile exchange, each party does not possess an ability to draw back and assess the larger picture. Being too close to daily experiences and operations prohibits the development of awareness about dysfunctional behavioural patterns. It is easy to underestimate an opponent's will by overlooking the propensity of one's attacks to stiffen others' resolve. In spite of short-term gains, longer consequences can be harmful and damaging. In situations of entrapment, immediate gains are easily reversed by future losses.

Irrational decisions continue to be made to conduct a violent struggle that has cost more than gains that one still hopes to obtain (Pillar, 1990). Even though they are no longer winning, it is difficult for adversaries to give up their original objectives. When the commitment is emotionally binding, each party is willing to tolerate costs and risks beyond acceptable levels.

Although desires of winning a war may dwindle, a destructive spiral of conflict attains a momentum of its own. As original causes behind antagonism become irrelevant to the persisting struggle, strategies shift from winning to not losing by sustaining the status quo. Reversing a chosen policy, along with the admission of deficiencies, is also difficult not only politically but also psychologically. The necessity to save face in the eyes of others and look strong becomes a driving force behind sticking to the existing course of action. Decision makers are more anxious about leaving an impression of being co-opted with harm to their domestic influence.

Irrational decision making stays rooted, along with a non-revocable commitment to losing causes, even though withdrawal presents a less perilous future. The benefit that may never be realized rationalizes the expended costs. Likewise, the visions, fixated on victory, act to undervalue the anticipated expenses, while exaggerating potential rewards. In addition, at this point, an increasing desire to damage an adversary overshadows the necessity to minimize one's overall losses.

The deception of one's own group members can be used to underestimate the extent of the sacrifice made to achieve victory. Unforeseen difficulties arise from desertions by allies and an opponent's stubbornness, but defeats are frequently concealed as mere temporary setbacks from public views for the mobilization efforts. Secrecy about losses hidden by a centralized leadership misleads the population or group members to believe that victory remains 'just around the corner'. Information guarded in the absence of transparency assists in disguising military setbacks occurring in remote areas, as happened to Japanese armies following Pacific battles during World War II.

The motives of messengers conveying any bad news are often questioned in an internal deception that is designed to hide weaknesses and boost morale. Ultimately, it can create an obstacle for ending armed hostilities. Even though the Pakistani army absorbed heavier losses and casualties in its 1965 War than its Indian counterpart, government reports had misguidedly glorified their military's admirable performance. This misinformation later provoked a backlash against an agreement on cease-fire and an initiative for mediated settlement since the public did not see the cessation of hostilities as necessary in a winning war.

In the Iran–Iraq war waged in the 1980s, a history of miraculous victories and courageous acts of heroism functioned as propaganda to distort objective reality and even the leaderships' own subjective assessments about the costs of suffering. Inaccurate historical records may shore up myths concerning the party's own invincibility (Blalock, 1989). Irrational decisions may be legitimized by ideological or some other standards that are external to the conflict. A nationalist cause's righteousness rooted in mythology contributes to the rationalization of one's own claims over an adversary's, fortifying a will to fight. The strength in the myth of invincibility stems from ideological simplicity. The pursuit of an absolute goal, for example, based on unchallenging values, is less likely undermined by the perceptions of setbacks.

Self-perpetuating decision-making rules

A failing course of action in entrapment persists due to the need to justify previously chosen investments (Brockner and Rubin, 1985). The expended resources are rationalized via the notion of 'too much invested to quit' in conjunction with a strongly felt need to recover past expenditures. Emotional obsession is made to validate irretrievable expenses, further expanding the gap between perceived and actual costs. It would surely be unthinkable to accept the accumulated sacrifices for nothing or an unworthy compromise. As is reflected in the Bush administration's policy towards the war in Iraq, a natural inertia reins in decision-making during the entrapment stage, at which point continued obligations may reflect active support for bottomless spending and troop deployments.

The determinants of entrapment include decision rules in which the degree of allegiance to the previously selected course of action increases automatically without more conscious efforts towards its reversal. Reflecting on an inevitable choice of a self-sustaining situation, the decision makers' expectations about the likelihood of goal attainment no longer influence views about continuing struggles. Future suffering may be considered relatively bearable and trivial in comparison with past investment in a very costly conflict.

Since an escalated commitment is not ingrained in a calculation of the appropriateness of keeping up the fight, the higher price becomes even more of a reason for carrying on the struggle. The increasing loss is able to justify both psychological and political sacrifices only if it yields a bigger reward. Typical entrapment decision making does not, however, consider the prospects for an optimal outcome. Actions are less motivated by rational reasons with a deepening degree of emotional attachment to the fight. The strength of the driving forces toward staying in entrapment is, in part, related to the degree of the desire to avoid the costs associated with having given up one's past investment.

The limitations on the number of decision choices in conflict entrapment are well illustrated by the 'dollar auction' game (Teger, 1980). The bidder's calculation is dictated by the rules of the game, indicating that the second highest bidder is obliged to pay the auctioneer the bidding amount for nothing in return. In the endless bidding war, the two competitors attempt to outbid each other whenever either of them is put in the subordinate situation. The second highest bidder is always entrapped in the dollar auction, due to the irretrievable amount invested in the unobtainable goal. This dynamic is continuously escalating the bidding. It is difficult to quit if the parties believe that the benefits of success and final victory are only garnered at the very end of the process. The unbearable costs can be transformed into 'investments' only if there is a prospect for victory.

Sustainability of entrapment

If the prolonged acceptance of costs is no longer legitimized or durable, any further devotion of resources to the goal, which is not likely to be achieved, can be interpreted as irretrievable. It is impractical to sustain undesirable struggles indefinitely, under growing pessimism, in the midst of unexpected difficulties. The necessity of ending a risky game may arise as a result of changes in balance between the subjective value of goal attainment and additional costs. When a substantial investment may not yield any valuable outcome, policy makers eventually have to grapple with the evidence of mistakes being made (Iklé, 2005).

The price ultimately reaches a threshold for making continued personnel and material devotion no longer bearable. The fatigue factor predominates, owing to difficulties in recruiting new members, declining logistical support, or the increasing vulnerability of a large population to an adversary's bombing campaign. The uneven distribution of expense among group members increases a potential for internal divisions, hurting the ability to fight effectively with enemies. The original belief systems, embedded at the time of conflict initiation, undergo modification. The decision relating to the US withdrawal from Vietnam in 1972 went through various adjustments in response to political, emotional, and financial costs.

Overall, the resilience of each group's cost absorption is affected by the level and nature of support that each garners from its constituents and external allies. Difficulties in ending the struggle come from a refusal to make concessions following long-term suffering. The continued reassessments of subsequent situations are essential to acknowledging the initial underestimation of the total costs and the duration of conflict. The Soviet retreat from Afghanistan in the late 1980s, for example, was seen as inevitable, owing to the invader's weakened ability and unwillingness to accept further absorption of massive expenses over a prolonged period of time.

Internal politics and group dynamics

The internal dynamics of a party, as affected by inter-group interaction, have an impact on conflict escalation and entrapment. The elite has to manage a difficult domestic political landscape while simultaneously responding to an international crisis. Internal factors of escalation include the selection of militant leaders, the ascendance of radical subgroups, the supremacy of extremist values or ideologies, and uncompromising organizational goals. In particular, the failure to effectively challenge a hard line faction is ascribed to intra-factional polarization among doves as well as the successful mobilization of partisan supporters in favour of hawkish factions.

Factions that bear an uneven share of the burdens of continuing struggles are inclined to look for ways in which to resist the prolonging of conflict. The patterns of gains and losses are directly connected to the morale of different segments of the population. In an enduring conflict, those who carry the greatest costs and receive the smallest benefits are likely to be the least powerful members.

Engagement in intense struggles with an external enemy becomes a safety valve for dissipating internal tensions. Indeed, aggressive actions are encouraged by the depiction of the enemy as a grave threat. Intra-group differences are often minimized in the midst of intense hostile inter-group exchanges. The efforts towards internal unity may focus on appealing to common goals against an external enemy. International conflict escalation distracts attention away from an internal challenge, contributing to rallying support behind the incumbent leadership.

However, it is difficult to keep unity upon facing an uphill battle which would eventually bring about a major defeat. By invading the Falklands and entering a war with Britain in 1982, the repressive Argentinean military *junta* was initially successful in diverting public attention from a devastating economic crisis and large-scale civil unrest. When Argentina had to confront a humiliating defeat, public enthusiasm with the war quickly evaporated along with a deepened mistrust of the ruling military elite. Despite its attempt to stay on by toying with long-standing sentiments towards the islands, the Argentinean military dictatorship lost its grip on power.

While increasing cohesiveness within a group can perpetuate external conflict, threats from outside enemies strengthen the control of coercive machinery by the authoritarian leadership. External threats are often utilized as an opportunity to manage internal tensions, even increasing an ideological bond. When the leadership is threatened or challenged by an immediate crisis, it takes more extreme actions to build a sense of solidarity, which may, in turn, create a false perception of psychological security within the group. Especially, a contentious interaction with an external enemy rationalizes extreme views within a group.

Relatively little in-group diversity tends to discourage raising any question about severe action especially in combination with organizational developments that restrict control over extreme factions. The rapid escalation of conflict can be more easily initiated and sustained by groups that have the strong cohesiveness. A lack of internal diversity in opinions is ascribed to a demand for conformity to exclusive belief systems. Initiating escalatory moves may depend on a strong consensus on the collective goals of defeating the enemy as well as a high level of grievances. Group members are pressured to adopt a hostile out-group image and develop a perception of an adversary's destructive motives toward them. The validation of group values reinforces a heightened commitment to the goal along with a stronger conviction in a victory.

Decision making, based on group solidarity, often promotes extreme choices by not permitting an opportunity to discuss an alternative course of action. Little internal diversity produces a similar response to events in drowning out dissident voices. The majority swamps a cautious, reasonable minority voice in seeking the homogeneity needed to concentrate on a fight with external adversaries. The fear of being labelled a 'traitor' also suppresses doubts, questions, and challenges about the legitimacy of contentious tactics. Meanwhile, the dissemination of information by media arouses negative evaluations of outsiders and institutes hawkish positions. Therefore, the intolerance of alternative views about the enemies, in part, ascribed to a lack of internal diversity, provides a basis for escalatory commitment to engage in more confrontational behaviour.

During escalation, changes in conflict orientation are likely to reflect the emergence of the militant leadership and the replacement of doves by hawks. The nature of partisan support and organizational goals go through dramatic alterations at different sub-stages of escalation. The new organizational objectives may help hawkish factions surge to implement the goals of defeating enemies. Above all, hawkish factions may feel a threat to their identity by accepting moderate positions. Mutual hostilities between factions may be directed toward causing harm to each other. In the 1994 Rwandan genocide, extremist Hutus assaulted and even massacred a number of moderate Hutus who did not join their violent campaign against the Tutsis.

In the Algerian civil war, two main guerrilla forces quickly emerged after the government intervened to cancel elections for the purpose of blocking the Islamic Salvation Front (FIS) Party's electoral victory in December 1991. The guerrillas initially targeted the army and police, but the insurgent movement began to diverge after some groups started attacking civilians. Eventually, the Armed Islamic Group (GIA), drawing support from the towns, declared a war on the FIS and its supporters when the imprisoned leadership of the FIS accepted the government's offer for negotiations in 1994. At that point, the other insurgent group, the Islamic Armed Movement (MIA) based in the mountains, was re-aligned with various smaller groups to form the FIS-Loyalist Islamic Salvation Army (AIS). Not only in Algeria, but also in Burundi and other African civil wars, factional differences often result in the restructuring of existing groups and the formation of new splinter groups that face the same adversaries, but employ opposing strategies and have different constituent bases.

In leadership struggle, contentious tactics are advocated as if to prove loyalty to group norms. A militant faction does not want to look weak or submissive, and so may step up coercive activities. The strong hand of militants, completely devoid of interest in resolution, is visible in inhumane attitudes that ritualize violence without any remorse. Such methods of brutality as beheadings, designed to impose maximum fear, have been adopted by radical insurgent groups in Iraq.

The threat from militant rivals in a leadership struggle forces the moderate to take a harsh position in support of escalation. The differences in decision making may not necessarily arise from the goals of, but from the choice of means for, struggle. Maintaining a costly fight is likely to bring about an increase in the number of hawkish members more committed to violent struggle. This change in the composition of a partisan group, or a decision-making body, expands a support base for more radical factions.

The impact of group radicalization

Various group membership characteristics re-define an intra-party political terrain in establishing relations with outside groups. In discussion about different priorities relating to a war, the relative influence of military and intelligence agencies fluctuates according to the degree of an emphasis on the necessity for coercive inducements. In inner fighting, extremist groups seize upon an external tension as an opportunity to outrival their moderate opponents with expanded resource bases and control over coercive institutions. In conducting their campaign of violence against the Sri Lankan state, the Tamil guerrilla leadership rejected and annihilated moderate Tamil politicians who sought a dialogue with the government via assassinations.

A widening conflict brings about structural changes in relation to group representation as a result of the reallocation of decision-making power and positions. A continuing fight gives more opportunities to those who are predisposed to intense violence and who express the total dedication to an exclusive group value. In addition, violent conflict presents militia group members with an opportunity for upward mobility especially in combat operations and for different kinds of leadership roles that are not available during peacetime.

Consequently, militant subgroups have vested interests in violent conflict that creates a new status and material compensation, even helping to develop a sense of new meaning for their lives. The incentives for upholding violent struggles are reinforced by the personalization of a group conflict that carries not only a new status but also honour. Members of Hezbollah in Lebanon, Hamas in Palestine, and Brothers in Solidarity in Egypt have developed a high level of principle and dedication, even surrendering their personal well-being to group causes. Especially for the underdogs, the martyr images, associated with suicide bombings and self-punitive tactics, such as hunger strikes during imprisonment, glorify the group's cause. At the height of their struggle against the policies of Conservative British Prime Minister Margaret Thatcher, imprisoned Irish Republican Army members chose to die from hunger strikes in 1981, further radicalizing their constituent base.

The widening participation of extremists generates rivalry between new and old militant groups over the radicalization of tactics adopted for total destruction of enemies with the creation of chaos. Numerous new splinter groups have been created, in Iraq, to radicalize the methods of fighting in a total war against common enemies, namely, the Iraqi government and US forces. With the formation of more groups, factional rivalry naturally develops animosities inside the insurgency movement. By directing its attacks toward the general population beyond Iraqi and US occupational forces, al Qaeda has further factionalized the civil war situation. The attacks by al Qaeda on other Islamic insurgent groups have even resulted in collaboration between other Sunni insurgents and the US occupation forces in western Iraq such as the Anja province.

The emergence of new radical groups and the prevalence of those in charge of a more intense means of violence generate newly aroused will at the height of an escalation phase. Even when moderate groups may have larger numbers of members, extremist groups can have a significant impact on conflict escalation with the use of more severe tactics. The entire group's goals can shift to the defeat and even annihilation of an opponent, along with the social endorsement of aggression. Escalation is most likely to be sustained by the rise of militant extremists in competition for leadership and their key decision making roles within a hawkish organizational setting.

Polarizing attitudes of the extreme leadership, accompanied by a radical shift in the public mood and the surge of militant groups, can catalyse counter-responses from the other party. The increased influence of a hawkish faction in one party gives the upper hand to the position of its counterpart on the adversarial side, making intransigence become more entrenched. Fluctuation in the management of long-term tensions between Israel and Palestine is, in part, traced to the difficulties related to controlling radicalized groups such as settlers, orthodox Jews and Islamic Jihad whose actions have often sparked off direct confrontation between the two opposing communities.

Part V
De-escalation
and Termination

De-escalation Dynamics

The initiation of a peace process may follow adversaries' acknowledgement of a stalemate, leading to their willingness to downsize and even abandon fighting. Motivational aspects of de-escalation represent a desire to end conflict, combined with some sort of cautious optimism or belief in the possibility of solutions through negotiation. The readiness for a new move is normally reached with the realization of a limited capacity to push for any gains through force or political alliances. Most importantly, an adversary's resistance contributes to difficulty in obtaining unilateral concessions. In addition, bold approaches can be adopted due to not only changes in an external environment but also the emergence of a new public opinion and a resurgence of a moderate political leadership in a power struggle.

In general, de-escalation is considered to entail a multidimensional process geared to rescinding the effects of conflict entrapment. This process is affected by the preceding conditions of conflict escalation that have changed interparty relations through efforts to destroy each other. This chapter investigates how and when de-escalation starts, eventually leading to conflict resolution.

What is de-escalation?

Transition toward de-escalation can be characterized by the adoption of new strategies following a perceptional adjustment derived from a modification of enemy images and stereotypes. In essence, confrontation and contentious tactics are substituted with conciliatory gestures. In de-escalation decisions, each party may have to rebalance goal hierarchies; some goals may even need to be sacrificed to accommodate the other's essential needs. Winning the struggle outright at this stage is regarded as unrealistic, owing to the exhaustion of resources. Scaling down aspirations is one of the indicators of seriousness in negotiating a settlement.

The identification of mutually shared goals brings about a shift from competitive to collaborative interaction. The potential for cooperative exchanges correlates to the exploration of common interests and values. The realization of mutual interdependence assists in reframing a conflict as a shared problem, in tandem with a search for superordinate goals. Seeking national unity is accompanied by an intense military struggle, for instance, in Mozambique and Angola. Breaking out of a vicious escalation cycle is essential to subduing the fear of the uncertainty surrounding new initiatives, as well as the resentments of loss or harm caused by past enemy conduct.

Psychological changes include a decrease in the negative expectations that are perpetuated by self-fulfilling prophecies and the predisposition towards hostile intent. A consistent de-escalatory move is geared to replace well-entrenched, heavily distorted 'enemy' images that have kept the struggle going. The formation of new attitudes would be based on information in support of changes in an opponent's hostile motivation as well as reduction in adversarial activities (Pruitt and Kim, 2004). Empathy is a prerequisite to eradicating psychological barriers ingrained in past grievances; surmounting an enemy's aggressor image helps remove difficulties in making concessions.

Interactive dimensions of de-escalation

The initiation of a de-escalation move needs to be separated from the management of escalation at a sustainable level. When full-scale adjustment is not feasible, conflicting parties may return to a less intense, more sustainable level of fighting. Renewed fighting can take place for the purpose of strengthening a bargaining position or making maximum gains prior to the termination of hostilities. During ceasefire negotiations designed to end the Korean War in 1953, for example, North Korea and its Chinese ally were engaged in intense battles with US and South Korean forces towards even small territorial gains (Boose, 2000).

For strategic reasons, a conflict can be carried on at its existing level in a more manageable manner without further escalation. In fact, long standing conflicts in Colombia, Kurdistan, Uyghur in China, Burma, Chechnya and many other places remain at a low intensity level in the absence of any visible signs of settlement. Each antagonist can be engaged in preparation for winding down a struggle or in buying the time needed to search for an opportunity to achieve a negotiated settlement. When vested interests generate inertia for the existing course of action, a switch to a new decision mode is difficult.

Decisions on continuing versus quitting in major armed conflicts between regional rivals (such as the series of Indo–Pakistan wars in 1947, 1965, and 1971; the Iran–Iraq war between 1980 and 1988) may necessitate complicated calculations originating from different types of balance sheet. Decision makers' choices are restricted by anticipated costs and diminishing resources, in conjunction with the accumulated hurts and sacrifices. High casualties and destruction certainly correlate to the strong desire to end armed conflict. If one party suffers more than the other, those absorbing heavier losses are more likely to be attracted to an immediate secession of hostilities.

De-escalation process

Each conflict's history contains different benchmarks that are context-specific, even though some are less clear, more subjective and ambiguous. A mix of various conditions characterize de-escalation in different circumstances of conflicts, ranging from the cyclical civil wars in Liberia (1989–2003), Sierra Leone (1991–2002) and Angola (1975–2002) to inter-state rivalry between India and Pakistan (since 1947). In a map of the conflict terrain, major 'landmarks' are comprised of the commencing and ending of physical violence, and other turning points that alter the character of the relationship between the parties. Various types of events and actions function as 'signposts' from which escalatory movements can be switched to the opposite, de-escalatory direction. The moves toward de-escalation are indicated by the concession and relaxation of punitive sanctions.

The impact of violence from escalation is likely to be reminiscent in each step toward de-escalatory interaction; mitigating past grievances is associated with undoing other harmful effects. In a linear, symmetric model of conflict dynamics, the abatement of intense, hostile interactions is accompanied by taking steps away from the preceding point of violence (Bonoma, 1975). Indeed, winding down from previous military escalation is considered to be traversing back over a number of already crossed thresholds such as the intensification of assault and occupation of territories.

An armed conflict between India and Pakistan (May to July 1999) in the Kargil region of Kashmir ended with the restoration of the previous status quo. Pakistani soldiers and Kashmiri militants captured Indian army posts, but Indian forces repelled the infiltrators and recaptured the posts. In the midst of international pressure on Pakistan to back down, India re-possessed Kargil. Whereas the territorial status quo was recovered with the cessation of armed hostilities, the incident can be seen as the re-ignition of the 1965 Indo–Pakistani War that also ended in stalemate.

In a more durable settlement, a de-escalatory move, from adversarial patterns of interaction to collaboration, entails a qualitatively dissimilar form of action visible during escalation—being typified by the substitution of denunciations and rebuffs with requests and proposals. In ending the 27 year-old civil war (2002), the Angolan government promised the members of guerrilla forces monetary incentives and job training for their demobilization as well as government positions for the leadership. The de-escalatory dynamic is characterized by the cessation of imposing rising costs on adversaries in tandem with the reinstatement of past pledges and remunerations. In an inverse form of de-escalation, preceding steps and policies are overturned to reduce the deleterious effects.

De-escalatory spirals invite reciprocal and incremental reduction in coercive action. As a hiatus, various steps can be halted to turn in a direction indicating tentatively heightened tensions. In general, however, previously adopted forms of behaviour need to be abandoned in reinstating a beneficial relationship. A de-escalatory spiral tends to be regarded as inverse to escalation dynamics, within which each round of exchanges corresponds to increasing damage to an opponent. In unwinding hostilities, sanctions are applied with a diminished scale over time in contrast with escalation involving the application of punishment at an increasing magnitude (Bonoma, 1975).

The inversion of all, or most, of the previous policies results in 'restoring' the earlier status quo such as some form of military disengagement. In a short lived crisis—especially one that has not involved major casualties and grievances—de-escalation and termination can be more easily accomplished by taking steps in such a manner as to turn around the direction of escalation dynamics (Kahn, 1965). Such downward steps as the withdrawal of troops are the converse process of the escalatory deployment of troops. During the Cuban Missile Crisis, the Soviets withdrew facilities and equipment for constructing their missile bases, whereas the American government eventually removed its missiles from Turkey. The Chinese invasion of Vietnam in 1979, meanwhile, was allegedly to 'teach lessons' in response to the Vietnamese military intervention in Cambodia, which toppled the Khmer Rouge regime accused of an estimated 1.5 million deaths through execution, starvation, and forced labour. Much of the military and political equation in Indochina did not change, however, being accompanied by China's quick withdrawal after its brief occupation of part of Northern Vietnam.

In contrast with the above cases, conciliation preceded by a protracted struggle is not likely merely to imply going back over past steps, because an accommodation process entails the development of different psychological and strategic patterns of influence. Even if high levels of coercive activities and violence are permanently withdrawn, emotional residues, as well as social and political legacies (following colonialism and ethnic atrocities), cannot be easily annulled by simply reinstating the pre-escalation state. Many psychological and structural conditions are not temporarily revocable nor are they easily subject to alteration without taking bold new initiatives.

In addition, retracing the initial, escalatory steps is basically not possible, for every conflict situation is created and recreated by a voluntaristic aspect of human behaviour often in an unpredictable manner (Mitchell, 1999). As exemplified by the continuation of decades-long civil wars in Colombia and Sri Lanka, temporary cessation of armed hostilities and negotiations did not bring about durable solutions in the event of renewed violence. This observation invites a thorough examination of circumstances under which adversaries are fully committed to a successful transition toward a normalized relationship.

Even when yielding and accommodation are introduced to invert such escalation tactics as intimidation, the contextual differences can be substantial enough to block any reinstitution of the old relationship. Simply undoing past steps may also be unproductive if it does not incorporate consideration of new opportunities and risks derived from the internal changes of each party. Given that de-escalation elements are likely to diverge, new types of initiative are needed other than simply invalidating the past occurrence (Mitchell, 1999). This is essential, in particular, for overcoming the legacies of brutal fighting to impose one's power over another.

Overall, a conciliatory process can be much more ambiguous than escalation, owing to the psychological and organizational impact of past hostilities on each protagonist and the relationships between them. In fact, one side's withdrawal of hostile intentions and strategies may not be interpreted by its adversaries as originally intended. The response of each party in de-escalation will often carry more subtle messages in contrast with the coercion and pressure more directly felt and expressed by antagonists in escalation.

The long-term consolidation of rewarding relationships can be a slower process than escalation, especially when it takes time to prevail over suspicion. In general, the time span for surmounting a high level of tension differs according to both internal conflict dynamics and its external context. In some situations such as the Cuban Missile Crisis, both the escalation and de-escalation phases were rapid and ended within a few weeks, compared with the almost year-long Berlin Blockade (between 24 June 1948 and 11 May 1949) that served as one of the first major crises in the early period of the Cold War. The methods for, and timing of, the introduction of various measures therefore affects either the accelerating or decelerating of a conciliatory process.

New situations prompted by the continuing struggle modify the dynamics of the conflict system as well as the parties themselves. In winding down the Suez Crisis, inverting intense military hostilities faced unexpected turns and diplomatic intervention. Egypt's decision of 26 July 1956 to nationalize the Suez Canal served as a pretext for a military attack on Egypt by Britain, France, and Israel on 29 October 1956. Even though the operation to take the canal was militarily quick, a ceasefire had to be declared eight days later, following the UN General Assembly's condemnation. An unanticipated threat of US sanctions and heavy international pressure brought about the withdrawal of the British and French troops within two months. While the attack on Egypt did not yield the goal of removing President Nasser from power, the British and their allies experienced a diplomatic fiasco with the collapse of the British Cabinet and the weakening of the French alliance with the United States.

Manifold actions, especially in long-term civil wars with the participation of multiple actors, are frequently inconsistent, suggesting that transformations do not progress in a unidirectional fashion (Bar-Tal, 2000). De-escalation may instead turn to a new path rather than moving backward to the beginning point of uprisings or clashes. Whereas unique markers and indicators exist for de-escalation thresholds, any new moves need to be adapted to different circumstances.

In protracted conflicts, therefore, diminishing the previous level of hostilities is essential, but climbing up 'a war-to-peace staircase' is likely to entail qualitative relationship changes (Hurwitz, 1991). The 1973 Yom Kippur War dramatically transformed relations among the major protagonists and their allies. The Israelis' continued military offence in violation of a ceasefire, largely negotiated between American and Soviet governments on 22 October, trapped the Egyptian Third Army east of the Suez Canal. In diffusing the crisis, the Nixon administration gained the upper hand by inducing Egyptian President Anwar Sadat to drop his request for Soviet assistance. Unwinding the war brought about the shift in the Egyptian allegiance to the Americans and conciliation with Israel, subsequently dividing the Arabic world with the destruction of its unity.

The conditions for de-escalation

Lowering intense conflict activities often takes place in the legacies of overt coercion and severe violence. In this context, structural elements in de-escalation are associated with a mutually damaging stalemate embedded in an unacceptable status quo. As decision-making reflects a leader's perceptions of structural conditions, painful stalemates have to be acknowledged and felt strongly by both sides (with the acceptance of desirability for non-coercive solutions). In order to act on their perceptions, decision makers have to be motivated to see the current costs and pending disasters as a psychological threshold.

An equilibrium in coercive capabilities between adversaries produces a long-term stalemate, consequently both physical and psychological fatigue. Emotional exhaustion and economic devastation are inevitable in the high cost conflict that can easily overwhelm any possible future gains. A costly dead-end stalemate, often called mutually hurting, produces the feeling that if we do not negotiate now, it will get worse. In a nutshell, a painful deadlock is more easily noticed when both parties find themselves entrapped in their attempts to advance their objectives in vain (Zartman, 2000).

The perception of mounting costs, combined with the fatigue of long struggles, results in a stronger desire for ending conflict. In addition, the infeasibility of winning encourages parties to increase the desire to look for ways to bail out of the fight. Overall, the small value of anticipated enemy concessions, in conjunction with a low probability of an adversary's retreat, diminishes the significance of any possible gain (Pillar, 1990). The attractiveness of goals is negatively correlated to increasing expenses reached at an unbearable level; priority is put on the minimization of loss vis-à-vis maximization of gains. The costs of conflict outweigh any possible benefit especially when unilateral gains may not be achievable even with additional investments.

The leaders ponder a major shift from the pursuit of victory to a search for a negotiated settlement under various circumstances. Particular conditions within both parties (related to motivational, resource, and fatigue factors) as well as relations between them (as affected by relative changes in fighting capabilities) must be met in order to move out of a stalemate.[1] Motivational aspects are weakened owing to waning internal support for continuing conflict and external pressure for ending hostilities as well as fatigue accompanied by increasing costs (Blalock, 1989). Such external conditions as the failure of alliance building and difficulties in dividing and co-opting opponents encourage the development of a conviction that a conflict cannot be won and is too costly.

International and internal political oppositions produce pressure for the de-escalation of conflict (such as the US war in Vietnam and the Soviet war in Afghanistan). The experience of severe costs, if not economic but political and moral, accompanied by a failure to contain the Intifada was often pointed out as a reason for the Israeli interest in the 1993 Oslo Peace Accord with the Palestinian Liberation Organization (PLO) led by Yasser Arafat. At the same time, the PLO also had to search for a different non-militant path after experiencing crucial setbacks in their diplomatic support base (presented by the break-up of the Soviet Union) and the severance of funding by moderate Arab states angered by Arafat's pro-Iraqi stance during the Gulf War (Lieberfeld, 1999).

The leaders' evaluations of power relations play an important role in the development of a conciliatory mentality. The perception of more or less equal power distribution may help parties agree to come to the negotiating table with a desire to control an entrenched battle. Not only a failure to impose unilateral solutions by a stronger party but also favourable changes in the power balance for a weaker party following many years of fighting serve as conditions for a negotiated settlement. A stronger party may be forced to reach the realization that defeating the other is too costly or not feasible any more.

Above all, an unequal shift in the power balance may give rise to an opportunity to reassess the cost of continuing stalemates. The protagonists may feel that it would be advantageous to enter a negotiation from a position of strength. For a weaker side, a continuing disparity impels interest in a settlement process that helps avert an impending military catastrophe (as exemplified by UNITA rebels in Angola after military setbacks in early 2002).

The loss of optimism for winning may justify at least cautious moves for a negotiated settlement. Egypt's defeat in the 1967 Six-Day war led to a yearning for victory, but yet another debacle in the Yom Kippur war in 1973 eventually led to a decision to give up the goal of regaining its lost territory through military means. A motivation to overcome the status quo and also evade the worst increases the craving for successful negotiation. The new perception of difficulties in a winnable conflict and pressure to forestall loss in a military campaign are further strengthened by the waning enthusiasm of allies (for example, the refusal of the Kremlin to provide offensive weapons for Arab states) or difficulties in keeping one's own alliance intact.

Leaders have different degrees of willingness to contemplate a peaceful resolution on the basis of their ability to further absorb the imposed costs and to weaken the enemy support base. The perceived risk of running out of resources increases a desire to put an end to the conflict. Paying too high a price following a recent or incipient national crisis increases incentives for settling conflict. External pressure or support in favour of negotiation can provide an excuse for expressing a willingness to seek a compromise.

In the 1965 Indo–Pakistani war, attacks and bold counter-attacks during the months of August and September eventually culminated in a stalemate characterized by each side holding some of the other's territory. The UN Security Council's call for an unconditional cease-fire ended the war on September 23. Mediation under the auspices of Soviet Premier Alexey Kosygin helped both warring parties agree to withdraw to the pre-war lines. Prior to this arrangement, Pakistan's military leader Ayub Khan had a strong desire to avoid driving the two countries into an all out war due to his country's near financial depletion. On the other hand, the Indian prime minister received a report from the commanding general that India could not possibly win the war due to a heavy frontline loss of tanks and other military hardware. Both sides became weary of the continuing loss and danger of being dragged into unrecoverable military disasters.

Rational decision makers are most likely to accept co-existence rather than being locked in a conflict for a prolonged period of time, eventually leading to catastrophe. In general, disasters approaching both sides more or less simultaneously create structural conditions for incentives to steer away from the existing course of actions. If the original goals are not easily attainable, it is more reasonable to pursue less ambitious goals with acceptable burdens. The assumptions of 'rational' policy makers centre on motivations for exploring less costly alternatives, being receptive to negotiations. Decision-making actors are inclined to look for favourable terms for ending the costly stalemate when they are perceptive of its hazards.

The convergence of interest among primary conflict parties in settlement rather than continued fighting serves as propitious timing. By taking steps to scale down conflict, protagonists can favourably react to new opportunities. The expected utility of terminating hostilities increases with the low probability of victory as well as small stakes for war (Goemans, 2000). The unbearable costs without any end in sight are likely to push decision makers to search for new options that carry a lesser cost and produce more likely gains than a continued coercive struggle.

Positive incentives for new initiatives

The perceived probability of heavy costs may not always initiate efforts to search for a more constructive course of action. The fear of defeat can keep the conflict going once a struggle is under way. If seeking a way out is difficult, a losing party 'would rather delay the moment of defeat and also want to hang on in the hope that something might turn up' (de Bono, 1985: 147). An ability to design an exit strategy without defeat is critical in encouraging a break in the status quo mentality.

A breakthrough ushering in new decisions would also be resisted by psychological difficulties stemming from discarding goals (instituted as indispensable or even revered). Once military means have been mobilized along with a call for sacrifice, it is difficult to dismantle them. The tendency to stay on course is reinforced by a strong desire for revenge as well as the persistence of a militant sentiment. Pride commonly precludes giving in to 'bullies' without a fight to the end. Psychological barriers include a collective group instinct to seek pleasure in demonizing and taking revenge on opponents as well as glorifying past wrongs which are condemned by not only an adversary but even by neutral observers.

The cognitive state of decision makers does not easily permit abandoning the cause committed to sustaining protracted struggles. Thus mental adjustment is needed for overcoming the psychological burdens of past damage. Pessimistic views about the current situation will strengthen the perception that the conflict is dysfunctional. While anticipated costs serve as a negative motivator for staying on the entrapment course, positive inducements (such as a return of lost territory in a war on the condition of reduced hostilities) produce an optimism about talks and hope in ending a deadlock. After years of failed attempts to destroy the IRA, the British government finally turned to negotiating tactics around 1990, believing that enough concessions such as acceptance of unification of Northern Ireland with the Republic of Ireland would draw substantial political support from moderate Catholics in the initiation of a negotiated settlement (Dixon, 2007).

Being accompanied by a benevolent cycle of an exchange of concessions, a strong willingness to seek mutual accommodation overshadows pessimism. Events confirming a new opportunity can bring about direct contact with people from the other side. This optimism may either increase or fade away at the initial stage of negotiations. The jolt to stimulate rethinking (following unexpected positive changes) generates an enthusiasm with exploring a way out to enter negotiation.

A sudden, unexpected visit by enemy emissaries can make a breakthrough in overcoming deadlocks or thawing entrenched rivalry. Right after he was elected in June 1988, Colombian President Andres Pastrana took a bold initiative to travel to the jungle for a meeting with the Revolutionary Armed Forces of Colombia (FARC) leader. He successfully persuaded the FARC leader to agree to new peace talks. One of the most dramatic examples in the Arab–Israeli relations was a conciliatory trip made by Egyptian President Anwar Sadat to Jerusalem in 1977. The trip was previously unthinkable, and the pleasant surprise played a key role in re-shaping Israeli public perceptions, resulting in the return of the Sinai to Egypt.

The intensity level of psychological pressure

As discussed above, negotiations may not be perceived as a better option than continued fighting prior to reaching an equally hurting stalemate with a deadlocked contest. The antagonists ought to be convinced that their present course of action constitutes an 'impending catastrophe'. Goals and strategies can accordingly be re-prioritized by new cost-benefit calculations. The failure of newly attempted aggressive initiatives cut through the rosy predictions with the consequent realization of sudden substantial costs.

The magnitude of current and future costs has different effects on the mentality and willingness of opposing leaders to initiate steps toward de-escalation (Salla, 1997). An enduring stalemate and imminent catastrophe create different levels of urgency. In reversing internal calculations, highly unexpected costs with large increments are more effective in overcoming entrenched inertia and undoing the emotional tides of hatred gathered during a long period of damaging struggle. In addition to the current expenses, foreseeable onerous future costs put an extra pressure on decision makers. In that sense, simply continuing a long-standing, low level of antagonism does not, in itself, propel a sense of urgency. A continuing bearable stalemate can be distinguished from a mutually catastrophic stalemate which constitutes a ripe moment for settlement efforts.

The decision not to go to any higher level of escalation generates a bearable stalemate, in conjunction with a belief in the absorbability of a steady accumulation of damages. Decision makers may consider that the marginal costs of staying on course in a potentially drawn-out impasse are manageable as long as the hope of victory has not completely evaporated. The nature of the stalemate is not clear cut in a low intense conflict with costs being dispersed over time.

The effects of some stalemates (such as declining battle capabilities for Angolan rebel forces prior to the peace agreement in 2002) might gradually increase pressure until a dramatic event takes place (the death of rebel leader Jonas Savimbi). In such situations as the Guatemalan and El Salvadoran civil wars, the new urgency was more strongly felt only after one of the adversaries sought a total victory with new offensives, but failed to overwhelm the other party with heavy casualties.[2]

In the midst of a deadlocked hurting stalemate, an imminent calamity creates a deadline for specific actions, diminishing decision making time. For instance, the encirclement of the Egyptian Third Army by the Israeli troops in October 1973 forced President Sadat to request U.S. President Richard Nixon to intervene through a CIA back channel. A flood of information about catastrophic disasters increases the time pressure with a deadline that the parties cannot afford to let pass. A painful deadlock may get only worse before any dramatic actions of seeking a way out are taken.

New initiatives can be more easily adopted by enticing opportunities (derived from the fall of leaders opposed to a peaceful settlement or even natural disasters). After the tsunami (triggered by a massive Indian Ocean earthquake) produced a heavy death toll in 2004, the Free Aceh Movement (GAM) and the Indonesian government developed cooperation for humanitarian assistance and eventually reached a peace agreement mediated by former Finnish president Martti Ahtisaari in August 2005.

A desire to end conflict gets stronger with a recently experienced or forthcoming catastrophe which has a cooling-down effect. Thus an unprecedented event or crisis can be seized upon, with new urgency, by decision makers to reduce a high risk confrontation. Fear of a looming calamity following a long deadlock may strengthen the desire to seek negotiation with adversaries more seriously by generating a sense of crisis with the demand for quick action. In a nutshell, the parties' willingness to moderate their behaviour may come from a large, unforeseen rise in damages rather than a steady accrual of loss felt by both parties.

Thresholds for de-escalation

Each conflict has a different threshold point for intolerable suffering since actors perceive a mutually hurting stalemate in a dissimilar manner. The de-escalation threshold for one conflict does not mean exactly the same conditions for reduction in other conflicts. Each actor may feel different sorts of pressure stemming from painful deadlocks, and has a different ability to endure suffering. In bloody conflicts with the Israelis, Palestinians have demonstrated a surprisingly high level of resilience despite their disproportionate casualties.

The tolerance level of the same type of loss or sacrifice differs according to group or national characteristics. Threshold points are higher when a party's main goal is to defeat or even destroy their adversaries, especially reinforced by a militant ideology of struggle. Some groups are more tolerant of loss because of their organizational structures (demanding total loyalty) and low respect for the value of human life. Extremist groups with an ideological commitment hold an ability and willingness to accept more suffering. Terrorist organizational cells and authoritarian states have far less difficulty in absorbing a high degree of civilian casualties and material loss owing to little internal opposition.

A tolerance level for pain can go up even for the same actors, especially when constituents are willing and prepared to take on heavy costs in a struggle for survival (World Wars I and II). The US 'war on terrorism' also raised the tolerance level of casualties higher than a previous engagement with a civil war intervention. This is contrasted with the American government's withdrawal from Somalia with the death of approximately 20 soldiers related to the ambush by local militia groups in 1993. The Reagan administration also withdrew from Lebanon in 1982 following the suicide bombing that killed about 200 US marines.

Ripeness and timing

Specific conditions within the overall conflict system are often considered appropriate for a successful de-escalatory initiative. In this perspective, new ventures alone would not bring about changes in conflict settings prior to the passage of certain stages of conflict. Particular systemic, semi-automatic conditions may have to be met for the start of de-escalation, since relationships of the parties are embedded in the overall conflict system.

In the absence of the right conditions for de-escalation, no single attempt or method would guarantee success. On the other hand, the moment of greater susceptibility to new initiatives is not necessarily a function of distinctive dynamics or the duration of the struggle. While certain conditions are too rigid to be met for de-escalatory moves within a given time frame, it is most likely that conflict situations are never totally resistant to being adjusted and re-arranged.

The questions surrounding ripeness are linked to the right timing of making a conciliatory gesture and initiating a sequence of de-escalatory moves. Ripeness is referred to as a precise moment or suitable time that an action needs to be taken to invite a desired change with a potential for an agreement. The appropriate timing assumes that both parties have developed the same or similar expectations about conflict processes and outcomes (Kriesberg, 1987). A propitious time for tension-reducing moves is accompanied by certain intra-party developments or alterations in an external context.

If particular action is not initiated at the proper time, it will be a missed opportunity. When everything happens sequentially, the conditions may not recur or would not be replicated owing to an irreversible series of events. The circumstances have to be susceptible to certain efforts to be effective in producing a desired outcome. Once the window of opportunity opens, an effective negotiation is necessary to move forward before it closes. The failure of the 2000 Camp David negotiation between Palestinian leader Yasser Arafat and Israeli Prime Minister Ehud Barak turned the clock back to the previous stages of the struggle.

In the context of moves for de-escalation, 'timing' signifies the proper moment for embracing particular strategies or actions so that the conflict will subside and reach some kind of fading stage. The appropriate set of circumstances for de-escalation comes after the adversaries jointly arrive at a point that they cannot afford a costly impasse any longer. The degree of ripeness is represented by the extent to which each party is ready to reduce and ultimately abandon its coercive strategies. There is a continuum between a less or more ripe period which reflects changes in the relationships between disputants as well as the costs and pain felt by them.

The choices of appropriate strategies at the right time are fundamental in converting an intractable conflict into a shared problem with a possible solution (Greig, 2001). Particular activities are more suitable for one point than another in conflict progression, especially with the assumption that events are likely to occur in sequence. It is expected that prior to ripeness, the other side may not react even if concessions or other appeasing moves are made. In fact, moves made at badly or inappropriately chosen times can be counter-productive, creating further difficulties in future settlement endeavours.

Ripeness is related to the concept of timing, circumscribed by certain psychological and structural conditions under which non-coercive solutions should be available and be recognized as desirable. The types of impediments to recognizing ripeness stem, in part, from perceptional failures to see objective external circumstances which demand new initiatives. The structural conditions (reflecting the natural sequence of a conflict's progression) generate a reality independent of the adversaries' actions and perceptions. In a perceptual threshold for ripeness, extreme tensions become so overwhelming that other concerns such as recovering past losses can be overridden.

The political and psychological effects of international events on decision makers and the public differ, in that perceptions are based on the subjective understanding of a natural sequence of events (Coleman, 1997). These perceptions do not remain the same over time with new experiences under different circumstances. Negotiating with an untrustworthy opponent is not perceived any more as a peril when no options are left.

The right time pertains to subjective judgements by those who desire to take on a de-escalation move; each adversary has their own cognitive maps of conflict terrains. Therefore, the other's moves are interpreted according to one's own cognitive maps. Timing for ripeness may be difficult if each side has different interpretations of conflict stages and thresholds along with the communication difficulties related to misinterpretations of the other's intentions. Given the diverse time perspectives felt by each party, some situations become more malleable for one party but unalterable for the other.

In fact, subjectively perceived ripeness may not necessarily be synonymous with an objectively identified hurting stalemate that sustains an undesirable status quo. Even if each side feels the negative consequences of an intransigent stalemate, such effects may not prompt a search for less costly options while expecting the other party to move first. In a deadlocked situation, some parties may not be ready to acknowledge a ripe moment for moving toward negotiation with less desire for a way out. A highly damaging deadlock should be felt painfully by every major party to break the inertia that has been perpetuated by the desire of recovering costs or being compensated for loss. The miscalculation of the efficacy of further military operations and the resistance to accepting compromise set back the chances for peace (Pillar, 1990).

Asymmetry in readiness

The degree of readiness to move away from an interlocked stalemate with impending catastrophes is reflected in the extent to which each side is willing to retreat from their positions. The perceived stalemate and felt hurt can raise the level of readiness to negotiate, in particular, with the experience of higher than expected costs (Pruitt, 2005). In reality, there are varying fatigue levels suffered by partisans. Different degrees of urgency might be sensed following a high rate of resource depletion. Therefore, the conditions might be ripe for one party, but not for the other. The susceptibility to change in the status quo creates diverse degrees of readiness, most significantly, influenced by varied organizational situations as well as dissimilar interpretations of entrapment.

The above discussion suggests that new initiatives may not be felt propitious in the identical manner at the same time. The perceptions of structural conditions in the decision-making processes are not likely to be the same because in most circumstances, parties may feel dissimilarly about moving toward disasters. Moreover, the leaders' perceptions of situations and interest in ultimate resolution can vary (von Heinegg, 2004). These variations have an impact on whether any unilateral de-escalation efforts will be successful in reducing antagonism. The shared perceptions should be developed by mutual understanding of a more objectively identified stalemate.

In spite of joint losses, both sides may develop a propensity that the other side yields first to make appeasing moves, believing that their opponents have a dire necessity to get out of the existing situation. Holding on to entrenched positions that the other party fails to break, each antagonist may resist making the first move sometimes for the reason that they will not look weak. In addition, certain anticipation based on past occasions of the opponent's concession making behaviour may serve as a psychological barrier to presenting concessions first. If the goals or level of commitments to de-escalation are balanced between the protagonists, those who have a conciliatory mentality are likely to move first.

The mutual perceptions of an impending crisis and knowledge about the other party's dreadful situation would help one of the partisans (in a more relatively advantageous position) initiate steps to reach out first. The decision also depends on who has viable, less costly alternatives to an entrenched struggle. In addition, motivation for de-escalation is positively associated with the reduced availability of new resources to carry on conflict. If one party has a promised or actual access to additional assets and funds (as well as political support from their allies), they are less likely to move first.

Those who recognize impending catastrophe more readily than the other tend to take steps toward unwinding exhaustive fighting. A party in a more desperate situation is likely to make initial and possibly greater concessions. In a one-sided stalemate, initiatives taken by a more distressed party can be favourably viewed provided that its adversary's goals are limited and self-controlled. A sufficient moderation of one side's goals spawns the other's optimism and interest in negotiation if the responding opponent's goals are modest, seeking co-existence. The strategies for diminishing animosity need to focus on who is moving first with what types of inducements on which issues.

A ripe moment is not likely to be applied to a one-sided hurting stalemate when only one party feels highly uneasy about the costs and risks involved in the prospect of failure (Zartman, 2000). A disaster may threaten one adversary more so than the other. In the event of an asymmetric experience of an unquestionable catastrophe with a growing imbalance in capabilities, a more advantageous side is likely to sit back, waiting for their enemy's plunge into self-destruction, and then move in to seize the triumph.

The application of ripeness to multi-party conflicts is far more complicated, since shared readiness among all the parties may be difficult to achieve. For instance, in ethnic conflicts in the Democratic Republic of the Congo, Burundi and Somalia, even if two or three major factions agreed to a cease-fire, others continued to resist a new move, creating intransigence in a settlement process. It was very difficult to engender a stable environment for settlement in Colombia due to the fact that the government had to negotiate with each of the three main guerrilla groups and had to control extreme violence by right-wing, narco-paramilitaries. Government negotiations with the FARC were, to a great extent, derailed by the attacks on the largest guerrilla organization by the right-wing paramilitary which began to act independently after its creation under the auspices of the intelligence agency and landlords.

Moves to de-escalation

Even if the chances of success are slight, attempts can be made to weaken and reverse a prospect for the currently unabated conflict's costly outcomes. On the other hand, failed moves carry certain risks of losing face. Once rejected, the proposal is stained, losing its fresh value. The initiative would be taken less seriously even if it is offered at a more auspicious time. A lack of bold endeavours may sound safe and risk free, but no efforts mean that we do not know which methods might work.

Even in unsuccessful attempts, new information, along with learning opportunities, could be gained for a more promising future plan. Thus the questions need to focus on how to create propitious situations in which new offers might be made (how to mature 'vine-grown fruit') rather than simply remaining inactive until a natural opportunity arrives ('waiting for falling fruit under a tree'). Reluctant parties can be convinced to move to de-escalation by signalling readiness to each other, eventually making a set of irreversible commitments to conciliation.

It may be argued that the pursuit of particular goals and strategies will never be suitable at a certain point in time. Indeed, there simply may not be a right or wrong occasion for moving effectively into de-escalation. Diverse strategies target long-term and short-term changes. Even when the immediate cessation of hostilities is not feasible, various tension reduction measures can still be introduced to prevent the institutionalization of hostilities, causing further difficulties for de-escalation readiness.

Different opportunities for de-escalation are explored by a variety of methods across a wide range of time. To establish any positive relationships, the dehumanization process should be stopped promptly (Visser and Cooper, 2003). Initiating and holding de-escalation moves on a firm ground may demand a longer time horizon when steps to ameliorate violence need to come first.

Indeed, initial strategies may focus on halting or reversing malignant escalatory spirals with a concentration on nonviolent interaction even though any ultimate resolution is not within reach.

Third-party intervention

The correct timing could be nurtured by diverse means of intervention designed for the reduction of tensions (Kleiboer and 't Hart, 1995). A ripe movement may arise when the adversaries see third party intervention as a face saving device and also when they have expectations of an intervener to produce a favourable settlement. External intervention in a de-escalation context is to dispose the partisans to re-evaluate their policies and set deadlines for new initiatives. The degree of ability to move a party in an intended direction depends on the leverage which an intervener has.

Not only military but also economic sanctions increase the pressure to end contentious strategies. For the purpose of moderating a conflict's intractability, external interveners can refuse the transfer of military or other materials to influence fighting capabilities. As part of a more aggressive strategy, NATO conducted very destructive bombing campaigns against the Federal Republic of Yugoslavia between March and June 1999 with a proclaimed aim of protecting Kosovo Albanians. A non-military external intervention also makes a big difference in terms of conflict outcomes with wider participation. For instance, the impact of international economic sanctions in the 1980s produced the demoralization of the white minority government and its supporters in South Africa.

The above intervention is contrasted with the lack of effective action in such cases in Sudan and Burma. As China emerged as a new global economic power, Western efforts to control human rights abuses through economic sanctions have become more difficult even though these are essential steps toward conflict mitigation. The failure of international action has emboldened the military dictatorships in Burma to further oppress opposition movements.

Third party intervention can bring not only material costs, but also psychological burden to change the motivations of entrenched parties. One way to control escalatory behaviour is to subject parties responsible for terrorizing a weaker opponent to broad condemnation by a larger society or the world as a whole. Sudden intense violence by military and paramilitary forces in Haiti brought about international sanctions and dispatch of UN contingents to end atrocities in 1994. The 1995 NATO bombing effectively stopped further aggression of Serbs in Bosnia-Herzegovina and prepared the way for settlement talks. This can be compared with a lack of attention to low intensity warfare (in such places as the Democratic Republic of the Congo) which killed astronomically more people than short term attacks in the former Yugoslavia.

International intervention could be used to prod a stronger party to take more moderate positions. Economic sanctions and forceful intervention can be designed to assist in ending violent struggle with a pressure for changing the behaviour of the prime antagonists. Peace enforcement is engaged in the control of violence while peacekeeping is oriented toward a tension reduction mechanism in support of mediation. Intervention tools designed for crisis management enhance confidence building even though the use of threats may occasionally need to be combined with fostering mutual trust. Separating warring parties is at least a minimum condition for controlling highly destructive violence (Carment et al., 2006). When government death squads target community leaders, observers of an international monitoring team might accompany vulnerable individuals to deter attempts at killing. Such 'protective accompaniment' may, in part, aim at reporting aggressive behaviour and human rights violations.

A third party can take on not only enforcing rules but also monitoring the implementation of a tentative agreement in a volatile situation. Economic assistance for reconstruction, personal sanctuary for some leaders, or even resettlement of refugees or displaced populations are commonly offered to increase stakes in a negotiated solution (Esman and Herring, 2001). When both sides are equally motivated, third parties should be in a position to straighten distorted facts and deliver a message or proposal. The elimination of misperceptions generated by a lack of communication is one of the most crucial roles of facilitation (Fisher, 2005). Some readiness to adopt a new strategy must exist on the part of partisans to successfully support external initiatives.

Not every intervention is effective, even further complicating the efforts of conflict mitigation. For example, the 1987 Indian intervention in the Sri Lankan civil war developed suspicion from all sides even though the Indians were initially invited to assist in the demobilization of Tamil militants. Tamil resistance against demobilization dragged Indian peacekeepers into direct armed clashes with the rebel group. The doubt about the role of external forces grew within the Sri Lankan society and government in the midst of killing villagers and other human rights abuses by Indian troops. Eventually Indian forces had to withdraw, leaving a security vacuum in the northern and eastern provinces of Sri Lanka which they were supposed to stabilize. Mistrust of foreign intervention by warring factions also accounts for the ambushes of UN peacekeeping contingents in Mogadishu, Somalia (1993) and attacks on African Union peacekeepers in Dafur, Sudan (2007). Foreign intervention is not likely to succeed without the external actor's investment and shared stake in the outcome as well as cooperation from local parties.

For a successful role in de-escalation, an intermediary should have persistence and perceptiveness in encouraging real change. A third-party motivation to assist in ending a violent conflict may be to prevent its spill-over effects. Disputes between allies are likely to lead a more powerful actor to intervene because of fears for the integrity of the alliance. American President George W. Bush tried to mediate disputes between the Pakistani and Afghan Presidents not to weaken their alliance in the war on terrorism. In the 1982 Falkland Islands crisis, US Secretary of State Alexander Hague made a futile mediation attempt to prevent war between the two American allies, Britain and Argentina.

Politics of de-escalation

Escaping from intractable conflicts may involve the establishment of new leadership more openly committed to embarking on fresh initiatives. While there are examples of policy changes under strong public pressure without any leadership change, abandoning past policies and adopting different ones is easier in a new political environment. Resistance to de-escalation comes, in part, from the tendency to refuse seeing the failure of old policies. Retracting prior statements for justifying the struggle can be seen to indicate an admission of political defeat. Even when leaders lose confidence and conviction over time, it always takes longer for them to admit past mistakes and failures.

Bringing fluidity to a deadlocked stalemate may follow the rise of a new leadership that does not have much emotional or ideological entanglement with the preceding events. The dysfunctional aspects of a conflict are more easily acknowledged by the emerging leadership which has alternative time frames and perspectives. The replacement of South African President P. W. Botha by F. W. de Klerk in 1989 was critical in the legalization of the African National Congress (ANC) and the release of its leader Nelson Mandela in 1990, opening the door for dramatic political transformation.

Incoming leaders have a freer hand to divert from the existing course of action and are not likely to be inhibited from terminating past policies that caused grievances to enemies. Emerging leaders are more detached from current operations upon which they did not decide, bestowing them with an opportunity to take a fresh look at the overall picture. In an initial 'honeymoon' period, leaders are also likely to have the luxury of removing not only unsuccessful policies but also the personnel previously committed to them.

Pulling away from disastrous policies is therefore far easier under the emerging leadership, in that new incumbents are not accountable for the failed policies of their predecessors (Gilmore, 2003). In particular, the leadership change, especially with major power shifts among factions, most likely signals changes in strategy, when the population has disliked past policies. Unforeseen flexibility might follow the selection of moderate factions, for example, Gorbachev in the Soviet Union. The ascent of reform-minded leaders on both sides, with a serious commitment to the mitigation of violence, provides fertile ground for the creation of a positive synergy.

If the new elite are less rigid and do not advance new demands, the adversaries feel more comfortable cooperating to reduce tensions, and express less distrust and resentment. Because they are distant from past events, the fresh leadership does not need to take responsibility for earlier incidents that draw the resentment of their adversaries. Optimism may not need to dissipate completely even when hard line leaders step in unless they have records of previous abuse.

Indeed, they may find it desirable or even necessary to seek negotiated solutions, once realizing the dire conditions on the ground. Adversaries are more likely to reach out to newly appointed policy makers and test their will to seek alternatives approaches with cautious optimism.

Internal politics

Difficulties in conciliation are understood in terms of intra-group politics as well as inter-group relations. Most political or social units are not likely to be unitary decision-making actors, as their choices are determined by the efforts to balance out opposing factional interests and manage institutional rivalry. Political divisions within each entity and rivalry for leadership complicate a switch to a new mode of actions. A lack of a coherent move can be attributed to the need for re-negotiation of intra-party positions in evolving conflict situations. The deepening violence in the Palestinian–Israeli conflict is, to a great extent, ascribed to internal politics such as the election of an intransigent hardline leadership (Israeli Prime Minister Ariel Sharon) and the prevalence of hawkish public opinion.

Internal political differences emerge over the methods, timing and tempo of conciliatory tactics. To a great extent, intra-party dimensions of ripeness are affected by the level of support for leaders committed to the moderation of a conflict. Bearing the burdens of embarking on a perilous process of ending protracted fighting opposed by powerful domestic institutions, the innovative leaders are likely to try to balance the political risks with unequivocal domestic gains.

Intra-elite rivalry can spill over to a wider struggle to determine positions on the course of new events. The leadership replacement may be accompanied by a rising level of anxiety among the rank and file as well as external pressure. The conciliation process can be hampered and stalled by internal political dynamics that give an upper hand to faction leaders with a vested interest in particular issues which may need to be bargained away. Internal politics involves the rearrangement of coalitions in support of a new cause.

The novel mood of a decision-making body within each party may coincide with the rise of a moderate leadership committed to a low or minimum preference for coercive strategies. This commitment to a new course of action can be made easier by shared feelings about the need for alternative strategies among the elite. Weak intra-party support is ascribed to a high level of internal mistrust as well as the absence of leadership cohesion. In moving towards a negotiated settlement, not only leaders but also followers have to be persuaded to perceive benefits rather than passively accepting existing or anticipated costs. Though an agreement can be reached between high level politicians, key constituents may still resist a conciliatory process. Effective control over extreme forces is more difficult in the absence of leadership unity.

In actuality, launching innovative sequences of policies is likely to undergo difficulties originating from differences of opinion among constituents and bureaucratic inertia. Fights between hawkish and dovish factions revolve around institutional competition with high political stakes. Internal politics related to the struggle between 'hawks' and 'doves' can put a hold on making any concessions necessary for reaching a final settlement. In order to undermine conciliatory tactics, the hawkish factions may agitate rank and file opposition, contributing to intransigence. Any compromise is perceived as betrayal for those who have been mobilized for the cause.

Various features of political systems play different roles in the outcome of internal negotiations. Authoritarian governments have a better control over their population than pluralistic political systems in which support by the majority of the public is essential to a crucial policy change (Goemans, 2000). In pluralistic democratic states, constituent interests (expressed in popular opinion or mass demonstrations) can shape the nature of policy making. Given the time constraints derived from electoral cycles, in addition, the elected officials face a difficult time developing a long-term perspective (Dixon, 1994).

As discussed above, any new move could be inhibited by the domestic conditions in each of the adversarial countries. The swings in a mood of pressure groups and public opinion limit the range of policy options. A drive for mobilization of support can be directed at the segments of the attentive public and their representatives. The opposition to the continuing course of actions would represent not only concerns about specific interests but also pressure for an improvement in general welfare (caused by continued spending in warfare and budget deficit). Even when the centralized decision-making elite (even a single ruler) determines goals and policies, they do not have a firm grip on every aspect of decision making, facing internal constraints.

Incompatible interests still exist even within the most centralized bureaucracy. It would be difficult to break through simple inertia long in place. Different agencies within each party are most likely engaged at diverse phases of conflict. While militant factions grab more power in executing coercive strategies, their role is very limited in ironing out ways to induce the other side to come to a negotiation table. By holding a greater authority in decision- making circles, the armed or intelligence units can oppose shedding coercive strategies despite a fruitless struggle with their enemies. Eventually when a peace process takes root, the control and demobilization of extreme elements in charge of security agencies and internal police forces are necessary to remove resistance against the negotiated settlement.

The art of coalition building

As a political project, coalition formation entails the negotiation of differences along with the recognition of multiple identities and interests within and across groups (Bystydzienski and Schacht, 2001). In order to develop and sustain any successful de-escalation dynamics, coalitions need to be built not only internally but also across party lines. The two level games of politics are composed of intra-party struggle, and its effects on the dynamics of inter-group relations and vice versa. Institutional competition, representation of constituent interests, and harmonization of diverse views need to be managed within a group. At the same time, this internal process is also affected by the party's relationships with the external party. Alteration in each party's positions might reflect implicit coordination among factions on both sides of adversarial lines whose main stake is to push for a peaceful settlement.

The moderate factions across parties see the benefit of compromise solutions, and are willing to take a risk of talking to their counterparts on the opposing side. In successful de-escalation, coordination among moderates across adversaries as well as a strong internal coalition for conciliatory policies is common. In order to weaken the hard-line opposition, reciprocal concessions might be made to strengthen the positions of the moderate segments within each party. The chances of a particular administration or political leader's success can be aided by the other party's 'strategic aid' through timely concessions.

Coalition building differs according to the relationships between the doves and hawks within a group as well as collaboration between the doves across party lines. The strength or weakness of a moderate coalition within each party may depend on leadership styles, power distribution among different factions, and the availability of the methods of controlling the extremists. The fortunes of moderate political forces are boosted by the existence of a charismatic or popular leader advocating cessation of violence and power distribution in favour of doves. The strategy of negotiating in the middle is essential to keeping a strong coalition in support of a compromise settlement. Too many concessions would be difficult to make at the beginning of negotiations not to give legitimacy to the hawkish faction's opposition.

In general, moderate factions play a key role in advocating accommodation, but each subgroup has divergent values and distinctive narratives. A larger coalition reduces the number of spoilers by isolating the die-hards defying compromise. Hawks would be put in a minority position with progression in the debates on how to end the conflict instead of attaining original goals. In the case of South Africa, Nelson Mandela and President de Klerk had big stakes in minimizing hard line challenges within their own ranks prior to building a broad constituent base for their proposals.

The support of de-escalation depends not only on the relationships between doves and hawks within a group but also the nature of mutual support between the doves across party lines. The negotiations of the moderates are likely to explore a shared position. As realists, moderates are less likely to take risks to make unpopular concessions for the sake of peace (Pruitt, 2005). Eventually a compromise is more likely to be formulated by new ties between moderate factions.

Once joint initiatives are introduced, moderates take a midpoint position falling between opposing viewpoints of the hawks and doves. However, enthusiasm is likely to wane with protracted efforts to narrow differences, posing real challenges to the prospect for peace. The post-Oslo Agreement process was derailed, in a large part, due to difficulties of holding a broad coalition together within each party during the prolonged discussion over implementation plans.

The moderation of behaviour and preservation of at least minimal trust among diverse factions across parties is a key to success. In nine years of tumultuous negotiations on the devolution of most central government power to a Northern Ireland Assembly (a crucial element of the Good Friday Agreement of April 1998), the British and Irish prime ministers played a crucial role in keeping a coalition intact along with facilitation of multi-party conferences as well as bilateral meetings. Their efforts to narrow differences over such contentious issues as disarmament of the Irish Republican Army (IRA) were critical in the formation of a power sharing government between Unionists and Republicans in early 2007. Reconciliation at a grassroots level, including various women, youth, business and labour groups was also initiated to provide a wide support for the moderate leadership's conciliatory efforts.

The terrain of factional politics

Inter-party collaboration among doves is needed for opening up communication channels with the utilization of informal diplomacy. In the efforts to surmount enemy images, doves can bridge emotional gaps created by distrust. Doves on both sides are willing to develop common values and perspectives that bind them together, while the moderates are likely to shape the key positions of their own party. Doves may try to salvage any derailment of a peace process by influencing public opinions even in an environment that is not friendly to conciliation.

The collaboration between doves across party lines may have to be rather implicit because they are vulnerable to accusations of being traitors within their own group. Too close an allegiance with any segment of the other side may invite questions about credibility and loyalty at home. In addition, tensions may arise, since each faction is also responsible for their own communities even though they want to develop a collegial relationship with their counterpart on the opposition.

When any violent acts are instigated by an adversary's extremists, hard-liners are likely to ridicule the doves, even endeavouring to de-legitimize their cause. The influence of doves tends to be considerably weakened by renewed violence. At the beginning of the massive air assaults in Lebanon in summer 2006, the majority in the Israeli peace movement community endorsed and advocated an aggressive military policy as retaliation against Hezbollah's provocations.

Intransigent hawks within each group are the most isolated and difficult to manage (Pruitt, 2005). In spite of a profound political distance between the hawks, they have common objectives of obstructing and demolishing a peace deal (given their quest for total victory regardless of the costs with a longer time frame). Hawks on either end of the spectrum do not communicate with each other in contrast with doves who are eager to develop informal contact.

The extremists would be deadly opposed to making concessions. Once rebellious 'rejectionists' are isolated or separated from the general public, they may depend on violence to derail any kind of compromise. Since militant radicals are more likely to be organized in a centralized fashion, they can offer a more decisive campaign to make their presence visible despite numeric inferiority. The role of fanatics is very destructive when they employ violent or other radical actions to strain an inter-party conciliatory mood.

Ethnocentric fanatics are even more of a serious threat if they have access to coercive instruments of the state (such as Hutu military officers engaged in campaigning for the extermination of Tutsis and moderate Hutus during the Rwandan genocide in 1994). Many right wing Israelis opposed any kind of concessions, and even praised the assassination of Israeli Prime Minister Yitzhak Rabin by one of their own members. Militant extremists are willing to depend on violence against even the moderates of their own party who are tolerant of an 'enemy'.

In contrast with the period of escalation, a belligerent hawkish leadership needs to be adjusted to the politics of negotiation after the loss of their prevalence. Right-wing paramilitary groups have often been supported by and closely linked to government policies of intimidating indigenous populations (in Guatemala and Colombia). However, they have been abandoned, for instance, in Colombia, once the government decided to scale down their aggressive operations. The militia groups engaged in atrocities against villagers have become a burden rather than an asset because they have to be brought to answer charges of human rights abuses.

As jobs and status are lost for those who have developed competence in coercive tactics, they may attempt provocative actions to regenerate violent escalation. For instance, negotiations in Northern Ireland were hampered for some time, owing to violent or criminal activities by IRA factions (Dixon, 2007). After the comprehensive Good Friday Agreement on power sharing was reached in April 1998, IRA bombing killed 29 people with hundreds of injuries in August. In addition, the IRA's lack of cooperation in the decommissioning process as well as their subversive activities generated mistrust among unionists in support of continued British rule, contributing to a significant delay in the implementation of the key provisions of the Good Friday Agreement.

The fanatical faction's willingness to take high costs is attributed to a blind commitment to an ideological zeal or nationalistic cause. The extremists would not be deterred by cost-benefit calculations. The loss of material support and even sacrifice of their own lives are accepted for the sake of future glorious victory. Ideologically motivated hawks do not show any interest in compromise, since their goal is not a negotiated settlement. Their extreme demands and deep mistrust of adversaries are rooted in their enemy stereotypes.

The politics of the middle

The conditions for conciliation may be ripe to the extent that there is a broad coalition in the middle of a political spectrum. The extremists need to be neutralized or controlled so that disruptive actions organized by zealots would not take place during the sensitive period of negotiation. In order not to instigate the hawks' sabotage, moderates might attempt to bring them into institutionalized debates. In addition, some minor details of peace accords or symbolic issues might be conceded to the demand of hawkish factions.

The numbers of ideologically committed hawks and fully dedicated doves do not change greatly regardless of evolving conflict situations. The number of moderate hawks and moderate doves as well as the centre continues to oscillate because subgroup boundaries either shrink or expand. In a transition toward de-escalation, some hawks in a leadership position (such as Yasser Arafat) may begin to take more pragmatic positions, eventually serving as moderates.

Each subgroup may be adjusted to their required roles at various points in conflict. At the initial stage of negotiation, the influence of doves and moderates produces an optimism that changes the public mood. In Northern Ireland, the Social Democratic and Labour Party (SDLP) representing moderate nationalists collaborated with their counterpart Ulster Unionist Party (UUP) to garner support for the Good Friday Agreement. Especially at the initial stage of inter-group contact, cooperation between SDLP leader John Hume and UUP leader David Trimble minimized the efforts to sabotage the initiatives organized by extremist groups such as the IRA. The smaller number of IRA armed radicals as well as Protestant extremists had to be isolated and sidelined in the political process. Unfortunately, electoral success by the Democratic Unionist Party's hawkish leader Ian Paisley and their Nationalist counterpart Sinn Fein's Gerry Adams, in the midst of difficult negotiation, laid many road blocks to the proper functioning of the Assembly and the Executive (designed to be responsible for self-rule) prior to early 2007.

The role of a moderate coalition

The size of a moderate coalition and the degree of its commitment to settlement are important for holding the process together (Kelman, 1993; Pruitt, 2005). As a matter of fact, allegiance to someone who symbolizes the community (Nelson Mandela) or past war hero (Yitzhak Rabin) is necessary to sustain the coalition over a period of time. Those who have sufficient hawkish credentials are more acceptable to most members of their group. In general, people tend to trust former hard liners who turned into moderates or even doves for the reason that they appear more credible to protect their group interests. At a low level of inter-party trust, moderate hawks may become more influential in determining the future of even enduring initiatives for cooperation (Schultz, 2005).

The moderates may look for ways to pacify hawks by giving way to some of their demands in averting destabilization. On the other hand, having an uncompromising hawkish partner in an alliance may result in putting self-limits on a pledge to search accommodation. In addition, the incorporation of a hawkish faction in a moderate coalition leads to a struggle to vie for power.

Despite various shortcomings, tactical alliances between moderates and hawks can be built upon domestic political convenience. When hard liners are in power, they may seek a moderate faction's support to justify their positions. This may soften their positions in an effort to accommodate some of the demands made by more moderate groups. Dovish Israeli politician Simon Peres accepted a membership in Ariel Sharon's cabinet, as foreign minister, after the Likud Party's victory in the 2001 election and then again at the end of 2004. While Peres was much criticized for joining the coalition government opposed to his own dovish stance, his participation in the second 'national unity government' along with other Labour party members was legitimized by the hawkish Likud party's support of 'disengagement' from Gaza.

When moderates on both sides fail to reach an agreement, the hard liners may re-gain their voice and even completely discard the conciliatory efforts. The reversal is accompanied by the reduced number of doves and dovish moderates. In the re-escalation, hawks dominate inter-party dynamics when the public have a pessimistic mood. The hawkish moderates and hawks may even take a new offensive against the 'deadly' opponent in a renewed escalation. Thus the roles of subgroups evolve in a response to the emergence of new external circumstances.

As ever larger numbers of moderates are pushed into the hard liner ranks, the hawks gain the upper hand. The radical factions are in charge of the course of conflict again. The enlarged size of the hawkish faction becomes an obstacle to renewed efforts for de-escalation. In the Palestine–Israeli conflict, the Oslo peace talks initially strengthened the size and role of the dovish factions on both sides, but the voice of doves was completely obliterated by a series of re-escalatory moves in the aftermath of failed Camp David negotiations (Quandt, 2005).

Palestinians are currently divided between moderate Fatah factions represented by President Abbas (based in the West Bank) and hard line supporters of Hamas Prime Minister Ismail Haniya and his cabinet (installed in Gaza). In the current Israeli–Palestinian conflicts, there is far less support for dovish positions than ten years ago when the optimism was driving a conciliatory initiatives in the Middle East. Palestinian suicide bombings and rocket attacks in Israel repeatedly invited the Israeli reprisal with much heavier lethal effects during the second Intifada's violent period (2000–2005). The assassination of Yitzhak Rabin and the election of Benjamin Netanyahu (critical of the Oslo Peace Accord), rightwing Likud Party leader, as Israeli premier in 1996 set the clock back toward the path of confrontation along with the flourishing of renewed Israeli settlements.

Notes

1 Decision-making factors interact with pre-existing structural conditions to induce certain types of behaviour.

2 In the 12-year civil war of 1980–92, a truce was declared in April 1991 after a major offensive launch by a leftist coalition known as the Farabundo Martí National Liberation Front (FMLN). Even though parts of capital city San Salvador were captured by the FMLN in 1989, a new willingness towards negotiation emerged in the aftermath of heavy casualties, in part, caused by government bombing in heavily populated areas.

Conciliation Strategies

10

De-escalation entails not only a whole range of conflict reduction strategies but also 'conflict coping' activities. The appropriateness of any strategy depends on the prevailing conditions at a specific point of a conflict cycle. In addition, a de-escalation process would often not be smooth especially in the event of the negative interference of a shifting external environment (Boose, 2000). Except in the situation of extreme power asymmetry, it is rare for a single party to wholly control the entire process. As the parties have different levels of aspirations, it is not easy for each to get exactly what they want. Sustaining the initiatives for de-escalation becomes more difficult under conditions of threat and actual use of violence.

The de-escalating process is not necessarily value-neutral, because it can eventually be judged in terms of how it is managed to bring about a satisfactory settlement to every party. Each partisan has their own sense of the feasibility about attaining an acceptable outcome in making decisions on when, how and whether to move into de-escalation at what costs. Various sets of inducements can be tailored to minimize differences in the issues considered important by the primary actors (who have diverse organizational characteristics and interests). In addition, the effectiveness of different inducements relies on how these have been introduced and in what time frame. An agreement on a cease fire or other narrowly focused hostility management measures, without an active engagement of adversaries in a conciliation process, tends to diminish the urgency and pressure needed for a more comprehensive settlement. This chapter reviews different types of conciliatory gestures, their applications, and effects.

Interaction patterns

Instead of sudden, dramatic changes in the relationship, a series of initiatives in limited boundaries can be built in a cumulative manner. At the initial stages of conciliation, low-key, unofficial channels might be helpful to transfer confidential messages to decision-making circles by a discreet intermediary. A gradual introduction of conciliatory gestures can be strengthened, following the other party's reciprocal moves. The treatment of Libyan leader Muammar al-Gaddafi as an international pariah by Western countries ended with his declaration of abandoning programmes on the development of 'weapons of mass destruction' in 2003, being rewarded by British Prime Minister Tony Blair's visit to Tripoli in 2004.

Prior to these events, Libya agreed, in 1999, to surrender two suspects accused of involvement in blowing up a Pan Am airliner over the Scottish town of Lockerbie in December 1988 and signed a deal to compensate families of the Lockerbie bombing victims with $2.7 billion in 2003. It took more than a decade for Colonel Gaddafi to thaw relations with Western powers after a series of confrontations that invited a range of retaliatory actions from the US shooting down of Libyan aircraft in 1982 and the death of 101 Libyans from the US bombing in 1986 to the 1992 UN economic sanctions imposed in the aftermath of the Pan Am bombing.

The elements of antagonistic and conciliatory moves may co-exist prior to reaching the final stage of de-escalation. Thus observable behavioural indicators for the de-escalation phase entail less visible acts of violence, but may not exclude frequent verbal accusations and protests in high stakes negotiation periods. In a long series of meetings with South Africa's white minority government between 1990 and 1994, the African National Congress (ANC) saw negotiation as another form of struggle replacing an earlier resort to armed resistance in their pursuit of ending the apartheid system. The adversarial bargaining was sometimes manifested in acrimonious, verbal exchanges between President F. W. de Klerk and Nelson Mandela.

Although fewer physical acts of coercion are revealed in non-adversarial dynamics, de-escalation may not be able to avert the exchange of acute accusations in a high stake settlement process such as the transition toward the creation of a new government after violent conflicts in Mozambique, El Salvador, and Bosnia-Herzegovina. The tactics of bullying and intimidation eventually need to be abandoned in the progressive movement toward de-escalation because they can be associated with mistrust and fear of renewed victimization. Threats or mild coercion have to be managed not to jeopardize efforts made to break out of a deadlocked struggle.

In spite of a decline in physical struggle, hostile comments, warnings, and denials may serve as a verbal smokescreen in order to take advantageous positions in bargaining and boost support from intra-party audiences. Verbal attacks and threats are likely to result from a bid for an immediate benefit rather than a demand for the opponent's total surrender. The interaction patterns are, in general, based on a contingent opposition between parties which seek an advantage at the initial stage of a negotiated settlement (Richmond, 2002). In such circumstances when each party wants to maximize gains prior to actual bargaining, contentious tactics are employed temporarily.

The communication patterns become more transparent and credible once significant sectors of each community are involved in de-escalation activities. After enough confidence and support have been built, more open initiatives can be made. In successful conciliation, public communication channels would eventually have to follow confidential contacts between the leaderships of adversaries even if specific facts or details of the offers might be concealed before the negotiation is over. The coordination of individual lines of action benefits from the exploration of shared schemes for the reciprocal exchanges of benign intentions (Applegate and Sypher, 1983).

The promise of further benefits can open up communication in conjunction with the exchange of rewards. However, intended actions are not necessarily interpreted in the same manner by protagonists. In a long cycle of conflict relationships, conciliatory overtures devised to move out of an entrapment may easily be treated as another ploy with the existence of deep suspicion. There is always a certain gap between one's own desired intentions behind a moderating course of action and the actual interpretation by others.

The conciliatory process is fragile and may easily break down when each party has an option to revert to contentious strategies. If the offer of concessions and accommodative bargaining remains constant with long-term conciliatory strategies, any setback is regarded as a hiatus. The reversal of coercive actions as well as persuasion needs to be designed in a way to encourage an adversary to negotiate with the goal of conciliation. While the deliberate exchange of punitive behaviour is not totally excluded in the midst of de-escalatory moves, most importantly, non-lethal means of conflict engagement enhance the odds for conciliation.

Whereas ambiguity in behaviour may be inevitable in a transition toward de-escalation, the uncertainty about each other's intentions impairs a lasting atmosphere of mutual assurance. Many initial steps become easily retractable and even reversed if an adversary's actions do not warrant any promise for non-antagonistic relationships. Since such measures as an unconditional release or return of political prisoners are not retractable, these moves at least carry some kind of optimism and hopeful future signs. Larger concessions can eventually be accompanied by a series of exchanges of good-will gestures. More significant actions involving considerable costs are likely to be taken at the later stage of de-escalation.

When both sides have mutually strong yearnings, the synchronization of a series of conciliatory moves can be made, if not explicitly, implicitly. Nonetheless, the real aims behind a response to a de-escalatory move would not always be clear even though a desire to slow or stop a competitive action might be shared to reduce costs. The identification of common interests facilitates increased predictability of each other's behaviour even in the absence of compatibility between major values.

Successful de-escalation ultimately depends on both parties' intent to curb exceedingly disparaging exchanges as part of efforts to create space for more serious endeavours to resolve contentious issues (Nation, 1992; Powell, 2004). There are various paths to move from an adversarial relationship to a more accommodating one. In a non-crisis situation, incremental, rather than dramatic, changes, with a longer time horizon might be natural for eliminating animosities on a persistent basis. Many small steps taken gradually have a cumulative effect in eventual trust building. This path would work only if adversaries have shared objectives and patience to bring about changes in leadership perceptions and public opinions on the adversarial side. Unfortunately, a serious setback might be accompanied by an overwhelming event that reverses everything achieved up to that point.

The initial steps for de-escalation generally start with moves oriented toward easing pressure. The level of a desire for better relations is manifested in the number and persistence of moves prior to the other's sufficient reaction. In contrast with an escalation that flares up quickly, any step in a de-escalation spiral is more likely to be cautious without dramatic changes in leadership thinking. In the absence of any spectacular events, a more gradual approach is regarded as safe; an initial conciliatory move is most likely to start with some caution due to a possible abuse of one's goodwill by an adversary.

The sustenance of any conciliatory move is dependent upon the reciprocal actions taken by an adversary (for example, a prisoner swap). In ending a civil war through negotiation, governments offer amnesty to guerrilla fighters and economic packages for their demobilization. The promise of concession can be made contingent on an adversary's specific actions. A continuing reward can be attached conditionally to the adversary's reciprocal actions for satisfying at least some demand by the initiating party. While the initiator may expect a certain action by a particular time, the retreat from the declared demand is regarded as a bluff.

Step-by-step de-escalation

In generating new dynamics of de-escalation, the adversaries may focus mostly on each other's positive, placatory statements or other signals, responding in kind. A series of incremental steps can be linked to each other, in an organic way, to accelerate an accommodating process. The public exchange of significant concessions is designed to serve each other's self-interests and cultivate a climate of mutual trust for negotiation (Osgood, 1962). The initiatives for the cessation of a nuclear test in the atmosphere by President Kennedy in June 1963 was accompanied by Soviet Premier Khrushchev's cooperative move for limiting nuclear tests. The amelioration of the conflict at hand is mutually rewarding, being aimed at an ultimate settlement along with a diminution of tension in the system.

Faced with difficulties to instigate reciprocal cooperation, a step-by-step approach would be needed to pull adversaries out from a deadlocked fight. This de-escalation spiral was described as the 'Graduated and Reciprocated Initiatives in Tension Reduction' (GRIT) by Charles Osgood in 1962. In an attempt to break conflict spirals, GRIT focuses on unilateral initiatives aimed at a series of cooperative moves, while publicly challenging the opponent to match de-escalations moves. A conciliatory concession normally commences with a small step at a time so that the gradual move will not risk the initiator's security. The intentions of revocation of positive actions are likely to be expressed either explicitly or implicitly if reciprocation is not forthcoming.

Compared to a tit-for-tat strategy (which returns rewards for rewards and punishment for punishment), GRIT depends on the tactics of unilateral, persistent initial concessions for drawing the other's attention to one's own good will. In fact, conciliatory initiatives are taken independently of the other's actions in the hope of severing locked-in competition. In GRIT, the actions of accommodation can be taken unilaterally with the assumption of the other side's similarly positive response. As a matter of fact, a unilateral gesture serves as an implicit, suggestive communication method to indicate the feasibility of further concessions in the event of an opponent's cooperation (Lindskold, 1983). Reciprocation, made by the other side, generates a new optimism to warrant the initiating party to launch a more promising conciliatory move. In a conciliatory spiral, optimism feeds each other's positive moves.

In graduated reciprocal reductions in hostilities, a small initial conciliatory gesture is supposed to invite the other side's response in kind with a snowball effect. Reciprocation of the first initial moves will likely invoke a second or third small gesture, further signifying one's willingness to improve relations. Even if a similar type of concession is not forthcoming, the initiator may move ahead to make a second unilateral overture, hoping the eventual reciprocation of the target's action. In the event of the target's reciprocation, further positive steps are essential to pushing more conciliatory moves—that is, the other's benign gesture needs to be matched by another slightly more positive move. In the end, the continuing pattern of conciliation replaces the former cycle of an escalatory spiral. Decrease in tensions, like an arms race in reverse, is supposed to be accomplished by the cumulative effects of a series of reciprocated actions (Lawler et al., 1999).

The unilateral moves can be announced to deliver a clear message with an open invitation of reciprocity. The continuing conciliatory gestures carried on for an extended period, even in the absence of an adversary's response, are based on the assumption that the other side may need time to measure the weight of the initiating party's original intention, prior to the formulation of their own responses. An immediate reciprocity is likely to be rare unless some informal understanding has been reached. Because the effects of a conciliatory gesture are context driven, the existence of a previous positive collaborative working relationship, even on a limited scale, prior to the recent escalation, would buttress an impetus for the conciliatory gestures.

It is not difficult to make a largely symbolic concession unilaterally on issues that would not endanger the initiator's security. This concession might be small, but has to be persistent with an irreversible commitment. An invitation to reciprocate is made in a subtle manner rather than being presented as an explicit demand. Eventually, gradual tension reduction builds a safe environment for taking more bold initiatives. The psychological effects of a series of unilaterally undertaken acts are supposed to erode perceptions of threats. In order to signal an adversary that the actions do not come from weakness or fear, firmness may be shown in other arenas while the conciliatory measures take hold or are even enlarged to shore up optimism.

The execution of graded sequences extending a series of unilateral concessions, no matter how the other side reacts, is critical in cracking an enemy stereotype attached to an untrustworthy, aggressive image. By following pre-stated plans, all conciliatory actions are geared to construct credible and trustworthy images by matching words with deeds. In the absence of knowledge about the other's intentions and great uncertainty, a gradual movement of concessions, from a low to high graded risk, would be a sensible approach. Even if the initial acts are not reciprocated, it really does not matter given the low stakes.

Such reciprocation retains a life of its own, forming a rhythm of concession making (Druckman, 1990). Being accompanied by a series of small, constructive commitments, the psychology of enthusiastic commitments is set in motion. The movement is difficult to stop when each side feels too much stake in the new process. Thus, more concessions are viewed by each side as further investment, increasing the significance of the continual exchange of benevolent actions (Brockner and Rubin, 1985).

In long-term hostile relationships, it is most likely that each side starts with a minor adjustment in their positions, in tandem with tentative actions aimed at enemy image changes. Each other's positive interaction is amplified through a feedback loop that is sustained by the success of de-escalation initiatives and their reciprocation. Through further feedback, a fresh series of actions produce a continuing alteration in behaviour and attitudes, enhancing confidence levels with the reciprocation of acts of reassurance.

Thus the GRIT policy's main objectives are oriented toward controlled reduction of tension with a careful selection of inducements based on appeals to the adversary's constituency. The key assumption is that threats often strengthen popular support for a more escalatory posture rather than intimidating the other's leadership or populace. A graduated reciprocation in tension-reduction helps diffuse international tension. GRIT has been used to illustrate the descending ladder of international hostilities during the Cold War, particularly tensions associated with the threat of nuclear holocaust.

In a high intensity conflict best exemplified by the US–Soviet arms race, a series of unilaterally chosen actions has been introduced in low risk areas, with a prior announcement, expressing a stronger desire to lower an intolerable level of tension. Whereas the other side is explicitly invited to reciprocation in a tension reduction process, one side may be more inclined to trigger, whether successfully or unsuccessfully, conciliatory moves setting an accommodative sequence. It takes a long time to dispel a protracted history of suspicion and distrust if reciprocation in tension reduction is bound to establish a firm ground for trust and credibility.

In winding down the Cold War period, Soviet President Mikhail Gorbachev adopted GRIT to spin down the spiral of expanded nuclear weapons production (Kenrick et al., 2005). In order to bring President Ronald Reagan to the negotiating table, Gorbachev took the initial step of a one-sided test ban to solicit the Americans to follow suit with a promise of continued suspension of Soviet nuclear tests. Despite the Reagan administration's refusal to reciprocate the Soviet move, Gorbachev's proposal warmed up American public opinion. By sensing a shift in the public mood, Gorbachev took his next step to invite US inspectors to verify Soviet arms reductions. The series of initiatives by Gorbachev finally enticed Reagan to reach an agreement on nuclear arms reduction.

Intra-party divisions can plague the efforts of commencing or sustaining an accommodative sequence. Especially if the adversarial party does not respond promptly with their own conciliatory tactics, it would be difficult for the proponent of tension reduction measures to overwhelm internal opposition. Internal criticisms may halt further progress after reaching a certain point of reciprocal exchanges. At this point, a new push, with more dramatic action, might re-generate a synergy for a series of new concessions. In one of the earlier GRIT attempts during the Cold War period, domestic criticism froze Soviet Premier Khrushchev's 'soft line' experiment following the 1963 agreement with the Kennedy administration to ban nuclear weapons in space.

Confronted by a tough competitor, one or two unilateral positive inducements might be introduced after the exhibition of firmness. Even though GRIT is a necessary step toward inducing a momentum for conciliation, counter-threats and unyielding responses are likely to be utilized against a bullying adversary who consistently returns to exploitative responses designed for unilateral gain. Even after mutual cooperation is established, a tit-for-tat strategy would still be employed from time to time in drawing essential concessions from a competitive adversary until the obtainment of full settlement (Pilisuk and Skolnick, 1968). Re-initiating coercive activities may serve as a tentative, retaliatory measure in the absence of an adversary's cooperative move. Faced with an intransigent opponent, thus, conflictive actions would not be totally abandoned even if cooperative actions constitute a prevailing strategy in pushing further for conciliation.

Conciliatory actions

Many forms of conciliatory gestures range from the public announcement of the failure of old policies and their removal to the initiation of benevolent policies rewarding the other side. Launching a new channel of communication along with a change in rhetoric can be accompanied by such symbolic actions as official or unofficial acknowledgment of at least some responsibility for past acts, modification or abandonment of the ideology of hatred as well as formal recognition of an adversary's legitimacy and their leader's right of representation. They may also involve the acceptance of claims and demands by an adversary and compensation for wrong doing.

In bringing about a fresh relationship between Eastern and Western Europe, German chancellor Willy Brandt offered an apology to the Poles, with such a worldly known gesture as 'Warschauer Kniefall' in which he knelt down at the monument to victims of the Warsaw Ghetto Uprising sacrificed during the Nazi occupation. His 'Ostpolitik' was aimed at encouraging change in an adversarial attitude through rapprochement. The conciliatory policies toward Eastern Europe were followed up with economic assistance and proposals for easing military tensions.

In an enduring rivalry, the initial gestures of de-escalation tend to come from the retraction and abandonment of policies and symbols associated with coercion. Interest in suspending hostilities may start with small steps such as verbalized or unspoken hints or requests for meetings and actual proposals. In fact, vague signals along with discrete contacts are helpful to conceal one's own conciliatory intent in public while 'testing the waters'. Such symbolic gestures as refraining from customary condemnation of an adversary can draw an initial recognition of the target party; other non-costly measures include an easing of travel restrictions. Eventually complete suspension or abatement of coercive sanctions may be accompanied by a temporary end to violence in a limited arena. Thus modes of behaviour representing conciliation entail the pause or termination of vicious military tactics such as bombing civilian targets as well as the cessation of military exercises.

The de-escalatory moves can be designed in a way to invite more open and clear communication in developing a higher level of shared understanding in lieu of continued adversarial exchanges. While trust building in overall relationships takes time, cooperation focused on an economic issue or the exchange of sports teams or cultural exhibits may lead to a thaw in long-term hostilities. The normalization of relations may have started unnoticeably or uncharacteristically, but its aim can be a gradual emergence of a strong bond. The trends in hostility reduction can become stronger with a change of officeholders or leaders, especially removal of those who have been responsible for past atrocities.

A failure to diminish mistrust is most likely to be associated with a lack of investment in relationship building supported by reconciliation efforts along with the admission of past guilt. The demands of 'comfort women', who were forced to serve as Japanese soldiers' sex slaves during World War II, were denied by the Japanese government which has been consistently refusing any official apology and compensation for the past wrongful acts. This denial has remained a continuing source of contention between Japan and its World War II victims even after more than 50 years since the war's ending. In abusive relationships, past experiences become a hindrance to establishing a foundation for new relationships.

Application of conciliatory measures

In making concessions and initial demands, the adversaries may have different referent points which serve as bench marks. The extent of the retreat is likely to be judged in terms of these bench marks. Informal discussion about solutions is encouraged by the abandonment of contentious goals or coercive actions (Hoffman, 2005). In violent civil or inter-state wars, the complete cessation of violence for a truce is denoted as a turning point in the relationship (Mitchell, 1999). The existence of common reference points facilitates coordination efforts for a conciliation process by adversaries. Transformations of relationships generally result from a sustained process of confidence building.

The rates and range of concession making vary at different stages of conciliation, influencing negotiation outcomes. Dramatic perceptual changes may follow unexpected behaviour, from antagonistic to conciliatory. While the existence of mutual eagerness for de-escalation brings about a quick de-escalation process, a mode of behavioural change can, in general, be incremental. In the post-civil war situations of Cambodia, Angola, Mozambique, El Salvador, and many other places, disarmament and demobilization of insurgents have taken a gradual approach until full trust is built. The involvement of more stakes pushes a conciliatory process up a continuing ladder from symbolic gestures, economic compensation for past harms, humanitarian assistance, release of political or war prisoners, withdrawal of troops and further confidence building efforts to the abandonment of occupied territories or granting of independence.

Some actions can perhaps be taken on a temporary basis while others are more or less permanent. A decrease in the negative mode of coercive activities can be embarked upon tentatively prior to an adversary's reciprocation. It is relatively easier to halt or completely remove cost inflicting policies with further conciliatory exchanges. However, it may take time to bring about benefit promoting changes which further facilitate a conciliatory mode of exchanges. Temporary withdrawal from negative sanctions is far less risky than a full strategy modification, since the direction within the same strategic mode can be easily reversed if there is no suitable reaction from the other side. In addition, it reduces resistance from hawkish factions which are sceptical of a restraint from high levels of coercion (Mitchell, 1999).

To accelerate the other party's conciliatory moves, accommodative messages (carrying 'positive forms of social influence') can be introduced, on a contingent basis, in proportion to the target's compliance. In order to induce the Soviet Union to withdraw their occupation troops, in 1955, Austria promised Moscow neutrality in the East–West conflict. In 1977 President Sadat of Egypt offered making peace in return for an Israeli withdrawal from the Sinai. The United States provided substantial economic and military aid for the purpose of moving Egypt away from the Soviet Union and signing a peace agreement with Israel.

The employment of rewards can induce cooperation, but it is essential to make clear that one has the intention and ability to retaliate. In fact, building a collaborative relationship is contingent upon the other's reciprocity of benevolent actions. Future decisions can depend on an adversarial side's response to a cooperative move. Once one's accommodative actions are abused, the party can become disillusioned.

In a strategy of reciprocating influence, a retaliatory threat is commonly re-introduced upon a lack of accommodating initiatives. If the other's intent is to abuse one's good will, it is better to retaliate quickly against an adversary's provocation. Reciprocation of competitive behaviour ought to cool off an adversary's expectations of further gains obtained by the pursuit of exclusive, unilateral interests. Mild retaliation is more likely to elicit cooperation, contrary to no retaliation or harsher retaliation.

Promises and rewards are generally withheld, reversed or reduced in the event of non-compliance, even if this change invokes a risk of re-fuelling renewed escalation. In the early 1980s, the Soviet Union threatened to withdraw from the Anti-Ballistic Missile (ABM) Treaty if the United States were to deploy an anti-missile defence system. In arms control, promises are often an essential tool to stimulate an adversaries' reciprocal arms reduction. When the adversary does not reciprocate moves for reduced military arsenals, unilateral arms control actions can be easily reversed.

The range of behaviour can be qualitatively compared among types of policies but, at the same time, quantitatively according to the extent of intensity. More specifically, the modes of action (comprised of the extraction of sanctions and reward conferring) can change quantitatively in either a negative or positive direction. A sequence of accommodative moves can be tuned toward de-escalatory sub-stages of interaction. Optimism is manifested in an upsurge in the proportion of accommodative messages. The other's compliance with one's own demand in a conciliation process would encourage further intensification of a positive mode of actions such as a guarantee of security. The acceptance of accommodation as a main strategy is seen as more shocking when it comes after long-term coercive actions that have created negative psychological effects.

The patterns of unilateral conciliatory tactics may start with refraining from making a coercive move such as an unconditionally declared cease-fire. In general, the withdrawal from negative sanctions such as a trade embargo or cessation of armed attacks can be considered far less costly than the provision of a new award such as economic assistance or territorial transfer. Even if concessions are made in one area (for instance, a favoured trading partner status), sanctions may still be imposed in other areas (such as a ban on the sales of technology to be used for military equipment). The sanctions could either be enlarged or diminished (as is seen in the tightening or loosening of the restriction on sales of advanced technology). The application of threats and coercion tends to rapidly decline once the exchange of rewards and mutual persuasion take hold.

Modes of introducing conciliatory actions

A reduction in the punitive mode of sanctions and an increase in the award mode of actions can be either simultaneously or sequentially introduced. The decisions may depend on the other's anticipated response to the initiator's move, the time horizon of the initiating actor, and the level of familiarity with the target party's motives as well as expectations based on past histories of such an exchange for de-escalation. Benefit-conferring measures are likely to be adopted when the initiator has not only strong confidence in the other side's positive response to the bestowment of an award but also a necessity to speed up the conciliation process.

A typical mode of starting off a de-escalation process is likely to be a withdrawal of past imposed negative sanctions along with a gradual reduction in coercive action (Mitchell, 1999). Reduction in a punitive mode of actions may not immediately be followed by a positive mode of actions such as granting a legitimate political status. In particular, the mode of action exclusively related to 'lessened coercion' can be preferred when the initiator is unsure about the prospect for future interactions.

In accelerating the elimination of a coercive line of cost inflicting policies, a brief halt in military offence can be sealed as a permanent cease-fire. The complete cessation of military hostilities can be accompanied by positive benefits (such as humanitarian relief aid) upon the adversary's corresponding move. More beneficial offers need to be further propelled to reach a more advanced stage when enough confidence has been built to generate its own inertia.

As opposed to sequential introduction, a benefit awarding mode of actions can be employed in overlapping sequences or simultaneously with diminished coercion. Decreased punitive sanctions and minor award conferring activities may persist until the eventual emergence of collaborative inter-actions. The upsurge of rewarding behaviour can go hand in hand with the lessened cost imposition if there is a strong will and commitment on the adversarial side to a peace process.

Response to conciliatory gestures

Effectiveness of any conciliatory initiative can be judged in terms of the target response and continuing sustainability of a positive mode of interactions.

The target side's behavioural response to the initiator's expectations and demands can indicate the success or failure of a particular type of influence attempt. Whether unilateral initiatives yield concessions by another, setting the stage for settlement, relies on the impressions given out.

This process is not necessarily rational, involving a high level of emotional anxiety that increases a potential for distorted perceptions. Expectations and desires held by adversaries play an important role in mutual behavioural patterns. The suspicion of motives behind one's offer (attributed to the extraction of undue concessions) might linger in the other side's mind. Overall, reversing the dynamics of an ongoing conflict demands extraordinary sensitivity to signals from the other side (Mandel, 2006).

Inter-action entails varied forms of tacit bargaining. A wide range of acts draws different degrees of attention from adversaries. In general, a benefit-awarding mode of de-escalation, derived from a more serious policy adjustment, is contrasted with a minor adaptation to the application of punitive measures. However, even a benefit-conferring mode of de-escalation is likely to yield an outcome with different degrees of success, since the target parties have diverse types of response to incentives. Each party may possess even opposing views of the nature of meaningful accommodation.

Decision makers have a wide range of reactions to the award of benefits and withdrawal of cost-imposing coercion under many different circumstances. Given its comparatively low cost and relatively simple logistical challenges, reversing on-going coercive activities would impress the recipient less than bestowing newly instituted rewards. The fear and distrust are supposed to switch to positive feelings, once the initial reduction in sanctions moves on to the benefit awarding mode. In general, gradual movements can provide time for the other side to adjust to a new mode of exchange.

The effectiveness of a variety of strategies and tactics to induce accommodation depends upon the circumstances of the delivery of conciliatory messages. In a contentious relationship, the reciprocation of concessions is not likely to be forthcoming if the other party thinks that the initiator acts out of desperation or if there is no genuine interest in cooperation (Patchen, 1988). In addition, a variety of motivational factors influence the choice among diverse types of responses to conciliatory gestures. Despite higher costs, the parties may refuse to signal any willingness to lower their commitment to fight until they are sure of the adversary's intentions. An enemy's conciliatory response may be seen as a gambit to soothe one's suspicion and earn more time in preparation for a renewed attack.

Reactions to unexpected concessions as well as sudden reduction in coercive activities are difficult to predict or gauge especially at the initial stage of de-escalation. A unilateral concession and expression of compromise may be misinterpreted by the other as a sign of weakness and retreat, inviting greater demands if an adversary seeks domination but not compromise. Hard line decision makers may erroneously believe that victory is around the corner, and may even further step up attacks with an attempt to bring the other party near to collapse.

On the other hand, fresh concessions can encourage an opposing side to more actively seize a new opportunity and relax their positions so that a compromise would be made feasible. This is inclined to happen if the other side's goal is to seek mutual coexistence. In general, successful new initiatives are supposed to create impressions of the initiator's trustworthiness. In addition, accommodating gestures are more likely to be effective in power symmetric relations than asymmetry with all other conditions being equal (Lawler, et al., 1999).

The signals embedded in conciliation can be easily misinterpreted especially when the concessions have been presented following a long period of sanctions. The effects of yielding differ, depending on whether to be seen as either coerced or voluntary retreat. Mere reversal of a cost imposition process is cheaper and safer for those who seek new relationships, but it may not be taken seriously by the target due to its status quo oriented nature. The removal of embargo, conditional cease-fire, or halt in bombing are conceived of as tactical, rather than strategic, changes. The modifications of old policies might be less persuasive without being accompanied by innovative moves such as dramatic gestures for an apology or conciliatory visit to an enemy territory.

Therefore, lessening or eliminating mutually costly sanctions can be simply attributed to a re-adjustment of strategies. Simply reverting the relationship to the previous status quo does not mean innovation, being merely seen as a tactical retreat. If the original imposition of coercion has been considered illegitimate or immoral, the reinstatement of the status quo alone is not likely to produce a perception of a meaningful turnaround. Reversion tends to have less impact on the adversaries' perceptions, since stopping something that should not have happened in the first place is not a cause for optimism or celebration (Mitchell, 1999).

The target would also be suspicious of the original motives of the initiator if benefits from withdrawing earlier policies such as economic sanctions are also advantageous to the initiator. The relief of costs for the opposing side can also be beneficial to the side initiating the move. Sanctions can carry costs for those who introduce them in terms of real expenditure of human and material resources. For instance, the US relief of sanctions on Libya was presented as a reward for the Gaddafi government's abandonment of nuclear programmes. However, since the programme was only at a primitive stage and since American oil companies have been beneficiaries, the removal of sanctions did not set an example of a promise of reward for other countries which pursue nuclear programmes.

More distinctive moves with unusual concessions are supposed to draw wide recognition, eventually eliciting similar actions by adversaries (Raiffa, 2002). In general, a benefit-awarding mode of de-escalation is considered a positive type of activity with implications for a more serious policy change than a minor adaptation to a given situation. Most importantly, authentic conciliatory gestures with specific, concrete offers are apt to be more visible than an ambiguous withdrawal of coercive messages.

The seriousness of the other's intention might be measured on the basis of the unilateral, unconditional and irreversible nature of de-escalatory moves (Mitchell, 2000). Irrevocable gestures made without any attached conditions are more prone to be accepted as being authentic. The recipients take more seriously any gestures, made in an open manner, whose significance cannot be easily denied in public. The target's calculations are also, in part, based on whether the past history of conciliatory offers by the other side has turned out to be mere deception or proved to represent genuine efforts. The ultimate credibility, of course, hinges upon whether the party backs up their words with reinforcing actions.

Perceptional change

In a long-term rivalry relationship, intransient policy-makers' perceptions are not easily altered even by clear conciliatory actions. The interpretation of any conciliatory initiatives is likely to be assimilated in closed, inflexible image of the adversary. In spite of his recognition of reduced Soviet hostility in the mid-1950s, for instance, hawkish Secretary of State John Foster Dulles during the Eisenhower administration did not abandon his negative perceptions of the Soviet Union. Cooperative moves such as the removal of troops in Austria and cutback in armed forces were attributed to Soviet internal weakness rather than goodwill initiated by new leader Khrushchev. It is very difficult to reliably demonstrate one's good intentions with cooperative actions to hardliners who demand nothing short of capitulation.

In understanding the complexity of de-escalatory dynamics, there are often gaps between the initiator's intentions and the receiver's perception. Due to its fixed enemy images of the Soviet Union, for instance, the Reagan administration initially paid little attention to a series of major concessions, made by new Soviet leader Mikhail Gorbachev, on arms control, troop withdrawal from Afghanistan, and unilateral troop reductions in Eastern Europe. Toward the late 1980s, Gorbachev even renounced the Brezhnev doctrine which prohibited political reform in Eastern Europe along with dramatic reduction in or virtual cessation of economic and military aid to Marxist allies in Mozambique and other parts of the world. Since these actions did not fit into the stereotypical patterns of Soviet behaviour, at first, American policy makers discredited these policies as mere public relations ploys cynically devised to modify the West's image of the Soviet leadership. Gorbachev's policies were re-interpreted, in the Cold War context, as a temporary retreat derived from Western strength and firmness rather than as desire for real change (Cashman and Robinson, 2007). It had taken several years to accept Gorbachev's policies as serious gestures and notice their real significance prior to the collapse of Communist governments in Eastern Europe.

Concession making ought to be carefully designed in order to modify enemy perceptions. It is a likely human tendency to easily discount small bits of offers coming at irregular intervals stretched out over time, since they are treated like mundane activities. In fact, dramatic pieces of information are more likely to produce pressure on the adversary to react, for spectacular events can certainly draw more attention of the adversary. Thus attractive offers descending all at once would be more effective in the conversion of attitudes than small concessions made piece by piece over an extended period. Equally, one-time extraordinary gestures alone would not be sufficient enough, under the weight of long term animosity, to overcome resistance against reduction in enemy images. Therefore, a spectacular event needs to be accompanied by the accumulation of less impressive and long term developments for lasting attitudinal transformation.

Politics for accommodation

Once de-escalation takes hold, parties can be mutually committed to irreversible and irrevocable changes. In order to avoid mutual loss, each side has to encourage the other to stick with the existing course of conciliation and keep providing mutually rewarding incentives. One party may retreat back to punitive tactics, out of impatience, inviting a negative conflict spiral with an opponent's ability to demonstrate their own coercive response. The resort to escalatory tactics might be rationalized on the grounds of a lack of behavioural changes and 'no choice'. This would shift the adversaries' goals back to seeking an advantage, irrespective of initial conciliatory intents and corresponding actions.

The risks involved in the discontinuation of a conciliatory line of policy are multi-fold; a rejection or withdrawal of a proposal for reduction in hostilities may be followed by a very sharp increase in conflict activities, further confirming the position of hard liners. The reinforcement of extremist positions would make it more difficult to initiate another round of conciliatory moves. The re-escalation of the conflict cycle may push high fatigue levels on both sides even higher.

The complexity of de-escalatory dynamics revolves around the fact that even well meant conciliatory moves often fail to launch a full-scale settlement process. Difficulties of communicating intentions come from 'noise', undercutting the efforts to stress the attractiveness of new offers. It is not unusual for each party to interpret opportunities and risks according to their own cognitive maps of various conflict stages and crossroads (Mitchell, 1999). Apart from this, the intra-party politics creates difficulties for initiating and positively reacting to an accommodative sequence.

Political strategies

The total abandonment of old strategies would be more convincing to the opponents, but it will be more challenging to sell to domestic opponents.

While lessening, but not completely abandoning, coercive action is tactically safe and politically more convenient in undermining internal resistance, it might not be taken seriously by an opponent who may believe that the stopgap measure does not carry sincerity, even to the benefit of the initiators more than the target. In the choice of de-escalation strategies, the balance between more benefit rewarding and sanction removing gestures can be tailored to the nature and extent of internal divisions of adversaries. In order to minimize the agitation of hawks on the other side, any types of visible efforts for positive relationship changes may have to follow immediately a lowered level of coercion.

Readiness for and continuing commitment to conciliation are, in part, affected by various types of conflict circumstances. Even if the target leadership is willing to take benign offers, they may not act more decisively in the absence of capacities to control the behaviour of potential spoilers. While forces organized for escalation need to be demobilized or weakened, new constituents or support bases have to be built for conciliation. The initiating leadership needs to rely on diverse channels of communication to influence not only an adversary's leadership but also their own rank-and-file constituents.

In the event of disunity among opponents, the rejection of friendly gestures may be ascribed to an internal power struggle. The move toward de-escalation can be hampered by the moderate's fear of losing power to hard line elements which seek net gains in missteps alluded to conciliatory postures (Blalock, 1989). Extremist, especially fanatic, groups (whose determination might have even been strengthened by a prolonged conflict) are very much concerned about their status during de-escalation. The acceptance of weak concessions by the moderate provides ammunition to conservatives who are eager to attack their internal rivals with their hawkish stance.

The fulfilment of conciliatory strategies, not wholly under any party's control, does not move in such a way as to produce one's intended effects. The internal aspects of conciliatory politics comprise the process of who gets what under which circumstances. Especially when each party's decision making is complex, their manifested behaviour tends to be multi-fold and often inconsistent. Not only the internal but also external surroundings of conflicts do not stay the same, requiring constant adaptation to new situations. A de-escalation course is not executed in a unidirectional fashion. It may take time to notice the genuine occurrence of transformative dynamics while the actual events are interpreted in a short-term time frame.

The role of communication

The presence of confidential channels, instead of public announcement, offers far more flexibility for both the initiator and target for transmitting conciliatory messages. Even if the target is interested in de-escalation, they may not be ready to respond for the reasons of internal politics. In case the target rejects new initiatives, it provides the initiator with the subsequent deniability of such a move. In the event of inability or unwillingness of official diplomats and formal representatives to communicate effectively, indirect channels are needed.

One path out of such a dilemma created by the lack of a direct contact between adversaries is the re-establishment of communication by a mutually-trusted third party who uses shuttle diplomacy to carry messages. Some form of third-party communication support is helpful at the high point of hostility where primary antagonists are reluctant to talk to each other in the midst of a continuing threat of repeated violence. Different channels especially in the absence of any reliable, direct communication mechanisms have diverse degrees of credibility with convenient means of deniability for any faltered initiatives. The third party intermediary can be seen as credible by having a direct and uninterrupted access to decision makers; they are more trusted by the partisans when they do not have self-interest in the outcome of the conflict.

Non-official channels are supposed to serve as vehicles for re-inventing a process to de-escalate intractable conflicts. 'Track two diplomacy' is differentiated from, but is supportive of, official or 'track one' diplomacy that is conducted by official state representatives (Price and Price, 2002). Non-official contacts can be made by entities in a private capacity within each party. Most importantly, informal contacts do not require psychological or political readiness as an essential condition for ultimate success in talks. An unofficial contact between informal representatives may eventually lead to the exploration of a workable alternative at an official level. Domestic controversies and cries of 'selling out' or 'surrendering' are avoided with the proposal made by intermediaries (instead of being directly presented by the leadership).

In reducing doubt about each other's motives, therefore, formal negotiations can be preceded by a preliminary period of back-channel, indirect communication (Kelman, 2002). In conciliation efforts, the hazard of looking weak and soft to the opponents needs to be outbalanced by the confidence in pre-negotiation contacts. Due to opposition in one's own camp, ascribed to the intolerant mood of any contacts with the enemy, the pre-negotiation period may remain entirely confidential. The risk of uncertainty coming from informal dialogue is much lower than in full-scale negotiation, provided that pre-negotiation contacts are kept confidential, not being exposed to the public. They could be even disavowed in the event of failure. On the contrary, progress made in pre-negotiation contacts undoubtedly fuels a higher level of optimism, leading to full-scale negotiation.

Communication strategies and trust

Various types of communication patterns are performed by one or more intermediaries whose functions differ in the chain of delivering messages. During the Iranian hostage crisis in 1979, Algeria acted as an intermediary, owing to the Iranian refusal to talk directly to the Americans. The negotiating was considerably slowed down by difficulties in the exchange of messages (Houghton, 2001).

Any proposals or counterproposals had to be translated twice, first into French for the Algerians, then into either Persian or English prior to being delivered to each side. Consequently, the questions and answers between Washington and Teheran had to go through a slow route.

Sometimes a communication chain may spawn two or more intermediaries who function as representatives of different protagonists. Due to the existence of severe hostility in a polarized conflict, no single third party may understand and gain trust from both sides. In such cases, a lower chain of two intermediaries can be formed at the initial stage of settlement efforts. Multiple intermediaries are more apt to assist in smoothing the delivery of contentious messages. Two or three liaison agents in the middle relay the messages of the responsible authorities on each end, as a communication buffer, to cushion pressure on the disputing parties.

The chains of communication are held tightly sealed when the parties are too antagonistic to acknowledge even an indirect contact between each other (Pruitt, 2003). The existence of complex chains furnishes a political cover for leaders interested in investing the prospects of a settlement with a sworn enemy. The complexity of a chain (comprised of at least two intermediaries) makes it easier to avoid directly contacting adversaries considered illegitimate, terrorist groups, with maintenance of secrecy. In a hostage crisis, a government leader does not need to admit any role in dealing with a hostile group or their host government by using the channel of a trusted intermediary (for instance, the Israeli government's indirect contact with the holders of their soldiers such as jihad groups or the Syrian government).

A broad system of communication can illustrate the manner to integrate all the decision making that goes into informal exchange of views (Burton, 1969). During the pre-negotiation period, the Irish and British government officials operated as a chain of intermediaries for various factions in the Northern Ireland conflict. Since hawkish parties, in particular, did not want to talk to their counterpart, the Irish government helped extend dialogue channels, for instance, reaching Sinn Fein closely associated with the IRA. The extremist group's concerns were delivered to the British government which, in turn, pulled the Unionist community, which wanted to keep the status quo, into the consultation network. In the long pre-negotiation period, starting in 1988 and continuing off and on, the Northern Ireland peace process was supported through indirect communication links, until the 1994 IRA cease-fire.

Parallel but complementary contacts constitute a communication nerve. The initial, higher level of communication paths was built at the meetings between the British and Irish Prime Ministers in 1985 to mark the beginning of an official Northern Ireland settlement process. At the same time, a series of meetings between moderate factions played an important role in the gradual development of the chains connecting groups within adversarial communities of Northern Ireland between 1988 and 1994 (MacGinty and Darby, 2002). It has taken nine years for a landmark, direct personal meeting to be held between the hawkish Democratic Unionist Party leader Ian Paisley and Sinn Fein leader Gerry Adams since the signing of the 1998 Good Friday Agreement.

Whereas complex networks of delivering and receiving various proposals offer synergy in multi-party peace negotiations, it can also produce severe message distortion. Details get lost, in preconceptions and wishful thinking, with the alteration of the fundamental meaning of messages. The longer and wider the network, the higher the likelihood of distortion and the greater the potential for misunderstanding. The sequence of communication in the middle is obviously shortened with the development of enough optimism, permitting a more direct contact between opposite camps at a distance (Pruitt, 2003). While direct information flow increases with a further decreased role of middle messengers, the intermediaries may stay on as neutral observers or in facilitative roles.

The direct exchange of views between the leaders needs to be expanded for mending the chasm at a wide level. In the early 1990s South African transition, for instance, many local peace committees were formed while the negotiation was going on between Nelson Mandela and F. W. de Klerk at a national level (Midgley, 2002).

Communication patterns in negotiation

Shortened distance in communication, with the gradual transformation of informal links into direct contacts, is accompanied by a transition from pre-negotiation to main negotiation phases. Success in negotiation lies in the full utilization of reliable channels for accurate understanding of the other side's goals, intentions, expectations, and the situation. Those who are competitively motivated may want to deliver unclear content to take advantage of an adversary's confusion. Such communication is likely to have negative effects on cooperation.

Improvement in the accurate interpretation of an adversary's messages is an essential step toward constructive exchanges. A structurally balanced form of communication is based on respectful and attentive listening about deep-rooted feelings, beliefs and experiences. At the end of successful exchanges, even hawkish factions might be enticed to moderate their deeply-held values with the acknowledgment of the 'genuine' reality.

The mechanisms for highly reliable and timely information beyond normal bureaucratic channels need to be established at times of crisis to control the perceived stakes in the outcomes. Flexible positions of the parties and a range of options would emerge from the mutually affirmed seriousness to defuse a catastrophic escalation. The operation of normal channels is undermined due to a sense of urgency (being pushed into a corner with a pressure for quick action) and high stake situations (facing humiliation). One way to slow the rate of action and reaction is to have sufficient time for mutual consultation and deliberation. In crisis de-escalation, for instance, the Berlin crisis of 1948-1949 and the Cuban missile crisis of 1962, the government's responses to their counterpart's demands were delivered through trusted channels between the leaders.

The quality in communication explains the feasibility of building a sufficient level of optimism and faith in moving into the direct final negotiations. Personal relationships established among leaders enhance confidence levels (shown in such examples as the informal lines of contact between Kennedy and Khrushchev in the aftermath of the Cuban Missile crisis). Stability of personnel smoothes negotiation, because it often takes a while for counterparts to get accustomed to each other's styles. Complex networks of consultation can be imposed on bilateral negotiations when mistrust and a lack of mutual respect stigmatize any efforts for problem solving. In the case of North Korea's negotiation with the Bush administration, the elements of crisis were controlled by the involvement of multiple parties, including South Korea, Russia, China, and Japan which have developed both direct and indirect links of exchanging information and views.

Ending Conflict 11

Diverse conflict ending processes manifest themselves in their different outcomes with implications for the future sustainability of relationships between adversaries. A deep frustration with the inability to negotiate a termination often reflects how difficult it is to resolve major conflicts on the international scene. Even in cases which are considered successful examples such as the end of the civil wars in Mozambique (1992) and Angola (2002), the independence of Namibia (1990) and the abolition of the Apartheid regime in South Africa (1994), it took several decades to reach a point where the protagonists began to have serious negotiations.

Every cycle of conflict episodes produces a new emotional and physical reality while leaving more victims and hard feelings behind. A renewed cycle of conflict may result in further entrenched positions, strengthening the existential elements of the struggle. Consequently, the emergence of new institutional structures and attitudes is essential to the transformation of a once seemingly intractable conflict.

This chapter covers diverse types and methods of conflict ending with discussion about conditions for sustainability. The courses of termination (revealed by the way conflict has been waged) have an impact on not only modes of outcomes but also their substantive nature. When some groups are left out or deprived of their essential needs, it creates a negative environment for amicable post-conflict relationships hampering the general atmosphere of reconciliation. Overall, the chapter is designed to review the strategies of conflict termination and their implications for a viable future.

The nature of conflict termination

The ending of a conflict is widely regarded as a condition for the cessation of adversarial activities with an explicit or implicit declaration of giving up existing efforts for the destruction of opponents. The result of conflict does not always leave clear-cut winners and losers. Drawing conflict to a close entails various types of costs as well as euphoria and feelings of relief (especially for those who are victorious). The outcome needs to be framed to generate the public or constituents' support if it does not deliver the original promises made by the leaders.

In contrast with armed struggles, the continuance and ending of a non-military conflict situation is not always obvious, reflecting the ups and downs of the relationships. For instance, Venezuelan President Chavez's denouncement of US President George Bush as 'the devil' in a September 2006 speech to the United Nations General Assembly brought about an informal skirmish and unpleasant exchanges between diplomats, but has not ended with particular incidents. Protests on social and moral issues (for instance, abortion) would also not be subject to clear ending points without essential agreements on value systems.

In truth, 'happy resolutions of macro social conflicts often do not occur in the real world', indicating that it is hard to meet ideal conditions for bringing an end to incompatibilities in values and interests (Blalock, 1989: 239). It is conceivable that conflict can end with or without mutual satisfaction. Even in a compromise solution, conflict situations leave one party worse off and the other better off, if not objectively, at least in their own estimation (Boulding, 1962). In this situation, compromise will never be permanent as a stopgap solution.

The degree to which each party feels that their goals have or have not been met tends to be asymmetrical. The extent of goal satisfaction reflects both the subjective feelings and objective conditions of reality faced by each party at the end of the conflict. Because of the need for a victory claim, the initial goals of conflict need to be reinterpreted or reformulated. The expectations of certain outcomes may be, in part, shaped by alterations in power relations after intense struggles.

New relations and rules are accompanied by a series of events which test each party's resolve and capacity to prevail. The character of future struggles is most likely related to the specific terms of the present fight's outcome. Redressing the grievances (derived from the effects of the current hostilities) becomes a goal of a new conflict.

A renewed struggle may also erupt with a sense of an unfulfilled entitlement. The rebel group's victory in the Democratic Republic of Congo (DRC) following President Mobutu's fall in 1997 led to another civil war, to a large extent, instigated by Rwanda and Uganda whose leaders felt betrayed by the new DRC government's policies. In other situations, the brutal treatment of a civilian population by occupying forces has fuelled further resistance.

The extinction of one conflict may leave the seeds of a future conflict. The negative consequence of the 1965 Indo-Pakistani war generated a growing resentment of the Bengali population in East Pakistan. The ethnic leaders accused the Pakistani government of re-directing large sums of money to finance the war in Kashmir. The rebellion for greater autonomy in East Pakistan resulted in the creation of the newly independent state Bangladesh after the military intervention of India in 1971.

In general, continuing mistrust and insecurity can be viewed as the causes of failed attempts to reach permanent peaceful settlement. When not every key party has been integrated in the settlement procedure, the remnant of disenchanted groups may be re-organized, violently transforming the old struggle into a new phase with the involvement of different players and issues. After the end of the bloodiest period of Colombian conflict waged by the military wings of the two main protagonists the Liberals and Conservatives (1948–1964), armed insurgencies have evolved into low intensity guerrilla warfare and multipolar violence by three different militant organizations.

In the absence of conciliation, a conflict may end with the cessation of nearly all direct relations between adversaries. Efforts to seek a mutually satisfactory result are opposed to the imposition of one's own preference on others via coercion. Even after the emergence of compromise, one of the parties may sabotage progress toward completion of peace talks in the absence of internal and external changes commensurate to progress at the negotiating table. Despite internationally mediated agreements in the early 2000s, the Tamil Tiger guerrilla leadership in Sri Lanka returned to even more atrocious fighting, proving that they are not a reliable negotiating partner.

For relationship building, cross-cutting ties need to be cultivated in the formation of superordinate goals. A new identity and symbols of power are frequently espoused after the demise of old systems. For instance, South Africa had to develop a new national identity after the elimination of the Apartheid system. In the aftermath of the collapse of the Soviet Union, the newly established states reconstructed their old ethnic myths with reference to ancient historical heroes in order to forge a common sense of destiny. To cement the unity of a multi-ethnic state, the Netherlands and Switzerland advanced a common civic identity despite permitting ethnic languages and other unique cultural traditions to flourish.

New values, institutions, and intricate social networks help opposing groups merge into a larger entity with emotional loyalty. In managing stable intergroup relations, major national organizations promote symbols of unity with shared identity regardless of differences in political affiliations, professional groupings, business associations, and trade unions. In a pluralistic society, these relationships develop a complex web of interdependence among multiple sectors of society, weakening the importance of the identity and membership of an exclusive social category.

Types of conflict ending

Three broad categories of conflict termination consist of one-sided victory, withdrawal, and accommodation. Unique conflict conditions promote either the imposition of one-sided will, retreat or compromise. Conflict may end, in the most drastic fashion, with unilateral destruction or mutual annihilation (Filson and Werner, 2004). Long-term animosities between two rivals with varying degrees of power disparities can be frozen without further provocations. Negotiated settlements generally rely on agreements reflecting the efforts of accommodation. These different types of conflict outcomes may not always be exclusive.

Imposition of unilateral decisions

When conflict is terminated through an exclusive victory in war or other types of coercive struggle, it obviously does not require intense negotiations to accommodate the other's needs. In the imposition of a unilteral decision, the victorious party has overwhelming power to determine the fate of the defeated (Mandel, 2006). If victory is achieved as a result of the total destruction of the other party's ability to compete or resist, the victor's preference may even be the dissolution of the defeated party's organizational structures or denial of a legitimate right to autonomy. The Ibo region in Nigeria was re-assimiliated following the Nigerian civil war in the late 1960s. The total destruction of one side weakens the capacity, morale, and will of the defeated to resist changes brought by the victors in at least short and intermediate terms. With an overwhelming sense of power, a winner gains confidence to control the destiny of their opponents.

In international conflict, victory may result in the annihilation of the vanquished, as experienced in genocide or military occupation. For instance, the political and military suppression of Tibet occurred as a consequence of the 1950 Chinese invasion. Likewise, the case of East Timor demonstrates that the weaker side's quest for independent political status can be cruelly suppressed through annexation. When East Timor declared independence in late 1975 after the end of Portugal's colonial rule, Indonesia invaded and occupied the territory. After 27 years of struggle, fortunately, East Timor was granted new statehood through the UN mandate in May 2002.

Imposed decision making is most likely to happen when at least one of the parties seeks to overwhelm their opponents in gross power asymmetry. The dominant party may not feel either normative or physical constraint in the ruthless treatment of the other. In this situation, one party is effectively applying coercion, both physical and psychological, against weaker, marginalized parties.

In case either assimilation or annihilation is difficult to adopt, owing to future political costs, in part, with the implications for the relations of the victors with other units in the international system, the victorious party may be interested in introducing new political and economic systems. A new international order was created, after World War II, with the massive US aid to reconstruct the economies of Germany and Japan, and also the Soviet implantation of a Communist regime in East Germany.

Political or military victory may result from a tipped balance following a long stalemate. The armed fighting between the Algerian government and various Islamist rebel groups (1991–2002) waned considerably after the surrender of the Islamic Salvation Army and the defeat of the rival Armed Islamic Group. On other occasions, the use of threats by a stronger party might be sufficient enough to cause the capitulation of a weaker party without any serious fight. In addition to psychological pressure, co-option and divide-and-rule tactics may be applied when the other party is split with a weak organizational capacity to resist. At its initial stage of war against the Taliban and al-Qaeda in Afghanistan, the US government bribed local warlords and armed factions in an effort to weaken the strength of Taliban loyalists. The current status quo is maintained, in part, by the tolerance of warlords' rule outside of the capital Kabul.

Withdrawal

When the process of ending conflict is protracted with the failure of each party to impose its own terms on the other, the cessation of hostilities in itself can be a new goal. In the event that the fight does not entail such a vital stake as survival, withdrawal is considered a more viable option than bottomless commitment to entrenched battles. If leaders perceive that they are not moving toward victory, abandoning the aim of seeking superiority becomes prevalent. Even seeking more effective means of fighting becomes counterproductive, under the conditions of increasing scrutiny from allies and unnecessary enemy making. These situations were exemplified by the French withdrawal from Algeria, Vietnam and other colonies as well as Portugal's decision to grant independence to Angola and Mozambique in the mid-1970s.

Instead of complete withdrawal, the parties may choose to keep their antagonistic relationships latent, as the past histories of the contest still linger. By avoiding engagement in direct contact, differences in the overall relationships would not be resolved. However, retreat from continuing fights would minimize the costs even though it means freezing the status quo. While parties may tolerate the existence of their rivals for the time being, they may look for future opportunities to improve their position vis-à-vis their adversaries.

Freezing of the status quo may follow the failure of contending sides to attain what they were seeking. When a continuing struggle does not yield what each party was longing for, the flames of conflict are likely to be extinguished through disengagement. Pulling out of antagonistic activities may occur when objects pursued by every side are not worth fighting any more. In the instances of the disappearance of the desired object, adversaries have nothing left over which to contend.

In a nutshell, complete withdrawal can be considered desirable in situations ranging from the high cost of violent struggle to the prospect for facing total defeat. Faced with destruction, the challenging parties are most likely to abandon contentious efforts in order to guarantee their survival or cut losses with some minimum guarantees of protection from future attacks. On other occasions, primary protagonists have strong incentives to avoid confrontation when comprehensive resolutions become attainable.

When decreased interaction follows the avoidance of further escalation, withdrawal does not require any efforts for conciliation, and at the same time, without forcing any new changes. The conflict outcome can be ambiguous, deficient of many substantive gains to either side. The mode of fighting and relative strength proven in the struggle give one party a one-sided advantage in claiming more. However, no one would be in a position to declare victory after the struggle is over.

Even in the power imbalanced situations of a contemporary conflict, it is difficult to pursue a clear-cut, unilateral victory given all the costs involved. The predominant US military power did not bring about the defeat of communist insurgents in South Vietnam. The Soviet war in Afghanistan led to the realization of the deadly capabilities of Mujaheddin guerrilla forces against the might of regular armies. As indicated by the above cases, the powerful party's desires to impose its aims by defeating the other prove to be too costly to satisfy.

In this situation, the consideration of cutting their losses can lead to giving up the costly engagements (especially when the conflict does not cause any threat to the withdrawing party's existential needs). Thus withdrawal is most likely in the event of imbalance between costs and gains. The US withdrawal from Vietnam, the Soviet retreat from Afghanistan and the Chinese withdrawal from Vietnam (after three weeks of invasion in late 1979) all illustrate the withdrawal of more powerful parties in a war with limited aims.

Negotiated settlement

The termination of conflict may involve tacit or explicit bargaining. In a negotiated settlement, compromise is an unavoidable component of conflict termination. Mutual concessions may follow the realization of difficulties getting what each partisan exclusively wants. The agreement may be reached due to a fear of re-escalation into another contest of strength which no one would be able to bear the cost of. Strong resistance from the other party with little power differentials is likely to induce compromise. In addition, if withdrawal is not an option because of an interdependent relationship, either geographic or economic, parties are pushed to talk.

Persuasion and mutual acceptance of legitimacy of each other's claims are reflected in a compromise settlement (Cloke, 2006). When differences are negotiated following a protracted period of fighting, conciliation may need to be involved in the resolution. A shift from hostility to acceptance is generated by reconciliation after each party comes up with its own terms of negotiation with the past. Each side may agree through persuasion that what they seek is not truly incompatible. New goals supplant the ends sought previously by re-interpreting differences in values between adversaries as insignificant.

With the existence of irreconcilability in major objectives, each may settle with a minimum compromise, and move on to the continuing negotiation, as evidenced in South Africa. Negotiation can challenge all the participants to protect their own interests while pursuing mutually agreeable goals. A transitional government demanded by the African National Congress paved the way for the creation of a new constitutional assembly and popular elections.

Bargaining may result in the settlement of some issues, while leaving other issues unresolved. Mutual satisfaction would emerge from win–win solutions where both sides enjoy gains without any loss to the other side. It is not unusual for parties to resolve differences in some essential areas such as immediate cessation of violence, and the synergy can produce an improved atmosphere for eventual resolution of more complicated issues. For instance, rebel forces and the government in Guatemala moved from an agreement on a cease-fire to the conclusion of the peace treaty that allowed wider participation in a new political process. The initial mistrust was diminished by the disarmament of rebel troops, easing the way to determine the contest between the government and opposition forces in electoral competition.

The end state of conflict

Whereas treaty signing and other ceremonial events may signal the end of hostilities, the exact ending point of conflict may not be so clear in the absence of mutual agreements and commitment to their implementation. A conflict is terminated more explicitly by an official peace accord with a clear cessation of armed fighting. In a social strife, an agreement may not be reached, but a conflict may lose steam when the government simply changes its legal codes, policies or declared stance toward marginalized groups.

Indeed, conflict may come to an end more implicitly in the event of withdrawal even without any official declaration. In this case, conflict termination is considered in terms of absence of provocative behaviour regardless of whether only one or both sides have officially accepted the existing conditions. When a struggle subsides quietly (for example, the 2005 Mohammed cartoon incident that inflamed the entire Islamic world), conflict may disappear uncharacteristically from public sight without any further noticeable events. Indeed, a particular struggle, void of resolution efforts, can become extinct without any visible changes in attitudes or relationships.

The termination of a conflict with or without mutual understanding and agreements has different implications for the sustainability of the outcomes. Even if one of the partisans declares the termination of conflict, the other side can refuse to accept the new status quo and continue to vow to fight even at a low intensity scale. In spite of the rejection of the end of war, the conflict can practically be deemed terminated without any visible strength on the defeated side to resist an imposed outcome.

From the victor's perspective, the occupation of an enemy territory means the termination of armed fighting, but the defeated side may consider it a beginning of guerrilla warfare. Effective resistance movements are sustained by a practice of hit-and-run attacks, sabotage and assault on the symbols of power. This occurred for the Chechen resistance after their being routed by Russian forces.

Even in the case of clear divisions between winners and losers, some conciliatory tones are critical to the reduction of resistance from the local population. In order to limit the scope of retribution, the leaders responsible for violence may be singled out while avoiding reprisal against the entire group. Past guilt and responsibilities for atrocious acts can be attributed to the dismissed political and military elite as well as a dominant group within society. In post World War II, the Nazi party, not the entire German population, was indicted for the horrors of the atrocities. That helped not to lay the seed of grievances among ordinary citizens. The removal of Serbian President Slobodan Milošević by popular demonstrations after the NATO bombardment and humiliating retreat from Kosovo assisted in lowering grievances among the population against the West, since the former leader was seen as the source of contention.

Lasting political acceptance is essential to 'peace' that winners desire to maintain (Iklé, 2005). In most circumstances, the defeated side is likely to reject a new status quo created at the end of conflict and deny the legitimacy of the victor's gains. A defeat in itself becomes an additional basis of grievances. When the loss of territory is part of the outcome, it often constitutes an issue to be addressed in a future war. In fact, the territorial loss in the aftermath of a war may create more difficulties for the defeated to accept the status quo. Southern Sakhalin was transferred to Japan following Russia's defeat in a 1905 war, but it was taken back by the Soviet Union after World War II. Japan refused to sign a peace treaty with the Soviet Union that could have officially ended their warring status. It has been considered symbolically important by the Japanese government not to accept the complete repossession of Sakhalin by Russia.

The nature of future conflicts is likely to be linked to the specific terms of the current struggle's outcome. The desire to overcome the shame of a defeat leads to the yearning for a future victory and preparation for another battle. In particular, inflicting harsh, punitive conditions on the losers such as slicing off territories or heavy reparations results in resentment that will generate future hostilities. As exemplified by Germany following World War I, a defeated party nurses grievances and awaits a future opportunity to engage an enemy. The Israeli imposition of severe sanctions along with its military operations in the Gaza Strip has led to endless new strife.

The sustainability of a post-conflict result, in part, depends upon acceptable settlement procedures. When the outcome is reached through negotiation, it reduces the likelihood of eruption of new violence compared to the imposition of unilateral gains achieved by coercive means. Negotiated settlements most likely bring about satisfactory outcomes with mutual accommodations (Avruch, 2003). Collaborative efforts are necessary for the creation of bigger pies to share. Concessions may be compensated by future gains if yielding promises a continuing exchange of goodwill. In addition, new options can be formulated to narrow the gaps between opposing positions.

Some form of mutual understanding and recognition of each other's values and needs is inevitable in responding to contentious issues. Long-term sustainability is more likely to be gained when adversaries have resolved their differences by reaching an agreement and have been successful in the mobilization of support for the settlement within their community.

Maintaining the status quo

Various types of conflict ending influence the conditions for establishing new relations between parties. The status quo may be maintained despite a desire for changing the motivation that instigated the conflict in the first place. The new rules, agreements, and contracts may simply be re-affirmed in support of the existing order. On the other hand, the continuing status quo does not completely deter the emergence of new attitudes and feelings in the aftermath of the struggle. In the negotiated settlements achieved by power symmetry, changes are not as dramatic as one-sided victory following either a war or revolution oriented toward the radical redistribution of land and other types of properties (Bell, 2006).

In instances where conflict is seen as a contest of power, the outcome may simply be freezing or changing superior relations. A series of Indo-Pakistan wars along with less intense armed skirmishes in Kashmir (since the two countries' independence from Great Britain in 1947) illustrate Pakistan's dissatisfaction with the territorial status quo and their failed attempts to change it in locked-in battles. A power contest can also be exhibited in hard bargaining. For instance, the outcomes of a labour settlement may reflect power balance at the negotiation table affected by physical actions on the ground such as strikes and the shut down of factories by employers.

In a militarily imbalanced conflict, bargaining has sometimes been employed to demand capitulation or justify the imposition of a stronger party's will. Two days after its invasion of Cyprus on July 20, 1974, Turkey halted their military advance temporarily but demanded at formal peace talks held in Geneva that the Turkish Cypriot community (comprised of about 18 % of the population living in 10 % of the island) be given 34% of the country's territory. When Greek representatives asked for two days of internal consultation, the Turkish government denied the time, and resumed its offensive to satisfy their own objectives (Callaghan, 1987).

When power relations are not certain without any sure measurement, initial fighting may test out each other's superiority. Even following intense casualties, neither side's domination may be established. The outcome of the Iran–Iraq war lasting ten years starting from 1980 did not establish either country's hegemony over the region. In this situation, the war's cessation re-confirms the existing status quo.

If withdrawal leads to freezing the pre-existing conditions, conflict merely serves as a failed attempt to change the power balance. Armed struggle may be terminated without bringing advantage to any side despite heavy casualties. The Korean War was completed without any American military advantage vis-à-vis North Korea. Whereas the Korean War produced no tangible territorial gains to either side, the Vietnamese guerrilla warfare ended with a stalemate prior to North Vietnam's military assault on the South in 1975.

Withdrawal may often be followed by containment policies, as exhibited between the first and second Gulf Wars. The end of the first Gulf War restored the status quo prior to the Iraqi occupation of Kuwait by leaving intact Iraqi domestic political situations after the recovery of territorial boundaries. However, further confrontation was accompanied by continuing economic embargoes and other sanctions besides the occasional US missile strikes on limited targets in Baghdad. The containment policy had checked Saddam Hussein's rule with international pressure, despite his public defiance against American policies, until the second Gulf War in 2003.

In general, withdrawal places a freeze on the new status quo, but it may not be held permanently in many cases. New conflicts can flare up again in the future when any of the parties is dissatisfied with the existing reality, and has the motivation and capabilities to start a new war. North Vietnam eventually invaded South Vietnam to unify the divided country after the US withdrawal. The initiation of the second Gulf War reflects the junior Bush administration's impatience with the status quo to leave Saddam Hussein in power and desire to establish a new American friendly government in the region.

As seen above, the cessation of struggle may not necessarily entail the resolution of the fundamental issues, while keeping the status quo. The active phase of the conflict may simply be frozen following a cease-fire without any settlement in sight. In other situations, conflict may have been settled, but collaborative relations are difficult to build. The peace settlement between Israel and Egypt brought about a cession of warring status between the two governments despite some occasional tension over Palestinian issues. The conformity with the current status quo (achieved by the September 1978 Camp David Accords) is largely attributed to the massive American aid flow to both countries. However, there have been little direct social contact and exchange among civilian sectors.

Establishing new relations and institutions

With the emerging realities at the end of a conflict, some settlements may bring about lasting changes in the relationships, leading to the creation of unified institutions and rules in which every party has a stake. At the conclusion of a civil war, the new elite may take control over the government or bring about changes in social order, creating shared institutions (Jeong, 2005). The end of a victorious armed struggle sometimes results in autocratic rules, as in the case of Eritrea.

Alternative values and institutions can be created in a way to establish interdependent relationships that are designed to prevent future conflicts (Kaufman, 2006). Parties are more easily integrated through the construction of common institutions along with efforts for the assimilation of minorities. In the aftermath of the US civil rights movement, segregation was made illegal to aid the integration of African-Americans into educational and other sectors of the society. In order to weaken a prospect for challenges of the majority Hutu population, the Tutsi leadership appointed a moderate Hutu politician to a presidential position, until he was replaced by former Tutsi military commander Paul Kagame in 2000.

While new rules may be forced upon a loser rather quickly, it can take time to bring about changes in normative values. The conversion results in the transformation of competitive relationships by accepting even opposing values and systems. The strategies of conversion include setting up even opposite social structures (communism being substituted by a capitalist economy and pluralist party systems) and replacing an old collective identity with a new one.

A different system can be exported with the imposition of one's values through military victory, exemplified by the end of the American civil war and World War II. In addition, one party may be willing to give in to an adversary under external pressure or due to the appeal of opposing values. Moral, normative victory gained through pressure and eventually persuasion contributed to the abolishment of apartheid in South Africa.

France and its European neighbours tried to assimilate Germany after World War II with incentives for economic and social cooperation (Iklé, 2005). Defeated adversaries might be granted financial assistance for rebuilding infrastructure along with respect for populations in the occupied territories (Flavin, 2003). The initiatives by the victorious party are more easily accepted if the newly imposed order is seen as beneficial by people in the defeated countries.

The transformation of an opponent may be accomplished by indoctrination as well as persuasion. The acceptance of an opposing side's values and systems can fundamentally alter the relationships between adversaries (Kriesberg, 1998). Ideological conversion of the Soviet Union brought the Cold War to a close (Odom, 2004). Mikhail Gorbachev and his colleagues believed that their system was not functioning, and had a desire for reform which eventually ended with the political and economic collapse of the Socialist system. Chinese students vividly demonstrated their yearning for Western values and systems by putting the Statue of Liberty in their protest of the autocratic rule of the communist party at Tiananmen Square of Beijing in 1989 though their protests were crushed.

While rejecting Western pluralistic democratic systems and human rights values, the Chinese leadership abandoned socialist economic systems and has actively courted foreign capital and jumped on the bandwagon of global capitalism with membership in the Word Trade Organization. They have been taking advantage of cheap labour under strict political control in competition for the world market. The conversion to a free market economic system changed Vietnam's relations with its former adversaries such as the United States. Even though the USA failed to bring down Communist rule in Vietnam militarily, they have been successful in affecting the leadership's thinking with the benefit of trade relationships.

While the above cases of transformation illustrate motivations for economic prosperity by the national elites, forced conversion has been devastating to the survival of tribal and other minority cultural groups throughout the world. The dominant institutions of capitalism and Western culture have served as agents of the superior. Religious and other value conversions, adopted as a means for hidden control and assimilation, have wiped out many indigenous life styles and their traditions that are compatible with nature.

Owing to its oppressive nature, European colonization in the nineteenth and early twentieth century invited resistance rather than acceptance. The colonial expansion re-moulded traditional social institutions to dis-empower and exploit inhabitants. Many historical examples, such as the European colonial conquest of Africa and the annihilation of native people in the Americas, reflect the fact that the imposition of cultures, values, and social systems served the interests of the conquerors. Likewise, religious conversion in the colonial period ended up being a means to control the subjugated people. Exclusive ideologies for the justification of human rights violation through state supremacy produce contentious conflict norms opposed to peaceful transformation.

An outcome matrix

In conflict termination, diverse circumstances exist, comprised of win–lose, win–win, and lose–lose. In a win–win outcome, satisfaction of everyone's needs does not produce a legacy of bitterness, helping to prevent future conflict. A mutually beneficial outcome is difficult to attain, though, when each party pursues their own exclusive interests with coercive forces. A unilateral victory may fulfil the desires of only a winner, but gains of one party are made at the expense of others. Each side can be a loser in a destructive fight for factional control especially when they confront a superior common enemy. For instance, the division between Hamas and Fatah armed members within Palestine weakened their ability to resist the Israeli occupation.

The outcomes of a conflict have an impact on the relationships between the main protagonists and other groups. The consequences of mutual destruction following a total struggle almost certainly strengthen the power status of other actors in the international system. The two world wars in the twentieth century led to the collapse of traditional European powers in conjunction with the break-up of their colonial empires.

The costs of abandoning goals consist of the loss of external allies who supported the cause as well as rising dissent among internal constituents. When Egyptian President Anwar Sadat made a unilateral peace deal with Israel, he antagonized the majority of Islamic constituents with the loss of his country's leadership role and reputation for championing 'Arab cause'. The Camp David Accords with Israel deprived Egypt of the Arab League membership for ten years in tandem with the relocation of the League headquarters from Cairo to Tunisia (1979–1989).

The expectations differ according to the party's motivations and intents. Even in a withdrawal situation, actors may have a different sense of victory. Despite either side's failure to change the status quo, Hezbollah may have felt a stronger sense of achievement despite heavier casualties. Given their far superior forces, the Israelis had higher expectations with the aim of complete annihilation of Hezbollah. The failure to eradicate the armed group's entrenched fighting infrastructure to strike Israel with rockets caused dismay with a call for the resignation of Prime Minister Ehud Olmert. For the militarily inferior guerrilla forces, successfully resisting the advancing regular army is a victorious outcome. By creating a sense of invincibility in response to the overwhelming military attacks, Hezbollah has generated new expectations for a future conflict especially among their supporters and constituents.

Even in a compromise settlement, internal differences are inevitable, owing to challenges to represent multiple, sometimes contradicting, concerns at the bargaining table. The degrees of satisfaction with an outcome are not monotonous within the same party, when an overall balance sheet of gains and concessions differs according to factional interests. High expectations derived from victory following the sacrifices of a long struggle create internal dissension for the distribution of positions or other prized tributes. The equality of access to decision making can be denied certain groups, reflecting an internal struggle in post-civil war state building.

How distant the actual outcome is from the expectation influences the perceptions of success. In a compromise acceptable to every side, any change in the status quo can be marginal and gradual because of difficulties to integrate all of the different interests. Despite the agreed settlement, the outcome may be imbalanced in terms of goal achievement for each party. The recognition of diverse levels of satisfaction with compromise is imperative when one party gets more of what they wanted while the other gets less. Nonetheless each protagonist may still feel that it is fair in a situation of limited options with the control of their grievance.

Most importantly, expectations vary according to the perceptions of power relations and the stake in a conflict. A weaker party tends to have a lower expectation in conflict outcomes than a stronger party. If a stronger party wants a total victory, nothing but an adversary's capitulation would be considered enough. Surviving a contest with an onerous foe is felt to be a triumph by a weaker party. The successful resistance may even generate confidence in their capacity to deter future assault.

Factors affecting conflict outcomes

The content of conflict termination (such as victory in an armed struggle, withdrawal, or negotiated settlement) is affected by evolving strategies of the contending parties and changing nature of goals as well as their power differentials (Kriesberg, 1998). The level of power imbalance has different implications for when and how conflict can be terminated. In fact, a decisive victory in armed struggles demonstrates great power disparity contrary to less eventful compromise from protracted negotiation.

The exercise of power and its utility in determining the outcomes entail the consideration of various opportunity costs (related to not only military uncertainties but also a risk of further human sacrifice, financial depletion and political costs). The gains in overwhelming an adversary would be compensated by the high level of opponent resistance and the political costs of actual employment of coercive force. The US government's decision to invade Iraq in 2003 certainly reflects miscalculations about the anticipated level of resistance against the American occupation by President Bush and his advisors.

Relative power differentials, modest versus considerable, have an impact on the parties' strategies and their expectations of conflict outcomes. Not only immediate disparities in coercive power capabilities, but also differences in economic resources to be mobilized in the future affect the calculation of relative power balance. Superior organizational skills and effective fighting capabilities may compensate, to a certain extent, relative nominal power inferiority.

Thus power differences are often more than the possession of the numerical amount of destructive military forces. The mobilization and deployment of coercive power by regular armies differ from the logistical and operational skills of armed insurgents. The effectiveness of guerrilla warfare against regular armies is hard to judge prior to actual engagement since the destructive capabilities of irregular armed combatants are hard to measure. Fierce resistance is more likely to be sustained on the home turf of extreme religious or ethnic movements.

In influencing the outcome of conflict, parties have relatively different capacities to fight with particular enemies. Their strength may have diverse adaptability to certain types of struggles, for instance, guerrilla warfare in mountainous or urban areas versus a contest between regular armed armies. At the same time, fighting capabilities as well as physical strengths are not the only factor in determining the outcome of a struggle with a specific adversary.

The level of morale affects the translation of numeric strength into actual logistical, operational abilities and tactical skills. Issue salience associated with different types of goals, essential and non-essential, also influences the extent of commitments to fight. The degree of confidence differs, depending on whom to fight against. American soldiers in Iraq are likely to have lower levels of motivation, compared with Islamic insurgents. Military superiority does not always guarantee success in a struggle against weaker but determined enemies. Withdrawal from a low stakes struggle with a staunch enemy is considered a less costly strategy. In fact, withdrawal can eventually follow a loss of interest in continuing fighting (Kriesberg, 1998).

One of the strong motivators for settlement decisions is a desire to avoid further sacrifice to be made for a lasting conflict. The gains from negotiated settlement can be compared to costs inherent in a loss after a sustained fight. The more necessity exists to make a victory claim for the justification of sacrifice, the more reluctance the elite has to give in to the other's demand. It takes longer to reach any kind of closure in situations characterized by a high degree of goal incompatibilities and entrenchment.

The degree of easiness to admit defeat is connected with the domestic political costs of discarding the goals as well as concerns over the prestige associated with a power status. In general, a conflict-ending stalemate precedes the final step toward settlement. It is displayed by resistance against concessions at a negotiating table or a final military assault prior to withdrawing troops in the cessation of warfare.

Other conditions for a protracted termination process include the opposition of domestic constituents as well as external allies to finishing a struggle. In the event that strong opposition to compromise is inevitable due to difficulties in meeting key constituents' essential demands, confidentiality is required. Internal strife against a moderate leadership might follow unpopular compromise, even challenging the basic premises of negotiating with an adversary. Bargaining processes can be tumultuous, with factional opposition, so internal negotiation is necessary to make decisions on types of concessions to be made.

Thus the loss of constituent support is involved in the calculation of costs in drawing conflict to a close. Extensive efforts may need to be made to build intra-party coalitions in support of particular conflict outcome. Internal politics need to be carefully managed for minimizing cleavages and controlling the assertion of narrow factional interests. The success in the acceptance of unpopular compromise may depend, in part, on the existence of a charismatic leadership with broad public appeal in support of settlement.

Each party has a different aptitude for early conflict termination, in tandem with the imbalance of costs. The level of subjective sensitivity to the same objective costs can be different. The insurgents care less about the number of deaths incurred from fighting than US and allied forces. The American general public would be less likely to accept high war casualties than populations in countries like Afghanistan that have become numb to seeing so much death.

Assessing conflict outcomes

In general, the imposition of superior power is the least desirable way of ending conflict in almost every situation, especially when its aim is often to deny legitimate rights of others or suppress their essential demand for survival. However, unfortunately, it is not unusual to observe that the end of conflict may even strengthen one party's grip over the other more firmly. After their military assault on the unarmed Tibetan resistance in 1957, the Chinese government has exercised a firm rule in Tibet with various measures to control the inhabitants' cultural values and education (Shakya, 1999). In fact, this example illustrates that conflict may even tighten a stronger party's control over every aspect of a weaker party's life as well as their dream for autonomy. It is indeed a sad fact that in a real world, many conflicts are often not terminated with justice.

Oppressive regimes are more likely to put a heavy burden on the civilian population after the crackdown on a rebellion as a means of reprisal. In the cases of the Khmer Rouge in Cambodia, Russia under Stalin and China during the Cultural Revolution, 'enemy classes' were systematically terminated by mass executions. In more recent experiences of civil wars in Sierra Leone, Uganda and other dysfunctional societies, warlords left a devastating impact on a social fabric with the indiscriminate killings of elders, rape of women and abuse of children. Terror has served as a means to strengthen the reign of the revolutionary elite or warlords over the population.

Thus we may need to acknowledge the unfortunate aspect of oppressive conflict outcomes against the ethical, universal standards which humanity seeks. In essence, conflict termination does not necessarily transform unequal relations and exploitative structures. When conflict is over, a lingering question remains as to whose justice has been served. In a true sense of conflict resolution, an egalitarian structure is more likely to develop a genuine sense of harmonious relationships than a hierarchical structure.

If conflict arises from an unjust and oppressive social structure, continued struggle is likely to re-emerge in the future unless marginalized groups have been completely wiped out and assimilated by a stronger party, as seen in many Native American communities or Australian Aboriginals. The deterioration of life, along with the availability of the means for struggle, strengthens the will to fight in the absence of non-violence culture. In general, an economic collapse and political chaos as well as ethnic tensions have been the main causes for civil strife.

When exclusive interests of privileged groups control the state system, oppressive institutional means are used to oppress the minority population's demand for autonomy under the name of sovereignty. Despite yearning for justice, most victimized groups often do not have equal ability to bargain for their own interests without external intervention. Especially, in international conflict, power, not compassion or justice, prevails except on rare occasions of public outcry or the trial of former warlords committed for atrocities at the International Criminal Court.

In an international system, regrettably, the use of military power especially by stronger countries has been permissible without much fear of its repercussions. Justice is a political, social principle bestowing an ethical ground which conflict resolution has to aim at although it may not be easily achieved with short term efforts. The end of conflict must be evaluated in a larger context of social progress, particularly in terms of the moral economy of the society where everyone's yearning for human development is respected.

Post-conflict relationship building

While reaching an agreement on specific measures signals the initial point of ending conflict, it does not preclude continuing oppositions. New institutions and procedures have to be set up to regulate competition in a more predictable manner along with the mitigation of social inequality and tension. The recognition of diverse social identities and call for justice need to be integrated for the development of the agreed boundaries of rules and arrangements. Peace-building cultivates capacity development which is needed for a response to sources of underlying violence (Alger, 2000). It is contrasted with peace-keeping of which primary concern is violence control for immediate safety.

Even though the physical destruction of war is more tangible, the effects of violent atrocities on the psychology of individuals and groups are profound. Indeed, post-conflict interactions can be inhibited by victims' direct experience of violent trauma, and legacies of grievance and enmity. Victims feel a loss of trust even in a safe and predictable world with the past experience of betrayal by neighbours, the loss of family members, and exposure to violence such as torture. These traumatizing experiences destroy people's spirit and impair their capacity to lead a healthy life. Healing is essential to curing psychological harm manifested in a variety of symptoms, including hopelessness, depression, and feelings of isolation (Jeong, 2005).

Sustainable reconciliation needs to be fostered by overcoming extreme animosity, fear, and stereotyping via remembrance and mourning. Each side will be able to see the human face of the other by breaking down the barriers of mistrust, and recognizing past wrong doing. Retribution is critical to restoring dignity and respect for victims in such instances as the existence of massive violence (Daly and Sarkin, 2007). Various aspects of reconciliation are supposed to heal fractured social bonds and to alter people's expectations of themselves and others.

Preventive strategies

There are diverse circumstances of intervention, ranging from flaring signs of struggles and street protests to full-scale armed fighting. The goals of intervention should be adaptable to a specific context such as a fresh escalation or the recurrence of violent exchanges. Intervention at the stage of escalation has to tackle such issues as how to actively control and limit the incidence and scope of antagonistic interactions. Preventive activities may include efforts to inhibit repetition of violent confrontations, for example, through some form of reconciliation.

In deterring escalation, preventive intervention may be geared toward effectively re-directing the postulated causal sequence from the initial point. In fact, intervention becomes, in itself, a crucial element in toning down volatile conflict dynamics. Negotiating preventively is generally better than waiting for or responding to the outbreak of violence. The causes of popular insurgence need to be moderated before the issues become more difficult to re-negotiate. While a traditional approach to preventive action mainly focuses on immediate conflict dynamics, intervention should also be able to identify any latent or long simmering discontent that has a potential for explosion.

The exogenous and endogenous variables can be contorted to influence either the dynamics of escalation itself or more imminent aspects of violent manifestations. A lack of local capacity prompts the necessity for deployment of intervention forces to support efforts to mitigate the adverse effects of humanitarian disasters on civilian populations. Moreover, crosscutting ties can be arranged to foster inter-group communication among potentially hostile groups, in an attempt to reverse a polarization process.

In a response to ordinary grievances, citizens and groups can be provided with access to avenues and mechanisms for resolving the range of disputes. Women and artists in Bosnia-Herzegovina organized various activities to bring diverse ethnic communities together. In addition, building or restoring crosscutting ties may focus on reconstruction of valuable production facilities and other infrastructure. The fear of economic devastation, along with the existence of close interdependence, tamps down the temptation to spark any uncontrolled incident (Jeong, 2005).

Neutrality is differently applied in a variety of intervention settings, ranging from the control of inflaming situations to monitoring of agreed rules as well as possible deal making. International organizations or sovereign states, neutral to the given conflict, can be endowed with diverse tasks from fact finding to military enforcement. While NATO was heavily involved in restoring order in the Balkans, the Organization for Security and Cooperation in Europe and UN agencies provided human rights monitoring teams to enhance security for returning refugees. The conditions for successful interventions are linked to enhancing the willingness of protagonists to engage in some form of conflict mitigation.

The contexts of a preventive diplomacy without enforcement functions are different from those of humanitarian intervention that need to be quickly arranged in the middle of escalation. In general, a crisis prevention approach is short-term, and is not intended to change the status quo. In order to avoid the recurrence of violent upheavals or catastrophic outcomes, however, medium and longer-term approaches are necessary to produce attitudinal changes. New procedures for the incorporation of the views of disenchanted groups can eventually be oriented toward structural changes with power sharing arrangements and economic equity.

The intervention methods are plural, being re-moulded by the unique roles of multiple sponsors. Beyond neutrality, the purpose of intervention encompasses the protection or support of particular groups such as refugees in Sudan and starving populations in Somalia. Tipping the balance in a struggle, as occurred in Bosnia-Herzegovina, is needed to bring about settlement later. Whereas some intervention is designed for promoting a desired outcome, others may be confined to a limited range of activities, like mediation (Bercovitch and Houston, 2000). Even after the cessation of armed struggles, continued external intervention is essential to overcoming the difficulties, for instance, in the post-civil war settings.

Fact-finding missions, inspections, monitoring, and consultations can constitute part of 'early warning systems'. The timing of intervention is affected by the technical capacity to identify deadly conflicts before they erupt. Indicators for the justification of intervention cover extreme threats to human life, a collapse of social order, and regional instability. Precipitating pre-emptive action may also reflect geo-strategic concerns, security interests, and refugee crises.

Ethos of conflict resolution and transformation

The main ethos in conflict resolution can be exploration of effective procedures which help reduce human suffering and minimize damage to social and natural environments. In this endeavour, it is essential to investigate what kind of process would result in a just outcome that is not only fair to participants but also meets the broader ethical concerns of a given society, and those of humanity. Reflecting on some of the above concerns, 'conflict transformation' emphasizes more than negative interaction dynamics of adversarial relationships (Mitchell, 2002; Botes, 2003; Lederarch, 2003).

Since conflict is a recurrent phenomenon, its transformation remains a key question. The development of synergies stems from concerted efforts to stop vacillating between controlled and destructive phases. Resolution strategies benefit from analysis of how the conflict has evolved with changes in the participants' behaviour, goals and attitudes (Mitchell, 1981). The best outcome of conflict is achieved when solutions are mutually satisfactory, self-sustaining.

Resolving conflicts is quite distinct from mere coping and management strategies that usually do not respond to the underlying causes (Burton, 2001). Negotiation about material interests is sometimes unavoidably entangled with concerns over differences in values and demand for recognition of identities. If ultimate resolution is difficult due to a deep split over the core issues, value incompatibilities need to be managed by the acceptance of differences.

Moving from transient compromises to more durable settlements tends to be slow especially when it takes time to bring about new levels of mutual understanding.

A vast range of activities produce cumulative effects on relationship formation. Even if resolution efforts are not adaptable or are ineffective, conflict may still be ameliorated by various initiatives to reduce destructive violence. Rare moments of positive personal contact between deadly adversaries might be able to stimulate critical movements to reverse the tide in violence by generating hope in a bleak situation. Even failed mediation attempts helped avert the brutality of the victorious government army at the end of the Nigerian civil war in 1970 by developing some understanding of dire situations in the rebel region through informal communication channels (Curle, 1986). Since any stage of conflict is either accelerated or decelerated by intervention, waiting for the arrival of particular circumstances is not necessary for resolution.

The basic premises of conflict management and settlement approaches are unlikely to pay attention to the weaker party's long-term needs in an equitable manner by ignoring 'the power relations on the ground' (Rouhana, 2004: 174). The 'power politics' perspectives of conflict settlement are oriented toward the status quo often with a compromise even on fundamental human concerns. On the contrary, the approach of conflict transformation has been proclaimed to work toward bringing 'reciprocity and equality' to unjust relationships in an asymmetric conflict. Various strategies of transformation are tied to generating the awareness of latent conflict conditions (Miall et al., 1999).

Thus asymmetric and symmetric conflicts have different paths to resolution. In an asymmetric conflict, consciousness raising and empowerment are essential to the conversion of an unbalanced relationship. The intensification of struggle is sometimes regarded as necessary to make hidden issues more visible. The new initiatives for enhancing human rights and community development have been more widely recognized as part of a process in support of 'just' conflict resolution.

In a nutshell, conflict transformation approaches are not prone to be satisfied with merely reframing positions in a search for a 'win–win' outcome. The manifested phenomenon at the site of conflict most often does not reveal the very nature of parties and relationships. Thus transformation is apt to highlight the wider social and political sources of a conflict in seeking to break the perpetuating cycle of oppression and resistance. The conversion of asymmetric, unbalanced relationships sheds light on the cultivation of the marginalized group's role in the negotiation of social values and relationships along with attitude changes of the dominant party. The alternative to transformation is a malignant cycle of institutional deformation and violence.

References

Abrams, D. (2005) 'A social psychological framework for understanding social inclusion and exclusion', in D. Abrams, J. Marques and M. A. Hogg (eds), *Social Psychology of Inclusion and Exclusion*. New York: Psychology Press, pp. 1–25.

Agger, I. (2001) 'Psychosocial assistance during ethnopolitical warfare in the former Yugoslavia', in D. Chirot and M. Seligman (eds), *Ethno-political Warfare: Causes, Consequences and Possible Solution*. Washington, DC: American Psychological Association, pp. 305–18.

Alger, C. (2000) 'Challenges for peace researchers and peace builders in the twenty-first century', *International Journal of Peace Studies*, 5(1): 1–13.

Allison, G. (1971) *The Essence of Decision: Explaining the Cuban Missile Crisis*. Boston: Little, Brown.

Anderson, B. (1991) *Imagined Communities: Reflections on the Origin and Spread of Nationalism*. London: Verso.

Anderson, M. (ed.) (2004) *Cultural Shaping of Violence: Victimization, Escalation, Response*. West Lafayette, IN: Purdue University Press.

Applegate, J. and Sypher, H. (1983) 'A constructivist outline', in W. B. Gudykunst (ed.), *Intercultural Communication Theory*. Beverly Hills, CA: Sage, pp. 63–78.

Audergon, A. (2005) *The War Hotel: Psychological Dynamics in Violent Conflict*. London/Philadelphia, PA: Whurr.

Avruch, K. (2003) 'Context and pretext in conflict resolution', *Journal of Dispute Resolution*, 2: 353–65.

Axelrod, R. (1984) *The Evolution of Cooperation*. New York: Basic Books.

Azar, E. (1986) 'Protracted international conflicts: ten propositions', in E. Azar and J. Burton (eds), *International Conflict Resolution: Theory and Practice*. Boulder, CO: Lynne Rienner, pp. 28–39.

Babbitt, E. (2006) 'Negotiating self-determination', in H. Hannum and E.F. Babbitt (eds) *Negotiating Self-Determination*. Lanham: Lexington Books. pp. 159–166.

Barkan, S. and Snowden, L. (2000) *Collective Violence*. Boston: Allyn and Bacon.

Bar-Tal, D. (2000) 'From intractable conflict through conflict resolution to reconciliation: psychological analysis', *Political Psychology*, 21(2): 351–66.

Bartos, O. and Wehr, P. (2002) *Using Conflict Theory*. New York: Cambridge University Press.

Bay, C. (1990) 'Taking the universality of human needs seriously', in J. Burton (ed.), *Conflict: Human Needs Theory*. New York: St. Martin's Press, pp. 235–56.

Bell, C. (2006) 'Peace agreements: their nature and legal status', *The American Journal of International Law*, 100(2): 373–412.

Bercovitch, J. and Houston, A. (2000) 'Why do they do it like this? An analysis of the factors influencing mediation behaviour in international conflicts', *Journal of Conflict Resolution*, 44(2): 170–202.

Berkowitz, L. (1990) 'Biological roots: are humans inherently violent?', in E. Glad (ed.), *Psychological Dimensions of War*. Newbury Park, CA: Sage, pp. 24–40.

Besancon, M. L. (2005) 'Relative resources: inequality in ethnic wars, revolutions, and genocides', *Journal of Peace Research*, 42(4): 393–415.

Binmore, K. (2007) 'Introduction', in Ken Binmore (ed.) *Does Game Theory Work?* Cambridge, MA: The MIT Press. pp. 1–22.

Bizman, A. and Yinon, Y. (2004) 'Intergroup conflict management strategies as related to perceptions of dual identity and separate groups', *The Journal of Social Psychology*, 144(2): 115–27.

Blalock, H. (1989) *Power and Conflict: Towards a General Theory—Violence Cooperation and Peace* (Vol. 4). London: Sage.

Bonoma, T. (1975) *Conflict: Escalation and De-Escalation*. Beverly Hills: Sage Publications.

Boose Jr, D. W. (2000) 'The Korean War truce talks: a study in conflict termination', *Parameters*, 30(1): 102–16.

Bordens, K. and Horowitz, I. A. (2002) *Social Psychology*. Mahwah, NJ: Lawrence Erlbaum Associates.

Botes, J. (2003) 'Conflict transformation: a debate over semantics or a crucial shift in the theory and practice of peace and conflict studies?', *International Journal of Peace Studies*, 8(2): 1–27.

Boulding, K. E. (1962) *Conflict and Defense*. New York: Harper and Row.

Bourdieu, P. (1991) *Language and Symbolic Power*. Boston, MA: Harvard University Press.

Brecher, M. (1998) 'Crisis escalation: a new model and findings' in F. P. Harvey and B. D. Mor (eds), *Conflict in World Politics*. Houndmills: Macmillan, pp. 119–41.

Brecher, M. and Wilkenfeld, J. (2000) *A Study of Crisis*. Ann Arbor: University of Michigan Press.

Brewer, M. B. (2003) *Intergroup Relations*. Milton Keynes/Philadelphia, PA: Open University Press.

Brockner, J. and Rubin, J. Z. (1985) *Entrapment in Escalating Conflicts: A Social Psychological Analysis*. New York: Springer-Verlag.

Bronfenbrenner, U. (1961) 'The mirror image in Soviet–American relations', *Journal of Social Issues*, 17(3): 45–56.

Brown, R. (1988) *Group Processes: Dynamics Within and Between Groups*. Oxford: Basil Blackwell.

Brune, L. H. (2006) *Chronology of the Cold War, 1917–1992*. New York: Routledge.

Brzoska, M. and Pearson, F. S. (1994) *Arms and Warfare: Escalation, De-escalation, and Negotiation*. Columbia, CA: University of South Carolina Press.

Burton, J. W. (1969) *Conflict and Communication*. London: Macmillan.

Burton, J. W. (1990) *Conflict Resolution and Prevention*. New York: St. Martin's Press.

Burton, J. W. (1997) *Violence Explained: The Sources of Conflict, Violence and Crime and Their Prevention*. Manchester: Manchester University Press.

Burton, J. W. (2001) 'Conflict prevention as a political system', *International Journal of Peace Studies*, 6(1): 23–38.

Burton, J. W. and Dukes, F. (1990) *Conflict: Practices in Management, Settlement and Resolution*. New York: St. Martin's Press.

Byrne, S. (2003) 'Linking theory to practice: how cognitive psychology informs the collaborative problem-solving process for third parties', *International Journal of Peace Studies*, 8(2): 29–44.

Bystydzienski, J. M. and Schacht, S. P. (2001) 'Introduction', in J. M. Bystydzienski and S. P. Schacht (eds), *Forging Radical Alliances Across Difference: Coalition Politics for the New Millennium*. London; New York: Rowman & Littlefield Publishers. pp. 1–18.

Callaghan, J. (1987) *Time and Chance*. London: Collins

Calvert, P. and Allcock, J. B. (2004) *Border and Territorial Disputes of the World*, 4th edn. London: John Harper.

Carayannis, T. (2005) 'The complex wars of the Congo: towards a new analytic approach', in R. M. Kadende-Kaiser and P. J. Kaiser (eds), *Phases of Conflict in Africa*. Toronto: de Sitter Publications. pp. 83–106.

Carment, D. et al. (2006) *Who Intervenes? Ethnic Conflict and Interstate Crisis*. Columbus, OH: Ohio State University Press.

Carnevale, P. J. and Leung, K. (2001) 'Cultural dimensions of negotiation', in M. A. Hogg and R. S. Tindale (eds), *Blackwell Handbook of Social Psychology: Group Processes*. Oxford/Malden, MA: Blackwell, pp. 482–96.

Cashman, G. and Robinson, L. C. (2007) *An Introduction to the Causes of War: Patterns of Interstate Conflict from World War I To Iraq*. Lanham, MD: Rowman and Littlefield.

Casmir, F. L. (1985) 'Stereotypes and schemata', in W. Gudykunst, et al. (eds), *Communication, Culture and Organizational Processes*. Newbury Park, CA: Sage, pp. 48–67.

Choucri, N., et al. (1992) *The Challenge of Japan before World War II and after*, London: Routledge.

Clausewitz, C. von (1984) *On War*. Rev ed Princeton, NJ: Princeton University Press.

Clemens, W. C. (2002) 'Complexity theory as a tool for understanding and coping with ethnic conflict and development issues in post-Soviet Eurasia', *International Journal of Peace Studies*, 7(2): 1–16.

Cloke, K. (2006) *The Crossroads of Conflict: A Journey Into the Heart of Dispute Resolution*. Calgary, AB: Janis.

Coleman, P. (1997) 'Redefining ripeness: a social-psychological perspective', *Journal of Peace Psychology*, 3: 81–103.

Coleman, P. (2000) 'Intractable conflict' in M. Deutsch (ed.), *Handbook of Conflict Resolution*. San Francisco: Jossey-Bass. pp. 428–450.

Connor, W. (2002) 'A prime for analyzing ethnonational conflict', in S. A. Giannakos (ed.), *Ethnic Conflict: Religion, Identity, and Politics*. Athens, OH: Ohio University Press, pp. 21–42.

Conteh-Morgan, E. (2003) *Collective Political Violence: Competing Theories and Cases of Violent Conflicts*. New York: Routledge.

Conway III, L. G., et al. (2001) 'Integrative complexity and political decisions that lead to war or peace', in D. Christie, et al. (eds), *Peace, Conflict, and Violence*. Upper Saddle River, NJ: Prentice Hall, pp. 66–75.

Cooper, J., et al. (2001) 'Attitudes, norms, and social groups', in M. A. Hogg and R. S. Tindale (eds), *Blackwell Handbook of Social Psychology: Group Processes*. Oxford/Malden, MA: Blackwell, pp. 257–82.

Coser, L. A. (1964) *The Functions of Social Conflict*. New York: The Free Press.

Cupach, W. R. and Canary, D. J. (1997) *Competence in Interpersonal Conflict*. New York: McGraw-Hill.

Curle, A. (1986) *In the Middle: Non-Official Mediation in Violent Situations*. Leamington Spa: Berg.

Dahrendorf, R. (1959) *Class and Class Conflict in Industrial Society*. Stanford, CA: Stanford University Press.

Dalai Lama (1997) *Healing Anger: The Power of Patience from a Buddhist Perspective*. Ithaca, NY: Snow Lion.

Daly, E. and Sarkin, J. (2007) *Reconciliation in Divided Societies: Finding Common Ground*. Philadelphia: University of Pennsylvania Press.

Davies, J. C. (1962) 'Toward a theory of revolution', *American Sociological Review*, 27(1): 5–19.

de Bono, E. (1985) *Conflicts: A Better Way to Resolve Them*. London: Harrap.

d'Estrée, T. P. (2003) 'Dynamics', in S. Cheldelin, et al. (eds), *Conflict*. London: Continuum, pp. 68–87.

Deutsch, M. (1973) *The Resolution of Conflict*. New Haven, CT: Yale University Press.

Deutsch, M. (1994) 'Constructive conflict resolution: principles, training, and research', *Journal of Social Issues*, 50(1): 13–32.

Dixon, P. (2007) *The Northern Ireland Peace Process*. London/New York: Routledge.

Dixon, W. J. (1994) 'Democracy and the peaceful settlement of international conflict', *American Political Science Review*, 88(1): 14–32.

Dollard, J., et al. (1939) *Frustration and Aggression*. New Haven, CT: Yale University Press.

Dovidio, J. F., et al. (2005) 'Social inclusion and exclusion: recategorization and the perception of intergroup boundaries', in D. Abrams, et al. (eds), *The Social Psychology of Inclusion and Exclusion*. Hove/New York: Psychology Press, pp. 245–64.

Druckman, D. F. (1986) 'Stages, turning points and crises,' *Journal of Conflict Resolution*, 30(2): 327–60.

Druckman, D. (1990) 'The social psychology of arms control and reciprocation', *Political Psychology*, 11(3): 553–581.

Dugan, M. A. (1996) 'A nested theory of conflict', *A Leadership Journal: Women in Leadership*, Vol. 1, pp. 9–19.

Eckert, R. and Willems, H. (2005) 'Escalation and de-escalation of social conflicts', in W. Heitmeyer and J. Hagen (eds), *International Handbook of Violence Research*. Kluwer Academic Publishers. pp. 1181–200.

Ellis, D. G. (2006) *Transforming Conflict: Communication and Ethnopolitical Conflict*. Lanham, MD: Rowman and Littlefield.

Esman, J.M. and Herring, J. (eds.) (2001) *Carrots, Sticks and Ethnic Conflict: Rethinking Development Assistance*. Ann Arbor: University of Michighan Press.

Fanon, F. (2004) *The Wretched of the Earth*. New York: Grove Press.

Faure, G. O. (2005) 'Deadlocks in negotiation dynamics', in I. W. Zartman and G. O. Faure (eds), *Escalation and Negotiation in International Conflicts*. New York: Cambridge University Press. pp. 23–52.

Fawcett, L. (2005) *International Relations of the Middle East*. Oxford: Oxford University Press.

Filson, D. and Werner, S. (2002) 'A bargaining model of war and peace: anticipating the onset, duration, and outcome of war', *American Journal of Political Science*, 46(4): 819–837.

Filson, D. and Werner, S. (2004) 'Bargaining and fighting: the impact of regime type on war onset, duration, and outcomes', *American Journal of Political Science*, 48(2): 296–313.

Fisher, R. J. (1990) *The Social Psychology of Intergroup and International Conflict Resolution*. New York: Springer-Verlag.

Fisher, R. J. (2005) 'Introduction: analyzing successful transfer effects in interactive conflict resolution', in R. Fisher (ed.), *Paving the Way*. Lanham, MD: Lexington Books, pp. 1–18.

Fisher, S., et al. (2000) *Working With Conflict: Skills and Strategies for Action*. London/ New York: Zed Books.

Flavin, W. (2003) 'Planning for conflict termination and post-conflict success', *Parameters*, 33(3): 95–112.

Försterling, F. (2001) *Attribution*. Hove: Psychology Press.

Franck, T. M. (2006) 'The power of legitimacy and the legitimacy of power: international law in an age of power disequilibrium', *The American Journal of International Law*, 100(1): 88–106.

Freire, P. (1998) *Pedagogy of the Oppressed*. New York: Continuum.

Freud, S. (1933a) 'Why war?', in *Collected Works*, vol. 16. London: Imago.

Freud, S. (1933b) *Collected Papers*, vol. 5. New York: Basic Books.

Galtung, J. (1990) 'International development in human perspectives', in J. W. Burton (ed.), *Conflict: Human Needs Theory*. New York: St. Martin's Press, pp. 301–35.

Gerzon, M. (2006) *Leading Through Conflict: How Successful Leaders Transform Differences into Opportunities*. Boston, Mass.: Harvard Business School.

Gilmore, T. N. (2003) *Making a Leadership Change: How Organizations and Leaders Can Handle Leadership Transitions Successfully*. Lincoln, NE: Author's Choice Press.

Gladwell, M. (2000) *The Tipping Point: How Little Things Can Make a Big Difference*. New York: Little, Brown.

Gleick, J. (1987) *Chaos: Making a New Science*. New York: Penguin Books.

Goemans, H. E. (2000) *War and Punishment: The Causes of War Termination and the First World War*. Princeton: Princeton University Press.

Golden, J. (2007) 'Conflicts around knowledge management: connecting complexity, conflict, and knowing to support knowledge-focused work', PhD dissertation, George Mason University, Fairfax, VA.

Goldstein, A. P. (2002) *The Psychology of Group Aggression*. New York: John Wiley and Sons.

Goodman, R. (2005) 'International institutions and the mechanisms of war: a review of solving the war puzzle—beyond the democratic peace', *The American Journal of International Law*, 99(2): 507–15.

Gordon, C. and Arian, A. (2001) 'Threat and decision making', *Journal of Conflict Resolution*, 45(2): 196–215.

Greig, J. M. (2001) 'Moments of opportunity: recognizing conditions of ripeness for international mediation between enduring rivals', *Journal of Conflict Resolution*, 45(6): 691–718.

Gudykunst, W. B., et al. (1989) 'Language and intergroup communication', in M. K. Asante and W. B. Gudykunst (eds), *Handbook of International and Intercultural Communication*. Beverly Hills, CA: Sage, pp. 145–62.

Gurr, E. R. (1970) *Why Men Rebel*. Princeton, NJ: Princeton University Press.

Hechter, M. and Borland, E. (2001) 'National self determination: the emergence of an international norm', in M. Hechter and K. Op (eds), *Social Norms*. New York: Russell Sage Foundation, pp. 186–234.

Hewitt, J. J. (2003) 'Dyadic processes and international crises', *The Journal of Conflict Resolution*, 47(5): 669–692.

Hocker, J. L. and Wilmot, W. W. (1978) *Interpersonal Conflict*. Dubuque, IA: W. C. Brown Co.

Hoffman, A. (2005) *Building Trust: Overcoming Suspicion in International Conflict*. Buffalo, NY: State University of New York Press.

Hogg, M. A. (2001) 'Social categorization, depersonalization, and group behaviour', in M. A. Hogg and R. S. Tindale (eds), *Blackwell Handbook of Social Psychology: Group Processes*. Oxford/Malden, MA: Blackwell, pp. 56–85.

Holsti, O. R. (1984) 'Theories of crisis decision making', in Robert Matthew, et al. (eds), *International Conflict and Conflict Management*. Scarborough, Ontario: Prentice Hall of Canada. pp. 65–83.

Horowitz, D. (2001) *The Deadly Ethnic Riots*. Berkeley, CA: University of California Press.

Houghton, D. P. (2001) *US Foreign Policy and the Iran Hostage Crisis*. Cambridge: Cambridge University Press.

Hurwitz, R. (1991) 'Up the down staircase? A practical theory of de-escalation', in L. Kriesberg and S. Thorson (eds), *Timing the De-Escalation of International Conflict*. Syracuse, NY: Syracuse University Press, pp. 123–51.

Idris, A. H. (2005). *Conflict and Politics of Identity in Sudan*. New York: Palgrave Macmillan.

Iklé, F. C. (2005) *Every War Must End*. New York: Columbia University Press.

Isenhart, M. W. and Spangle, M. (2000) *Collaborative Approaches to Resolving Conflict*. Thousand Oaks, CA: Sage.

Janis, I. L. (1982) *Groupthink: Psychological Studies of Policy Decisions and Fiascos*. Boston, MA: Houghton Mifflin.

Jeong, H.-W. (2005) *Peace Building in Post-Conflict Societies*. Boulder, CO: Lynn Rienner.

Jervis, R. (1976) *Perception and Misperception in International Politics*. Cambridge, MA: Harvard University Press.

Jones, A. (2006) *Genocide: A Comprehensive Introduction*. London/New York: Routledge.

Jones, T. (2001) 'Emotional communication in conflict', in William Eadie and Paul E. Nelson (eds), *The Language of Conflict and Resolution*. Thousand Oaks, CA: Sage Publications. pp. 81–104.

Jones, W. and Hughes, S. H. (2003) 'Complexity, conflict resolution, and how the mind works', *Conflict Resolution Quarterly*, 20(4): 485–94.

Kahn, H. (1965) *On Escalation*. New York: Praeger.

Kaufman, S. J. (2006) 'Escaping the symbolic politics trap: reconciliation initiatives and conflict resolution in ethnic wars', *Journal of Peace Research*, 43(2): 201–18.

Kellett, P. M. and Dalton, D. G. (2001) *Managing Conflict in a Negotiated World*. London: Sage.

Kelman, H. C. (1972) 'The problem solving workshop in conflict resolution', in R. L. Merritt (ed.), *Conflicts Between People and Groups*. Urbana: University of Illinois Press.

Kelman, H. C. (1993) 'Coalitions across conflict lines: the interplay of conflicts within and between the Israeli and Palestinian communities', in S. Worchel and J. A. Simpson (eds), *Conflicts Between People and Groups*. Chicago, IL: Nelson-Hall, pp. 236–358.

Kelman, H. C. (2002) 'Interactive problem-solving: informal mediation by the scholar-practitioner' in J. Bercovitch and J. Rubin (eds), *Studies in International Mediation*. New York: Palgrave Macmillan. pp. 167–93.

Kenrick, D. T., et al. (2005) *Social Psychology: Unravelling the Mystery*. Boston, MA: Pearson.

Khadiagala, G. M. (ed.) (2006) *Security Dynamics in Africa's Great Lakes Region*. Boulder, CO: Lynne Rienner Publishers

Klar, Y. et al. (1988) 'Conflict as a cognitive schema: toward a social cognitive analysis of conflict and conflict termination', in Wolfgang Stroebe et al. (eds), *The Social Psychology of Inter-group Conflict: Theory, Research and Application*. New York: Springer-Verlag, pp.73–88.

Kleiboer, M. (1996) 'Understanding success and failure of international mediation', *Journal of Conflict Resolution*, 40(2): 360–389.

Kleiboer, M. and 't Hart, P. (1995) 'Time to talk? Multiple perspectives on timing of international mediation', *Cooperation and Conflict*, 30(4): 307–48.

Kriesberg, L. (1987) 'Timing and the initiation of de-escalation moves', *Negotiation Journal*, 3(4): 375–84.

Kriesberg, L. (1998) *Constructive Conflicts: From Escalation to Resolution*. Lanham, MD: Rowman and Littlefield.

Kruse, L. (1986) 'Conceptions of crowds and crowding', in C. F. Grauman and S. Moscovici (eds), *Changing Conceptions of Crowd Mind and Behaviour*. New York: Springer-Verlag, pp. 118–139.

Lawler, E. J., et al. (1999) 'Unilateral initiatives as a conflict resolution strategy', *Social Psychological Quarterly,* 62(3): 240–256.

Leatherman, J. (2003) *From Cold War to Democratic Peace.* Syracuse, NY: Syracuse University Press.

Leatherman, J. and Webber, J. (eds) (2006) *Charting Transnational Democracy.* New York: Palgrave.

Lebow, R. and Stein, J.G. (1994) *We All Lost the Cold War.* Princeton: Princeton University Press.

Lederach, J. P. (2003) *The Little Book of Conflict Transformation.* Intercourse, PA: Good Books.

Leng, R. J. (1983) 'When will they ever learn? coercive bargaining in recurrent crises', *Journal of Conflict Resolution,* 27(3): 379–419.

Lieberfeld, D. (1999) *Talking with the Enemy: Negotiation and Threat Perception in South Africa and Israel/Palestine.* New York: Praeger.

Lindskold, S. (1983) 'Cooperators, competitors and response to GRIT', *Journal of Conflict Resolution,* 27(3): 521–32.

Littlejohn, S. W. and Domenici, K. (2001) *Engaging Communication in Conflict.* Thousand Oaks, CA: Sage.

Lobell, S. and Mauceri, P. (2004) 'Diffusion and escalation of ethnic conflict', in S. Lobell, et al. (eds) *Ethnic Conflict and International Politics: Explaining Diffusion and Escalation.* New York: Palgrave Macmillan. pp.1–10.

Lorenz, K. (1966) *On Aggression.* New York: Harcourt, Brace, Jovanovich.

Lulofs, R. S. and Cahn, D. D. (2000) *Conflict: From Theory to Action.* Boston, MA: Allen and Bacon.

MacGinty, R. and Darby, J. (2002) *Guns and Government: the Management of the Northern Ireland Peace Process.* Basingstoke, England: Palgrave/Macmillan.

Mack, R. and Snyder, R. (1971) 'The analysis of social conflict', in C. G. Smith (ed.), *Conflict Resolution: Contributions of the Behavioural Sciences.* Notre Dame, IN: University of Notre Dame Press, pp. 3–35.

Mandel, R. (2006) *The Meaning of Military Victory.* Boulder, CO: Lynne Rienner.

Maoz, Z. (2006) 'Network polarization, network interdependence, and international conflict, 1816–2002', *Journal of Peace Research,* 43(4): 391–412.

Marshall, M. G. and Gurr, E. R. (2005) *Peace and Conflict.* College Park, MD: Center for International Development and Conflict Management, University of Maryland.

Marx, K. and Engels, F. (1947) *The German Ideology.* New York: International.

Maslow, A. H. (1971) *The Futher Reaches of Human Nature.* New York: Viking Press.

McAdam, D., et al. (2001) *Dynamics of Contention.* New York: Cambridge University Press.

McCarty, N. and Meirowitz, A. (2007) *Political Game Theory: An Introduction.* New York: Cambridge University Press.

McDermott, R. (2001) *Risk-taking in International Politics: Prospect Theory in American Foreign Policy.* Ann Arbor: University of Michigan Press.

McGrath, J. E. and Argote, L. (2001) 'Group processes in organizational context', in M. A. Hogg and R. S. Tindale (eds), *Blackwell Handbook of Social Psychology: Group Processes.* Oxford/Malden, MA: Blackwell, pp. 603–27.

Miall, H., et al. (1999) *Contemporary Conflict Resolution.* New York: Polity Press.

Midgley, J. R. (2002) 'Guests overstaying their welcome: the demise of the peace accord structures in South Africa', *International Journal of Peace Studies.* 7(1): 77–89.

Minahan, J. (2002) *Encyclopedia of the Stateless Nations: Ethnic and National Groups Around the World.* Westport, CT: Greenwood Press.

Mitchell, C. (1981) *The Structure of International Conflict.* London: Macmillan.

Mitchell, C. (1999) 'The anatomy of de-escalation', in H.-W. Jeong (ed.), *Conflict Resolution: Dynamics, Process and Structure*. Aldershot: Ashgate, pp. 37–58.

Mitchell, C. (2000) *Gestures of Conciliation: Factors Contributing to Successful Olive Branches*. New York: Palgrave Macmillan.

Mitchell, C. (2001) 'From controlled communication to problem solving: the origins of facilitated conflict resolution', *International Journal of Peace Studies*, Spring 6(1), pp. 59–69.

Mitchell, C. (2002) 'Beyond resolution: what does conflict transformation actually transform?', *Peace and Conflict Studies*, 9(2): 1–24.

Morgan, P. M. (2005) 'Deterrence, escalation and negotiation' in I. William Zartman and Guy O. Faure (eds), *Escalation and Negotiation in International Conflicts*. New York: Cambridge University Press. pp. 53–80.

Nation, J. E. (ed.) (1992) *The De-Escalation of Nuclear Crises*. New York: St. Martin's Press.

Neumann, J. and Morgenstern, O. (1944) *Theory of Games and Economic Behavior*. Princeton University Press.

Nishida, H. (2005) 'Cultural schema theory', in W. Gudykunst (ed.), *Theorizing About Intercultural Communication*. London: Sage, pp. 401–18.

Nossal, K. R. (1984) 'Bureaucratic politics and the Westminster model', in Matthew, Robert et al., *International Conflict and Conflict Management*. Scarborough, Ontario: Prentice Hall of Canada. pp. 120–127.

Odom, W. (2004), 'The sources of new thinking in Soviet politics', in Niølstad, Olav (ed.) *Last Decade of the Cold War: from Conflict Escalation to Conflict Transformation*. London; Portland, OR: Frank Cass. pp. 135–158.

O'Kane, R. H. T. (1996) *Terror, Force, and States: The Path from Modernity*. Aldershot, UK: Edward Elgar.

Olzak, S. (2006) *The Global Dynamics of Racial and Ethnic Mobilization*, Stanford, CA: Stanford University Press.

Operario, D. and Fiske, S. T. (1999) 'Integrating social identity and social cognition: a framework for bridging diverse perspectives', in D. Abrams and M. A. Hogg (eds), *Social Identity and Social Cognition*. Oxford/Malden, MA: Blackwell, pp. 26–54.

Opp, K.D. (2001) 'Social networks and the emergence of protest norms', in M. Hechter and K. Opp (eds), *Social Norms*. New York: Russell Sage Foundation.

Osborne, M. J. (2004) *An Introduction to Game Theory*. New York: Oxford University Press.

Osgood, C. E. (1962) *An Alternative to War or Surrender*. Urbana, IL: University of Illinois Press.

Pammer, W. and Killian, J. (2003) *Handbook of Conflict Management*. New York: Marcel Dekker.

Parsons, T. (1951) *The Social System*, London: Routledge.

Patchen, M. (1988) *Resolving Disputes Between Nations: Coercion or Conciliation?* Durham, NC: Duke University Press.

Paul, T. V. (ed.) (2005) *The India–Pakistan Conflict: An Enduring Rivalry*. New York: Cambridge University Press.

Pilisuk, M. and Skolnick, P. (1968) 'Inducing trust: a test of the Osgood Proposal', *Journal of Personality and Social Psychology* 8: 122–133.

Pillar, P. R. (1990) 'Ending limited war', in E. Glad (ed.) *Psychological Dimensions of War*. Newbury Park, CA: Sage, pp. 264–73.

Powell, R. (2004) 'Bargaining and learning while fighting', *American Journal of Political Science*, 48(2): 344–61.

Price, T. F. and Price, L. A. (2002) 'Multitrack diplomacy', in Harvey J. Langholtz and Chris E. Stout (eds), *Psychology of Diplomacy*. Westport, CT: Greenwood Press. pp. 97–126.

Pruitt, D. (2003) 'Communication Chains in Negotiation Between Organizations', Occasional Paper #3, Sabanci University Program on International Conflict Resolution, Istanbul.

Pruitt, D. (2005) 'De-escalation in asymmetric conflicts', Presentation delivered at Festschrift Workshop in honour of Christopher Mitchell, George Mason University, Fairfax, VA.

Pruitt, D. and Kim, S. H. (2004) *Social Conflict: Escalation, Stalemate, and Settlement*, 3rd edn. Boston, MA: McGraw-Hill.

Putnam, L. L. (2004) 'Transformations and critical moments in negotiations', *Negotiation Journal*, 20(2): 275–95.

Putnam, R. D (1988) 'Diplomacy and domestic politics: the logic of two-level games', *International Organization*, 42(3): 427–60.

Quandt, W. B. (2005) *Peace Process: American Diplomacy and the Arab–Israeli Conflict Since 1967*. Washington, DC: Brookings Institution Press.

Rabbie, J. (1993) 'A behavioural interaction model', in K. S. Larson (ed.), *Conflict and Social Psychology*. London: Sage, pp. 85–108.

Raiffa, H. (2002) *The Art and Science of Negotiation: How to Resolve Conflicts and Get the Best Out of Bargaining*. Cambridge, MA: Belknap Press of Harvard University Press.

Rapoport, A. (1966) *Two-Person Game Theory: The Essential Ideas*. Ann Arbor, MI: University of Michigan Press.

Rapoport, A. (1990) 'The problem with gains-maximizing strategies', in E. Glad (ed.), *Psychological Dimensions of War*. Newbury Park, CA/London/New Delhi: Sage. pp. 91–115.

Reicher, S. (2001) 'The psychology of crowd dynamics', in M. A. Hogg and R. S. Tindale (eds), *Blackwell Handbook of Social Psychology: Group Processes*. Oxford/Malden, MA: Blackwell, pp. 182–208.

Reiter, D. (2003) 'Exploring the bargaining model of war', *Perspectives on Politics*, 1(1): 27–44.

Richardson, L. F. (1967) *Arms and Insecurity*. Chicago: Quadrangle.

Richardson, L. (2006) *The Roots of Terrorism*. London/New York: Routledge.

Richmond, O. P. (2002) *Maintaining Order, Making Peace*. New York: Palgrave.

Robinson, S. P. (1996) *The Politics of International Crisis Escalation: Decision-making Under Pressure*. London: I.B. Tauris.

Rosenthal, U., et al. (2001) 'The changing world of crises and crisis management', in Rosenthal, Uriel, et al. (eds) *Managing Crises*. Springfield, IL: Charles C. Thomas. pp. 5-27.

Ross, M. H. (2007) *Cultural Contestation in Ethnic Conflict*. Cambridge: Cambridge University Press.

Rouhana, N. N. (2004) 'Identity and power in the reconciliation of national conflict', in A. H. Eagly, et al. (eds), *The Social Psychology of Group Identity and Social Conflict: Theory, Application, and Practice*. Washington, DC: American Psychological Association, pp. 173–88.

Rubenstein, R. (2001) 'Basic human needs: the next steps in theory development', *International Journal of Peace Studies*, September 6 (1), pp. 51–59.

Rummel, R. J. (1975) *Understanding Conflict and War, Volume 1: The Dynamic Psychological Field*. London/New York: John Wiley and Sons.

Salla, M. (1997) 'Creating the ripe moment in the East Timor conflict', *Journal of Peace Research*, 34(4): 449–66.

Sandole, D. J. (2006) 'Complexity and conflict resolution', in N. Harrison (ed.), *Complexity in World Politics*. Albany, NY: State University of New York Press, pp. 43–72.

Saunders, H. (1999) *A Public Peace Process: Sustained Dialogue to Transform Racial and Ethnic Conflicts*. New York: Palgrave.

Scharff, D. et al. (eds) (2007) The *Future of Prejudice: Psychoanalysis and the Prevention of Prejudice*. Lanham, MD: Rowman and Little Field.

Scheff, T. J. and Retzinger, S. M. (1991) *Emotions and Violence: Shame and Rage in Destructive Conflicts*. Lexington, MA: Lexington Books.

Schelling, T. C. (1960) *The Strategy of Conflict*. Cambridge, MA: Harvard University Press.

Schneider, D. J. (2004) *The Psychology of Stereotyping*. New York: Guilford.

Schultz, K. A. (2005) 'The politics of risking peace: do Hawks or Doves deliver the olive branch?' *International Organization* 59: 1–38.

Segev, T. (2007) *1967: Israel, the War and the Year that Transformed the Middle East*. New York: Metropolitan Books.

Shakya, T. (1999) *The Dragon in the Land of Snows*. New York: Columbia University Publishers.

Sharp, G. (1973) *The Politics of Non-Violent Action, Part One*. Boston, MA: Porter-Sargent.

Sherif, M. and Sherif, C. (1953) *Groups in Harmony and Tension*. New York: Harper and Bros.

Singer, J. D. (1990) Models, Methods, and Progress in World, Boulder: Westview press.

Singer, J. D. (1999) 'Prediction, explanation, and the Soviet exit from the Cold War', *International Journal of Peace Studies*, 4(2): 47–60.

Soeters, J. L. (2005) *Ethnic Conflict and Terrorism: The Origins and Dynamics of Civil Wars*. London/New York: Routledge.

Sterling-Folker, J. (2006) 'Game theory', in J. S. Folker (ed.), *Making Sense of International Relations Theory*. Boulder, CO: Lynne Rienner.

Stetter, S. (2007) *Territorial Conflicts in World Society*. London/New York: Routledge.

Tainter, J. (2007), 'Forces of reaction and changes of scale in the world system of states', in R. Brian Ferguson (ed), *The State, Identity and Violence: Political Disintegration in the Post-Cold War World*. London: Routledge. pp. 68–88.

Tajfel, H. and Turner, J. (1986) 'The social identity theory of intergroup behaviour', in S. Worchel and W. Austin (eds), *Psychology of Intergroup Relations*. Chicago, IL: Nelson Hall, pp. 7–24.

Talentino, A. K. (2005) *Military Intervention after the Cold War*. Athens, OH: Ohio University Press.

Taras, R. and Ganguly, R. (2005) *Understanding Ethnic Conflict: The International Dimension*. New York: Longman.

Teger, A. (1980) *Too Much Invested to Quit*. New York: Pergamon.

Tetlock, P. E. and McGuire, C. B. (1985) 'Cognitive perspectives on foreign policy', in S. Long (ed.), *Political Behaviour Annual*. Boulder, CO: Westview. 'tHart, P. and Boin, A. (2001) 'Between crisis and normalcy', in Uriel, Rosenthal, et al. (eds), *Managing Crises*. Springfield, IL: Charles C. Thomas. pp. 28–46.

Tillett, G. and French, B. (2006) *Resolving Conflict: A Practical Approach*. Melbourne, Australia: Oxford University Press.

Ting-Toomey, S. (1985) 'Toward a theory of conflict and culture', in W. Gudykunst, et al. (eds), *Communication, Culture and Organizational Processes*. Newbury Park, CA: Sage, pp. 71–86.

Tormey, S. and Townshend, J. (2006) *Key Thinkers from Critical Theory to Post-Marxism*. London: Sage.

Turner, J. C. (1981) 'The experimental social psychology of intergroup behaviour', in J. Turner and H. Giles (eds) *Intergroup Behaviour*. Chicago, IL: University of Chicago Press, pp. 66–101.

Turner, J. C. (1982) 'Towards a cognitive redefinition of the social group', in H. Tajfel (ed.), *Social Identity and Intergroup Relations*. New York: Cambridge University Press, pp. 15–40.

van Evera, S. (1999) *Causes of War: Power and the Roots of Conflict*. Ithaca, NY: Cornell University Press.

van Evera, S. (2001), 'Hypotheses on nationalism and war', in Brown, M. et al. (eds), *Nationalism and Ethnic Conflict*. MIT Press, pp. 26–60.

Vertzberger, Y. (1990) *The World in Their Minds: Information Processing, Cognition, and Perception in Foreign Policy Decisionmaking*. Stanford, CA: Stanford University Press.

Visser, P. and Cooper, J. (2003). 'Attitude change', in M. A Hogg & J. Cooper *The Sage Handbook of Social Psychology*. London, UK: Sage Publication. pp. 211–31.

Volkan, V. (2006) *Killing in the Name of Identity: A Study of Bloody Conflicts*, Charlottesville, VA: Pitchstone.

von Heinegg, W. H. (2004) 'Factors in war to peace transitions', *Harvard Journal of Law and Public Policy*, 27: 843–76.

von Neumann, J. and Morgenstern, O. (1944). *Theory of Games and Economic Behavior*. Princeton: Princeton University Press.

Walt, S. (2000) 'Rigor or rigor mortis?', in M. Brown, et al. (eds), *Rational Choice and Security Studies*. Cambridge, MA: MIT Press.

Waltz, K. (2007) *Realism and International Politics: The Essays of Ken Waltz*. London/New York: Routledge.

Wehr, P. (1979) *Conflict Regulation*. Boulder, CO: Westview Press.

Winter, D. G. (1973) *The Power Motive*. New York: Free Press.

Wright, Q. (1942) *A Study of War*. Chicago, IL: University of Chicago Press.

Wright, S. C. and Taylor, D. M. (2003) 'The social psychology of cultural diversity: social stereotyping, prejudice, and discrimination', in M.A. Hogg and J. Cooper (eds), *The Sage Handbook of Social Psychology*, London/Thousand Oaks, CA/New Delhi: Sage, pp. 432–57.

Zartman, I. W. (2000) 'Ripeness: the hurting stalemate and beyond', in P. Stern and D. Druckman (eds), *International Conflict Resolution after the Cold War*, Washington, DC: National Academic Press, pp. 225–50.

Index

page references followed by f indicate an illustrative figure; n indicates a note

diffuse conflict, 130-2
dispute, definition of term, 6-7
dollar auction game, 170-1
Dollard, John, 48
Druze, the, 60-1

early warning systems, 243
East Timor, 94, 228
economic factors, 7-8, 15, 18, 44, 236
   Asian financial crisis, 36, 103
   assistance for reconstruction, 195, 212
   black market, 149
   deprivation, relative, 49-51
   deterioration, 35, 50; collapse, 93, 240
   labour, division of, 53
   sanctions, 139-40, 144, 151, 206
   stratifications, 53-4
Egypt, 58, 121, 127, 174, 183, 184, 187,
   188, 214, 234, 237
   see also Israel, Six Day War
Einstein, Albert, 45
El Salvador, 4, 92, 100, 188, 204n, 206
embedded conflict, 126-8
end of conflict see termination
entrapment, 97f, 98, 102, 154, 167-71
   self-perpetuating decision making and,
     170-1
   sustainability of, 171
environmental issues, 17-18, 23, 26,
   146
Eritrea, 61, 150, 235
escalation, 37, 38, 84, 86, 91, 97f, 137,
   142, 147, 175, 242
   controlled, 166-7
   deterrence and, 164-6
   dynamics of, 154-7
   internal factors, 171-4
   modes of, 109-10, 110f; crisis mode,
     162-4
   mutual, 98-9
   non-military, 161
   psychological aspects, 157-8
   spiral, 158-62
   see also de-escalation
ethical standards, 240, 241, 243
Ethiopia, 61, 149, 150
ethnic factors 12, 13, 15-16, 17, 28, 49, 61,
   93, 94, 97, 139, 149, 193, 201, 240
   collective memory, 47
   cross border relationships, 119
   expression of demand for autonomy,
     25-6, 227

government discrimination against
   minorities, 60-2
   multi ethnic states 58-9, 227
   multicultural societies, 56-7
   tangible and symbolic issues, 26
   see also genocide; language; state,
     contemporary systems
ethnic cleansing, 4, 57
ethno-nationalism, 35, 150
ethos of conflict resolution, 243-4
Europe, 14, 28, 56, 60, 112-13, 242
Europe, Eastern
   collapse of communism, 50, 95,
     108, 218
   conciliation with Western Europe, 212
evil, images of, 76-7, 156, 160
extremism, 63, 82, 129, 147, 153, 156,
   171-2, 173-5, 189, 198, 219, 202, 222
   fanaticism, role of, 201, 220
   radicalization, 13, 36, 149, 174-5
   see also terrorism

Falklands War, 65, 73, 162, 172, 195-6
Fanon, Frantz, 49
fatigue factor, 171, 184, 191
fear, projection of, 157
female soldiers, 122
focal conflict, 129-30
France, 16, 58, 86, 114, 124, 131, 155,
   183, 229
Freud, Sigmund, 45, 46-7
functional/dysfunctional conflict, 52-3

genocide, 28, 37, 44, 57, 78, 86, 126, 173,
   201, 228
Germany, 59, 164-5, 229, 232, 235
   Berlin blockade (1948), 72, 107, 108,
     183, 223
   Dresden (1945), 78
   Munich crisis (1938), 71-2, 143
global warming, 17-18
globalization, 28
goals
   hindering goal seeking behaviour, 48
   incompatibilities, 11-12, 24-5, 43,
     83, 239
   mapping, 21f, 22
Graduated and Reciprocated Initiatives in
   Tension Reduction (GRIT) (Osgood),
     209-10, 211
groups
   decision making, 84-6, 173

groups—cont'd
hawks and doves, 198, 199, 200-1, 202, 203
inter-group dynamics, 149-50, 197-8, 199
internal politics and group dynamics, 171-4, 197-8, 199, 211
mobilization and role of groups, 96-7
radicalization, 13, 36, 149, 174-5
veto groups, 23
Guatemala 4, 92, 102, 148, 151, 188, 201, 231
gypsies, 48

Haiti, 194
halo effect, 82, 87n
hawks and doves, 198, 199, 200-1, 202, 203
Hezbollah, 22, 49, 118-19, 142, 145, 162, 174, 200, 237
Hindus, 75, 168
Hiroshima, 78
Holocaust, 40
human nature see behaviour
human needs, 28-9, 51-2
see also deprivation; ethical standards
human rights, 13, 18, 129, 147, 236, 242
abortion rights, 28
see also civil rights
humanitarian forces, use of, 39
Hutus and Tutsis, 15-16, 45, 78, 119, 126, 173, 201, 235

identity
formation, 55-7
politicization of, 57
images, 76-7, 218-19
imperialism, 46
India, 56, 75, 195
caste system, 46
Pakistan's relationship with, 60, 106, 121, 129, 130, 181; 1947, 180, 233; 1965 war, 162-3, 169, 180, 186, 227; 1971, 180, 227
Punjab, 63n
indigenous populations, 17, 23, 60, 61, 201, 236, 240
Indonesia, 17, 36, 61, 103, 188-9, 228
information, inaccurate, 169-70
inhibiting factors, 94-5
institutions, 8, 35, 44, 47, 234-5
see also organizational behaviour

interests, definition of, 26-7
intervention, 112, 148, 241-3
instinct and, 47
third party, 38-9, 194-6
intractable conflict, 12-13, 28, 104-6, 194, 196
Iran, relations with
Britain, France and Germany, 86
Iraq, 169, 180, 234
USA, 12, 83, 122, 140, 142, 221-2
Iraq, 60, 87, 152, 169, 180, 185, 234
2006-7, 119-20
insurgency, 63, 174, 175, 239
occupation of Kuwait, 80-1, 83, 234
search for weapons of mass destruction, 8
US invasion of, (2003), 4, 8, 83, 84, 85, 117, 170, 175, 234, 238
victimization of Palestinian refugees, 48
Ireland, Northern 4, 13, 16, 104, 187, 200, 201, 202, 222-3
Irish Republican Army (IRA), 23, 104, 174, 187, 200, 201, 202, 222
Islam see Muslims
Israel, 13, 201, 203, 214, 234, 237
Palestinian conflict with, 4, 38, 52, 62, 104-5, 109, 111, 124, 158-9, 189, 197, 200, 203, 232, 236
Six Day War (1967), 47, 127, 141, 155, 185
Syria's relationship with, 12, 116n, 162, 222
Yom Kippur War (1973), 83-4, 108, 109, 121, 127, 184, 185, 188
issues, points of disagreement, 25-6

J-curve (Davies 1962), 50
Japan, 59, 105, 112, 142, 164, 213, 229, 232
Janis, Irving, 84
justice, 240-1
Jordan, 63

Kant, Immanuel, 18
Kelman, Herbert, 29
Kennedy, John F., 208, 211, 224
Korea, North, 13, 18, 40, 83, 86, 98, 105, 106, 121, 122-3, 124, 137, 142, 162, 224, 234
conciliation with South Korea, 110, 180
Kosovo, 16, 48, 58, 59, 150, 194, 232

Kurds, 17, 60, 61, 87, 120
Kuwait, 80-1, 83, 234

language, 16, 28, 56, 101, 168
large conflict systems, 127, 128, 131-2;
    curvilinear path of, 106-8, 107f
latent to manifest conflict, 91-7
Latin America *see* individual countries
leadership, 147, 153, 172, 184-6, 192, 196
    militant, 171, 173-4, 175, 201, 202
Lebanon, 118, 142, 145, 162, 174, 189, 200
Liberia, 102, 181
Libya, 206, 217
Lorenz, Konrad, 46

Macedonia, 39, 101, 112
macro-conflict dynamics, 107f
Mandela, Nelson, 104, 196, 199, 206, 223
mapping, 20, 21-2, 21f
    actor analysis, 22-4
Maslow, Abraham, 51
Marx, Karl, 52, 53
mass killing, 4, 39, 126, 146, 148, 194
    see also genocide
memory *see* collective memory
migration, 28
militancy *see* extremism
moderation, 202-3
morale, 239
Morocco, 58
Mozambique, 4, 100, 102, 140, 180, 206,
    218, 225, 229
multicultural societies, 56-7
Muslims
    Algerian guerrilla forces, 173, 229
    attacks on Christian Africans, 62
    Bosnia-Herzegovina, 4, 39, 111
    cartoon controversy, Denmark, 114
    intercommunal violence, 60
    issue of headscarves, 15, 155
    misconceptions about Islam, 82
    radical groups, 36
    riot in France (2005), 16
    self-determination, 128-9
    social marginalization, 121
    Turkish, 56
    see also terrorism

Namibia, 225
nationalism
    ethno-nationalism, 35, 150
    solidarity, 58, 63n

state and, 57-9
Syrian Christians, 63n
ultra-nationalism in Europe, 14
NATO, 39, 107, 112, 194, 232
Nepal, 112, 149
Netherlands, 227
Nicaragua, 28, 92
Nigeria, 228, 244
Nixon, Richard, 148, 188
non-violence, 3, 14-15, 144, 146-7, 150,
    152, 161, 240
nuclear power, 122, 140, 142
nuclear weapons, 18, 40, 78, 86, 98, 105,
    107, 122-3, 137, 142, 208, 210, 211,
    214
see also arms race; Cuban missile crisis

objectivity, 9-10, 21, 25, 26, 64
oil, 59, 61, 93
organizational behaviour, 145, 146-7
    bureaucratic inertia, 198
    bureaucratic organizations, interplay
        of, 86-7

Pakistan, 18, 60, 86, 106, 121, 129, 130,
    156, 181, 195, 233
    1947 war, 180
    1965 war, 162-3, 169, 180, 186, 227
    1971 war, 180, 227
Palestine
    conflict with Israel, 4, 38, 52, 62,
        104-5, 111, 124, 158-9, 189, 197,
        200, 203, 232, 236
    Hamas, 22, 49, 174, 203, 236
    Palestine Liberation Organization (PLO),
        23, 185
    victimization of refugees in Iraq, 48
peace keeping, 241
    compared to peace enforcement, 195
    UN peacekeeping, 39, 40, 195
peace zones, 39
phases of conflict *see* stages of conflict
Poland, 28, 122, 143, 164-5
    Brandt's apology, 212
    Solidarity movement, 55
polarization, 37
Portugal, 228, 229
post-conflict relationship building, 241
principles of conflict resolution, 39-40
prisoner's dilemma game, 67-8, 70, 71
psychological factors, 10, 11, 145
    cognitive consistency, 79-81

Nixon, Richard; Reagan, Ronald
Uzbekistan, 61, 95, 101

values, 9, 12, 23, 53, 112, 132, 160, 227,
    233, 235
  value differences, 27-8, 35
veto groups, 23
Venezuela, 226
Vietnam, 49, 83, 121, 152, 171, 185, 229,
    230, 234, 236
  Chinese invasion 1979, 182,
    230, 236
Von Neumann and Morgenstern, 66

Wales, 58
Weber, Max, 52
World Bank, 5
World Trade Organization, 8, 236
World War I, 114, 162, 166, 232
World War II, 59, 72, 83, 112, 114, 124,
    164-5, 169, 213, 229, 232, 235
Wright, Quincy, 138

yielding, 32-3
Yugoslavia, former, 16, 18, 35, 47, 58,
    128, 145, 194

Zimbabwe, 57